Python Illustrated

Not another boring Python book, learn programming the fun way

Maaike van Putten

Imke van Putten

<packt>

Python Illustrated

Written by Maaike van Putten

Illustrated by Imke van Putten

Portfolio Director: Kunal Chaudhari

Relationship Lead: Tushar Gupta

Project Manager: K. Loganathan

Content Engineer: Deepayan Bhattacharjee

Technical Editor: Irfa Ansari

Copy Editor: Safis Editing

Indexer: Manju Arasan

Proofreader: Deepayan Bhattacharjee

Production Designer: Ajay Patule

Growth Lead: Mansi Shah

First published: February 2026

Production reference: 1180226

Published by Packt Publishing Ltd.

Grosvenor House

11 St Paul's Square

Birmingham

B3 1RB, UK.

ISBN 978-1-83664-633-4

`www.packtpub.com`

Contributors

About the authors

Maaike is a software consultant and trainer with a passion for sharing her expertise to empower others in their careers. Her love for software development shows in the numerous software development projects she participated in and the many certifications she obtained. She has designed and delivered a broad spectrum of training courses catering to beginners and seasoned developers in Java, Python, C# and many other languages and frameworks. Next to that, she has authored multiple books and online courses through multiple platforms reaching over 500,000 learners across the globe.

Imke is a multi-talented content creator, co-teacher, and the creative force behind much of the illustrated content in *Python Illustrated*. With her unique combination of technical insight and artistic skill, she makes coding concepts fun, visual, and accessible to everyone.

Beyond her work in tech education, Imke channels her creativity and empathy into a variety of pursuits. She sews, designs, and runs wheelchair skills workshops that empower people with tools for independence, a mission deeply rooted in her own lived experience. Her passion for helping others navigate the world with confidence reflects the same care and thought she puts into making programming approachable.

About the reviewers

Dr. Seán Kennedy is a university lecturer with over 20 years of experience in teaching. His Ph.D. is in IT and he is OCP certified in Java. For the past 14 years, he has taught advanced Java on Ericssons' bespoke Master's program. He has co-authored two books with Maaike van Putten: *Learn Java with Projects* and *Java Memory Management*. Outside of work, he enjoys tennis, walking, TV, and nature.

Ricardo Bánffy is an experienced engineer living in Ireland, with a long career in varied engineering and management functions in areas ranging from advertising and aerospace, all the way to web applications. He is still looking for what to do that starts with Y and Z, for the sake of completeness. Owning a yacht would be a stronger candidate if Ireland's weather were nicer.

Ricardo has been reviewing books about Python and many other interesting topics, and enjoying it immensely. If you are reading this, maybe you should try it someday.

I'd like to thank first and foremost my handlers at Packt. God knows what I've put them through and their endless patience saved the day more than once.

Join us on Discord!

Read this book alongside other users, developers, experts, and the author himself.

Ask questions, provide solutions to other readers, chat with the authors via Ask Me Anything sessions, and much more. Scan the QR or visit the link to join the community.

`https://packt.link/deep-engineering-python`

Join us on Discord!

Read this book alongside other users, developers, experts, and the author himself.

Ask questions, provide solutions to other readers, chat with the authors via Ask Me Anything sessions, and much more. Scan the QR or visit the link to join the community.

`https://packt.link/deep-engineering-python`

Table of Contents

Chapter 5: Iterating with Loops 125

Chapter 9: Understanding Inheritance 261

Preface

> *"They said magic isn't real, but that was before they typed their first Python script and watched as the impossible became possible."*
>
> *- Me, Zia (portrayed in the picture below)*

Okay, I might be setting the expectations a little bit too high there. However, you've made a great decision choosing Python. You could arguably not pick a more versatile and developer friendly programming language. Python has a relatively easy syntax that looks a lot like plain English.

Ignore her for now. On top of that, you can do a lot of things with it, just to name a few:

- Web development
- Desktop tools
- Data analysis
- Artificial intelligence (AI) and machine learning
- Automation of all sorts of repetitive tasks
- Scientific computing

The community that uses it is amazing. You'll find that most of the questions and problems that you're going to run into have been answered by some friendly stranger on the web. Next to that, there is so much made that you can use with Python. We sometimes say it has a "rich ecosystem". This means that many ready made bits and pieces of code are available for you and that will help accelerate development of whatever it is you're creating.

Before we can get there though, we'll need to understand the basic syntax. And that's what this book is for.

Who this book is for

Anyone who wants to learn Python without wanting it to be boring can benefit from this book. This book aims to be the most accessible and fun book to teach you Python. It should be a light read, without compromising the quality or depth of our explanation. But I'm aware that fun is not for everyone.

If you know another language already, this book might be easy for you. That's why I try to make it interesting with humor. If you are new to coding, this book will probably be hard. That's why I try to make it lighter with humor.

What this book covers

Chapter 1: Get Your Computer Ready to Code Python

You'll prepare your computer for Python. Setting up Python is easier than catching a laser pointer (which is surprisingly hard). By the end of the chapter, you have everything installed and written your fi rst lines of code.

Chapter 2: Understanding Variables and Data Types

In programming, we often need to remember something. This is where variables come in. The chapter deals with how to create variables and what different data types there are. This way, you can keep track of the data needed in your program.

Chapter 3: Working with Conditional Statements

I can't help you make diffi cult decisions for you, but I can help you understand how to make diffi cult decisions in code. After this chapter, you'll be writing if, elif, else code to control the fl ow of your program.

Chapter 4: Using Lists, Tuples, and Dictionaries

In this chapter we'll deal with collections, ways to store multiple values in one variable. This is great for organizing our data and opens up a whole world in which we can deal with more complex types.

Chapter 5: Iterating with Loops

Loops let you repeat actions in your code. By the end of this chapter, you'll be able to avoid some duplicate code and automate more tasks.

Chapter 6: Writing Functions and Using Built-In Functions

This chapter is going to open up a whole new level of code organizations. Typically not the easiest concept, but if anything is like magic, it is this chapter. We are going to create our own little magic spells! These magic spells are called functions. When working with real projects, files get too big easily. We can split up files to organize functionality in separate files. These are called modules. Inside one module (yes file), we can import another module (uhuh file) to use the functionality. We will also see some common built-in modules and functions once we understand that module concept.

Chapter 7: Handling Files and Exceptions

Learn to open, read, and write files, so you can manage files. You'll be able to store and retrieve information from your programs with ease.

Chapter 8: Creating and Using Classes

This chapter is going to be a tough one! You'll take your first steps into the world of object-oriented programming. Think of classes as blueprints for your own custom types. You'll learn to create objects that can have attributes and behaviors.

Chapter 9: Understanding Inheritance

Why reinvent the wheel when you can inherit it? This chapter is going to build on the previous one and focus on better code organization. You'll discover how to build new classes that borrow features from existing ones.

Chapter 10: Debugging Our Code

Even the best of us miss a jump now and then. This chapter teaches you how to find and fix errors in your code, ensuring your programs land on their feet every time.

Chapter 11: Next Steps

Now that you've caught the red dot, what's next? I'll guide you on how to continue your Python learning, explore advanced topics, and maybe even catch that elusive laser pointer for good.

To get the most out of this book

My human says this all the time: coding is something you learn by doing. Of course, just reading this book will give you some insights. But to make the most out of it, it's highly recommended that you code along.

In the chapter, you'll find coding examples. These are also on the GitHub repository:

`https://github.com/BrightBoost/python-illustrated`

You can use git properly, or just copy them from there and paste them in your editor. At the end of each chapter, you'll find a list of exercises and a quiz to test your understanding of the topics discussed. The answers and explanations are in the back of the book (and on Github of course, so you can run and verify them easily).

Get in touch

If you are stuck and can't continue your learning to code ambitions. Please don't be stuck. Reach out to me, as long as I can handle the load and it doesn't get too busy, I'll help you get unstuck.

And don't ever be afraid to ask stupid questions. There's no such thing. It's stupid to not ask the question.

Free benefits with your book

This book comes with free benefits to support your learning. Activate them now for instant access (see the "*How to Unlock*" section for instructions).

Here's a quick overview of what you can instantly unlock with your purchase:

DRM-Free PDF Version

Download DRM-free PDF and ePub copies of this book.

7-Day Packt Library Access

Get 7-day unlimited access to 8,000+ books and videos. No credit card required.

Available for first-time Packt+ trial users only.

Next-Gen Reader Access

Read this book on Packt Reader with progress sync, dark mode and note-taking.

How to unlock

Scan the QR code (or go to `packtpub.com/unlock`). Search for this book by name, confirm the edition, and then follow the steps on the page.

UNLOCK NOW

Note: Keep your invoice handy. Purchases made directly from Packt don't require one

Share your thoughts

Once you've read *Python Illustrated*, we'd love to hear your thoughts! Scan the QR code below to go straight to the Amazon review page for this book and share your feedback.

`https://packt.link/r/183664633X`

Your review is important to us and the tech community and will help us make sure we're delivering excellent quality content.

Introduction

Hi, my name is Zia.

Yes, I'm a cat.

You might think that cats have no business writing books on Python. Well, you're wrong. If you own a cat, you might know that we love to be on your keyboard. Partly because it's warm (yes, it feels really good, not going to lie), but also because we love to type all sorts of things.

My human is a teacher in the tech space. She accidentally taught me Python while I was on her lap during her lessons. Fast forward to now, and I'm employed (100% remotely, of course) at a big tech company. I cannot tell you which one because I've signed an NDA. Also, I always use my human filter on Zoom and they cannot know I'm a cat. I've tested the waters with HR, and exposing that secret would get me fired.

Oh right, one more person I need to introduce.

Wiesje is here too. It's a Dutch name, you'd pronounce it something like Weesha. She is the cutest dachshund dog, and I'm proud to say that she's my cousin. Not sure why, but she doesn't seem to share the joy of us being related and can come across a little grumpy.

Once you get to know her better, you'll find that she's actually very sweet. She can't code Python yet, so she'll join you in the learning process.

Anyways, Python is easy, and I can teach you. But wait... What even is Python? Python is a programming language. A programming language is a set of instructions that can be used to communicate with computers. Just like how we use English to talk to each other, we use programming languages to tell computers what to do. Python is one of the easiest languages to learn and use, which makes it great for beginners.

To give you some more concrete examples, here are a few things you can do with a programming language:

- Automating repetitive tasks such as renaming files
- Making applications, for example a calculator
- Creating a game, just to name something... a number guessing game

Spoiler alert! We are going to do all of these things in this book (and more of course). Here's an overview of the things we're going to do:

- Get your computer ready to code Python
- Understanding variables and data types
- Working with conditional statements
- Using lists, tuples, and dictionaries
- Iterating with loops
- Writing functions and using built-in functions
- Handling files and exceptions
- Creating and using classes
- Understanding inheritance
- Debugging our code
- Next steps

Okay, time's valuable, let's get started getting your computer ready to code.

1

Get Your Computer Ready to Code Python

To make the most out of this book, it's best to follow along on your computer. But you can't just go ahead and write code on any computer; it's often required to get your computer ready to go. You do this by installing some necessary programs. We'll start by making sure you're ready to code. After this chapter, you'll have written your first line of code and run your first program. Exciting, isn't it?

Exploring Python features

Before we get too excited and jump into the installation straight away, let's take a sneak peek at what Python can do. Think of this as sniffing around before committing to the full pounce.

In short, here is why you'd want to learn Python as your programming language:

- Python's syntax is designed to be readable and straightforward. For a programming language, it's simple. It's like a warm sunbeam on the floor: inviting and comfortable.
- From web development to data analysis, Python wears many hats. Or should I say, many collars? It's a language that can be used for many different purposes and is therefore a great pick.
- Python has a supportive and loving community. An active community means tons of libraries and frameworks to play with. If you get stuck, there's practically always someone who has asked the same question before. And if not, they're rushing to answer your question on Stack Overflow. Stack Overflow is a forum that is used to solve mostly coding issues.

Setting up your system can be tricky and even a little frustrating if it doesn't take the happy path directly, but I promise you it's worth it!

Technical requirements

What do you need to run Python? Well, if you really, really had to, you could even learn it on your phone, tablet, or Chromebook. It's not ideal, but if you're motivated enough, you can make it work. At the end of this chapter, I will show you how to set that up. I just wanted to start by telling you not to be discouraged by not having fancy gear; we can make this work with almost anything. Just skip to the end of this chapter if that's you.

While phones and tablets might be possible, they're far from ideal for coding Python. A bit more of a mainstream setup for learning Python is some sort of personal computer. Ideally, you have a laptop or PC with the following specifications:

- Windows, macOS, or Linux as the operating system. Yes, even that old laptop in your closet might do.
- 8 GB RAM is comfy, but if you have 4 GB RAM and an extra splash of patience, it can work as well.
- An Intel i5 or equivalent processor is nice. Of course, anything faster is even better. An i3 will work too, but be prepared for some extra coffee breaks while things load.
- 2 GB of free disk space should suffice. That's like, what, a dozen cat videos?
- Install rights – sometimes, when it's a laptop from work or school, you might not be free to just go ahead and install applications without permission. If you can't install, hop to the end of this chapter, where I discuss how to use Python in the browser.

As you can tell, there's some flexibility here. I'm a big fan of using whatever you have. Once it gets more serious and you have the budget, upgrade your laptop. Python is not too heavy, but some of the programs we use for writing our Python code are. Not having the recommended laptop but using a more basic Python editor instead can be a perfectly fine solution to get started.

If you follow the steps, your system should be ready. The following installation steps are for Linux, macOS, and Windows laptops. For all of these steps, understanding and being able to use the terminal is important. Let's talk about that first.

The terminal

In movies, you might have seen scenes where hackers are doing their magic work, breaking into some sort of system. The application that they typically use when doing this is the terminal.

We might be less cool than those villains or superheroes in the movies, but we will use the terminal as well. When writing and running code, you'll be using a terminal every now and then, or in some cases quite often.

At this point, you might not know what a terminal even is. In the next image, you can see a picture of a terminal.

A terminal is a different way of controlling your computer. As a user, you are used to giving your computer instructions with the mouse and the keyboard. For example, if you want to open your mailbox, you can click on the application icon. This mouse click is an instruction your computer understands, and it will proceed to open the mailbox.

By typing text in the terminal, you can also give your computer instructions. As a bonus, it makes you look like one of those cool hackers from the movies. The terminal is the application that you are using to type these commands; it's sometimes also called the command line.

Here are some things you can do with the command line:

- Create, edit, and delete files
- Install applications
- Run applications
- Check versions
- And a lot more!

We'll be using the command line to install Python, add Python libraries, and run Python files. In order to use the command line, you'll have to know which commands to use. It's very possible that you don't know any. No problem! I will tell you what to type and what it means as we go.

Opening a terminal

Before we install Python, we'll need to check whether Python is already installed. To do that, we'll need a terminal. How to open a terminal depends on the system you're using.

For **Linux**, depending on your distribution, you can use the shortcut *Ctrl* + *Alt* + *T*. If that doesn't work, you can open the application menu (sometimes called **Activities**) and look for the applications. There, you can search for terminal. Click on the terminal icon. That should open the terminal.

For **Windows**, there are two built-in terminals: the command prompt and PowerShell. Either one of those is fine. You can open the command prompt with the shortcut *Windows button* + *R*. Or, you can type `cmd` in the search box in the start bar. If you don't have a search box in the start bar, you'll have to click on the Windows icon first and type it in the search box that pops up as part of the menu. Again, the terminal should open.

Lastly, for **macOS,** I like to use the Spotlight search. This can be done by pressing *Cmd* + *Space*. This brings up a search box. In there, we can type `Terminal` and press *Enter*. If that doesn't work, you can use Launchpad. Click the Launchpad icon in your dock and use the search bar at the top to look for **Terminal**. Click the Terminal app and it should open.

Now that you have the terminal open, let's give it a spin.

Speaking the terminal's language

The terminal might look like a dark and scary place, but it's really just a simple conversation with your computer. You type a command, press *Enter*, and your computer responds. Each command is like a magic word that makes something happen. The terminal is in a certain folder on your computer. This is like when you have File Explorer or the Finder application open; you are in the folder that you see.

On mine, in the image with the command line, we are at the location ~. Which means that I'm currently in my home directory. The home directory is known as the default user folder. If you're not sure where you are, you can ask the terminal where you are. Here's how it's done on macOS/Linux. In the terminal, type the following:

```
pwd
```

Then press *Enter*. This `pwd` stands for "print working directory." In my case, you can see I'm in the user's home directory, the user folder. This is the default folder where I am when I start the terminal like this.

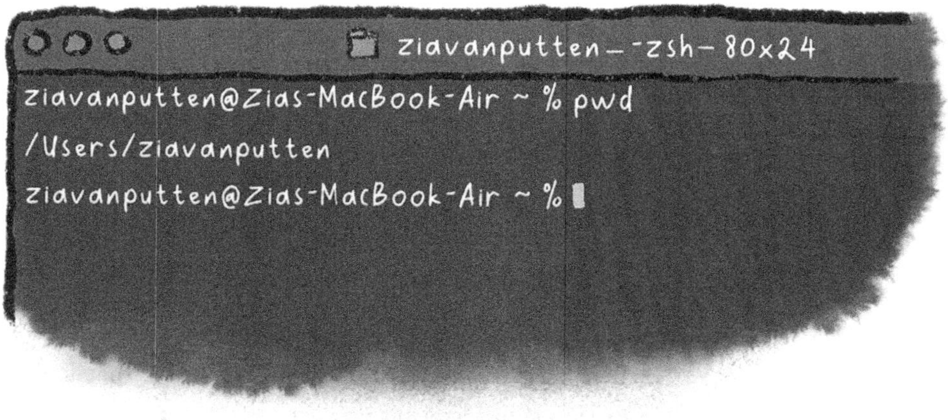

On Windows, you can see the directory by looking at the terminal window. It tells you where you are.

If you want to change the directory, you can. There are three things you can do when it comes to changing directories: step inside a folder, step up a folder to the parent directory, or go to a complete path that starts from the root of the file system. You change the directory with the `cd` command. After the command, you specify where to go.

You can step inside a folder that is in the directory where you are. You can do this with the following:

```
cd foldername
```

The `cd` stands for "change directory." After executing the command, you're in the subfolder with the name `foldername`. You can go to the parent folder. This is done with the following:

```
cd ..
```

You can go to a location that you know the absolute path of. The absolute path starts from the root of the filesystem. This example is for Windows:

```
C:\Users\Zia
```

This example is for Linux and macOS:

```
/home/zia
```

If you want to know which files and directories are in the directory that you are in, there's a command for that too. On **macOS/Linux**, type `ls` and press *Enter* to see a list of the files and directories. On **Windows**, type `dir` and press *Enter*.

Don't worry if this is new; you'll get the hang of it with practice. It's time to find out whether Python is already installed on your system using the terminal!

Is Python already purring on your system?

We can check whether Python is already curled up inside your computer – yes, I just mean installed. In the terminal, type the following commands and press *Enter*. These commands are like asking, "Hey computer, do we have Python here? If so, which version?"

On Windows, it is probably not installed:

```
python --version
```

If that doesn't give a number, try the following:

```
py --version
```

On macOS/Linux, there might be a different version – for example, 2.7. In order to find that out, run the following:

```
python --version
```

If that doesn't give a version number that starts with a 3, try typing the following:

```
python3 --version
```

If you need to add the 3, that's no problem; `python3` ensures you're using Python 3. It's like making sure your human is opening the right can of food (clearly tuna), not the old sardines.

The syntax of Python 2 is very different from Python 3; you really need to have Python 3 installed for this book. Don't worry if it's not installed – we'll walk you through it.

Understanding the response if Python is found

If Python is installed, you'll see something like this:

```
Python 3.12.6
```

If that's the case, purrfect! This means Python is already lounging around, ready to play. You might wonder what these numbers mean. Let's break it down:

- **3**: The major version. We need Python **3**, as Python 2 is like an old scratching post: still there, but not as much fun.
- **12**: The minor version. Each minor update brings new features.
- **6**: The micro version. These are small fixes and tweaks.

So, `Python 3.12.6` tells us you're using Python version 3, update 12, patch 6.

Using the right version of Python is important because code written for Python 3 might not work in Python 2. Also, newer versions have cool features that we'll use in this book.

For our adventures, we need **Python 3.10** or newer. If your version is older, some of the exciting things we'll do might not work.

Understanding the response if Python isn't found

You might get a message such as the following:

- 'python' is not recognized as an internal or external command, operable program, or batch file (Windows)
- command not found: python3 (macOS/Linux)

Don't worry! This is not an error. It just means Python hasn't moved in yet. We'll invite it over in the next section.

Windows users: a tiny hiccup

Sometimes on Windows, typing `python` might open the Microsoft Store. That's your computer's way of saying Python isn't installed, or it's not set up quite right. No biggie – we'll sort it out soon. Let's close the Microsoft Store for now, and I'll talk you through it in the rest of this chapter.

So, if Python is already installed and up to date, you're ahead of the game! If not, we can install Python. It's easier than convincing me to chase a laser pointer.

Installing Python

Now, let's get Python installed on your machine. This works a little differently for each operating system. Let's walk through it.

First, these are the steps for **Windows** users:

1. We'll start by downloading Python:
    - Go to the official Python website: `python.org`
    - Click on the **Download Python 3.x.x** button. There are many versions that will work, but I'd recommend grabbing the latest stable release. The x.x is not literal; I just cannot include it in a book because the numbers change so fast.

2. Now that we have the executable downloaded, we can run the installer:
    - Open the downloaded `.exe` file.
    - **Important**: Check the box that says **Add Python 3.x to PATH**. This makes it easier to run Python from the command line.
    - Click on **Install Now**.
3. Verify the installation:
    - If you have the Command Prompt still open, close it.
    - Open Command Prompt (search for `cmd` in the **Start** menu) (again).
    - Type `python --version` and press *Enter*.
    - You should see something like `Python 3.x.x`

Yes, Wiesje, we'll do **macOS** too. There are different ways to do it. You could use Homebrew if that's set up. You can find out whether you have it by running the following:

```
brew --version
```

If that gives you something such as `Homebrew 4.5.13`, it has been set up.

In that case, it's just a matter of doing the following:

1. Open the command line and type the following:
    - `brew install python3`
2. Verify it's installed by doing the following:
    - Type `python3 --version` and press *Enter*.
    - You should see the version number.

But if you don't use Homebrew, you can just download Python and install it:

1. Download Python:
    - Go to `python.org`
    - Download the latest Python 3 installer for macOS.
2. **Run** the Installer:
    - Open the downloaded `.pkg` file.
    - Follow the installation steps.
3. Verify installation:
    - Close and reopen Terminal if it's still open; otherwise, just open it.
    - Type `python3 --version` and press *Enter*.
    - You should see the version number.

Last but not least, let's talk about how to do it for **Linux** users. Most Linux distributions come with Python pre-installed. But it's often Python 2, which, while still lovable, is not what we're going to use.

1. Update the package lists:
    - Open Terminal.
    - Run `sudo apt update` (for Debian-based systems).
2. Install Python 3:
    - Run `sudo apt install python3`
3. Verify installation:
    - Type `python3 --version`
    - You should see the version number.

If that doesn't work, you can download the installer package from `python.org`, like Windows and macOS users, and proceed to install that. After installing, the version number should show when entering the following command in the terminal and pressing *Enter*:

```
python3 --version
```

At this point, we're ready to use Python. Exciting adventures are ahead – let's move on and write our first program!

Writing our first program

It's time to actually start coding. Traditionally, programmers start with a "Hello world!" program in whatever new language or framework they start using. But since I'm a cat, let's make it more relevant. Python only needs one line of code for the first program, and that makes it one of the shortest first programs you can write. If you ever try a language such as C++, Java, or C#, you'll really appreciate how straightforward Python is. Let's see the steps for creating our first little program.

First, we need to create a new file. You know how Word documents have the `.docx` extension, text files have a `.txt` extension, and ZIP files have a `.zip` extension. A Python file has its own special extension as well, the `.py` extension. Let's create a file and call it `hello.py`.

How do we create a file with this extension, you might wonder? Well, there are multiple options again. I'll walk through one option for each operating system that we've been talking about. It's easy to start by opening a text editor. If you have downloaded Python from the website, it probably came with a program called IDLE, which is great for this. Otherwise, you can use Notepad (Windows), TextEdit (macOS), or any basic text editor that your system has. Type the following line in this file:

```
print("Hello humans.")
```

Next, we're going to save the file as `hello.py`. Make sure it's saved with the `.py` extension and not `.txt`. Sometimes, it accidentally saves as `hello.py.txt`. This is still not correct, and that will not work. Also, for TextEdit (macOS), you don't have the option to choose the right extension – go for `.html` for now.

(If you're struggling for an unnecessarily long amount of time with the extension, you might consider just leaving it, as we'll take another approach soon. You can download the file from my GitHub instead.)

Then there's one extra thing you need to do: you want to make sure it's plain text, otherwise the quotes will be the wrong quotes. What do I mean?

" is not the same as " . Do you see the first ones curling a little? You don't want those curly ones. So what we need to do is to go to the top menu bar, to **Format** and choose **Make plain text**.

Then, lastly, we can rename the file and just modify the extension. On Windows, you'll need to enable adding the extension to the file name to be able to do that (don't mind the warning about changing the extension that follows – we really want `.py`).

Running your first Python program

In order to run our program, we're going to need the terminal again. So, let's open the terminal as a first step. We have an additional challenge before we can run it: we need to find the file. Let's start by asking ourselves the question, where is the file saved? Let's say that, on my laptop (macOS), it's stored here:

```
/Users/zia/Documents/pythoncourse
```

The easiest way to go there is by entering the full (absolute) path in the terminal, like this:

```
cd /Users/zia/Documents/pythoncourse
```

Let's make sure we're in the correct folder by asking where we are:

```
pwd
```

If you want to see the files that are in there, you can run the `dir` command for Windows and the `ls` command for macOS and Linux.

Now that we're in the correct location, we'll run the program. We do this by typing the `python` command, this time not followed by `--version`, but by the name of the file. So please go ahead and type `python hello.py` for Windows and `python3 hello.py` on macOS/Linux. Next, press *Enter*.

We should now be able to see the output. The output should be `Hello humans.` printed in your terminal. And that's it! I suppose congratulations are in order; you've just written and executed your first Python application.

So far, we've been using tools that our computer has. And that's fine – it will work. However, there are nicer tools to work with Python. Let's talk about these tools, called IDEs, next.

Working with an IDE

As we have seen, writing code in a basic text editor works... But it's as if you're eating dry kibble when you could have had tuna. The tuna in this case would be the IDE. **IDE** stands for **Integrated Development Environment**. This special application, meant for coding, offers features such as syntax highlighting, code completion, and debugging tools.

It's a little bit like choosing between Word and Notepad for writing books. Notepad will work, but it's nicer to use a slightly more elaborate writing tool. Just like you have different applications that you could use for writing a book, there are different excellent options for writing Python. Here are some great choices that you can install on your computer:

- PyCharm (by JetBrains)
- IDLE
- Atom
- Sublime Text
- Visual Studio Code

If you have a somewhat more basic machine, it might be a great option to work with IDLE. If you downloaded Python from the python.org website, this probably came with it. In your programs, you can search for IDLE, and the editor will open.

For this book, I'll be using Visual Studio Code. It's typically a bit more lightweight than PyCharm, but when I'm developing web applications with Django (a Python framework), I do prefer PyCharm. When I'm writing a quick automation script or teaching a course, I'll always opt for Visual Studio Code.

Introducing Visual Studio Code (commonly called VS Code)

VS Code is a great choice for an IDE in general. It is free and relatively lightweight for your computer. It supports so many languages and frameworks. You won't have to worry about frameworks yet; that is what we'll use when we make more complex applications, such as web apps, later. It consists of a basic application that can be extended with many (free) plugins, called extensions. With the right extensions, VS Code is a really great tool for writing Python. Let's walk you through how to install it.

First, we need to download it.

- Visit `code.visualstudio.com`
- Download the version for your operating system.
- Now that it's downloaded, it's time to install VS Code:
- Run the installer and follow the prompts.
- After it's installed, open VS Code.

We'll install the Python extensions later – that's our last step. But let's take a moment to enjoy the view and explore what VS Code looks like.

What's where?

When you first open VS Code, you might feel a bit like when I moved to my new house – so many places to explore! Let's break down the main areas. VS Code is quite heavily focussed on the **activity bar**. This is the vertical toolbar on the very left. (It's shown in the picture on the next page.) In here, you'll see different icons:

- **Explorer (files icon)**: Access your files and folders here. This is where you'll have an overview of all the files in your project.

- **Search (magnifying glass)**: Search for text across your entire project. If you have lost some lines of code and you don't know in which file they are, you can search across multiple files here.
- **Source Control (branch icon)**: Manage your code versions with Git. Don't worry if you don't git... uhh get... that yet.
- **Run and Debug (bug with a play button)**: Run your code and debug errors. This is the place that helps you catch bugs. I don't mean spiders and mosquitoes, but tiny mistakes in your code. We call those bugs too.
- **Extensions (four squares)**: Find and install extensions to add new features. This is where we'll go in a little bit to fine-tune VS Code for helping us to write and run Python.

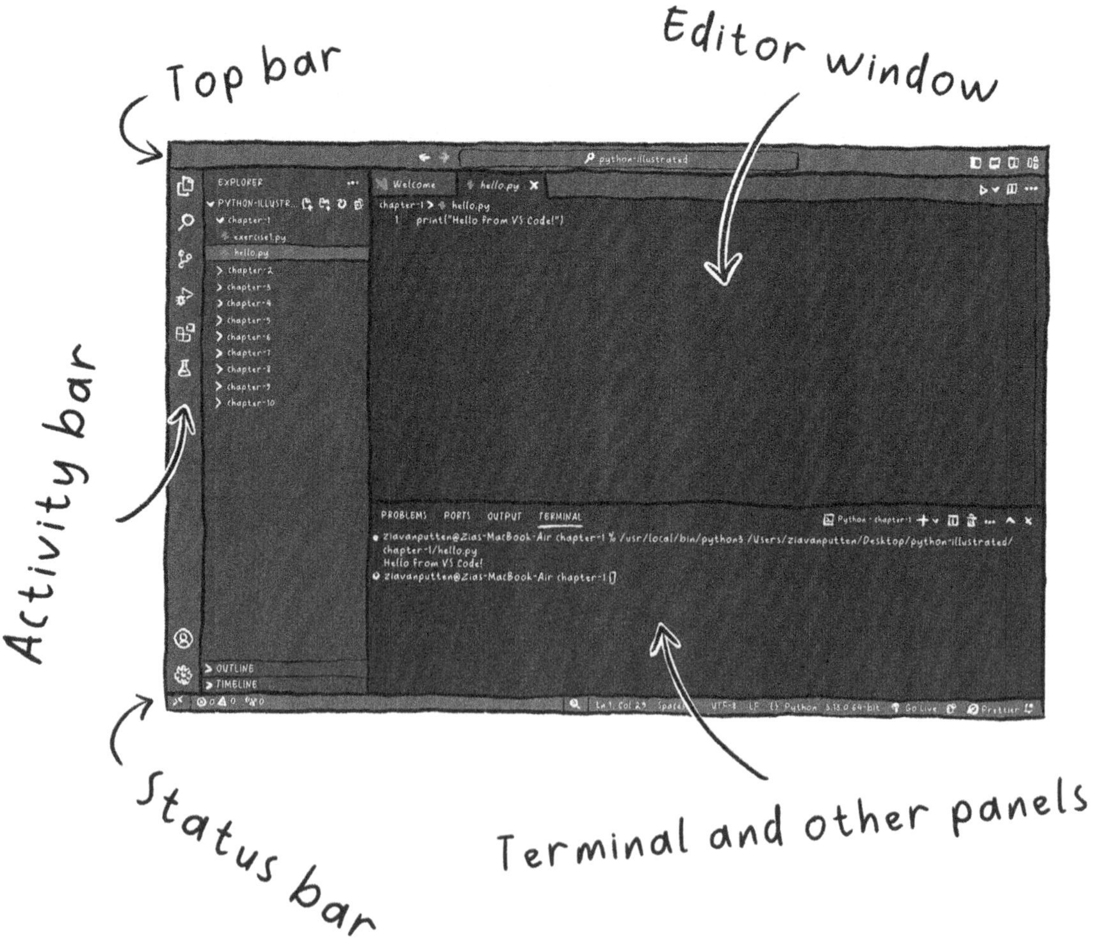

Depending on changes within VS Code and extensions you have installed, there could be more or fewer icons. But in general, whenever you click on one of these icons, a panel next to it (called the sidebar) will open with some more options or show information. If we move a little further to the right, we get the main area. This is the **editor window**. The central area where you'll write your code. You can open multiple files in tabs, just like browsing the web.

If you run your code, the focus will shift to the bottom. This bottom area houses the built-in terminal, debug console, output, and problems tabs. You can toggle this panel with shortcuts or menu options. I'm quite a fan of the built-in terminal; it's so nice not to have to change windows, but just access it right where I was working already.

If we move down a little further, we'll find the **status bar**. This is the strip at the very bottom. It shows useful information such as the current programming language, line and column numbers, and the Git branch (again, don't worry if this doesn't mean a lot to you yet).

There are some really cool things to say about VS Code, such as the command palette. This can be accessed via *Ctrl* + *Shift* + *P* (Windows/Linux) or *Cmd* + *Shift* + *P* (macOS). This is a feature that's a lot like a magic wand. You can type commands to do almost anything without touching the mouse. There are also a lot of great shortcuts and features, but I don't want to spend too much time on them, even though I'm very enthusiastic.

Alright, alright. Just this – there are lots of handy shortcuts. In the top bar, you have the regular menu. Next to the name of the options, you'll see the shortcuts. I'll share how to use VS Code as we walk through the book. Oh, and this: you can personalize VS Code as well. Go to **File** > **Preferences** > **Settings** (Windows/Linux) or **Code** > **Settings** > **Theme** (macOS). There are a lot of options here; you can change the theme to get a look and feel you're comfortable with.

One of my personal must-haves is auto-save. I don't want to have to save manually all the time. You can enable auto-save by going to **File** > **Auto Save**. This saves your files automatically after a delay. If files are unsaved, they have a little dot behind the title in the tab. If you want to be in full control, don't enable it.

Let's wrap up our VS Code setup by installing the Python extensions that we'll need. First things first, let's open up the right view. Click on the Extensions icon in the Activity Bar (this is the one that looks like four squares).

Here, we can browse extensions and install them. In the search bar on the extensions sidebar, search for `Python`. Open the one by Microsoft and click on **Install**. If you have made a Python file in VS Code already, it may have prompted you to add the extension, and it's possible that you already have it.

Creating and running a program with an IDE

Let's recreate our `hello.py` program in VS Code. In order to do this, we'll open a folder first. We have different options to do this. If you click on the file icon, there's probably an **Open Folder** button that allows you to navigate to a folder that you'd like to open. It's probably best to create a special folder for the examples in this book. Let's say you choose the name `python-illustrated`. You'll navigate to this folder (or create it on the spot), select it, and click **Open**.

Then, when the folder is open, make sure to be in the **Explorer** view by clicking on the files icon on the left. Next to the name of the folder, you will see icons. One of them is to create a new file. You can also right-click the mouse and choose **New file** in the Explorer view. Name the file `hello.py`.

It should open in the main area, the editor. In there, type the following:

```
print("Hello from VS Code!")
```

Make sure that it's saved (there should not be a dot beside the name of the file in the tab, which indicates it's not saved). Now we're ready to run the program. Of course, why have only one way to run the program? We have several ways:

- **Option 1**: Right-click in the editor window and select **Run Python File in Terminal**.
- **Option 2**: Press *Ctrl* + *Shift* + *P* (Windows/Linux) or *Cmd* + *Shift* + *P* (macOS) to open the command palette, type `Run Python File`, and select the option that pops up. If the shortcut doesn't work, open the terminal using the user interface of your operating system.
- **Option 3**: Add the Code Runner extension. Use the play button icon in the top-right corner of the editor. If you have the extension already, you'll see the play button in the top-right corner.

Any of these ways should show the terminal within VS Code with the following text:

```
Hello from VS Code!
```

And that's it. You're all set for this book.

Before we move on, let's talk about what to do when you don't have a computer on which you can install Python.

Alternatives for when you can't use a computer

Maybe you're on the go, or perhaps your pet parrot spilled water on your laptop (it happens). Or, you have never had a PC or laptop. As long as you have a device with a browser, you can use any of these alternatives.

It all comes down to online Python interpreters. Not all of them are free, and they have different options. Some allow you to create an account where you can store and manage full projects (those are typically paid). There are basic online interpreters where all your progress is lost with a page refresh. These are typically free.

- **Repl.it**: Visit `repl.it` to write and run Python code in your browser. You'll have to sign up for an account.
- **Google Colab**: This one is great for data science and machine learning, accessible via `colab.research.google.com`. However, it is perfectly fine for most of the examples in the book.

There are also mobile apps that you can install. Current examples of these are as follows:

- **Pythonista (iOS)**: A full Python IDE for your iPhone or iPad
- **QPython (Android)**: Allows you to run Python scripts on your Android device

These alternatives aren't pawfect, but they'll do.

And there you have it! We are all ready for it. Remember, every great coder started with a simple "Hello world!" or, in our case, "Hello humans." If you want to try something, just do it. Experimenting and playing around are great ways to learn unexpected things. Coding is something you'll learn. As most people know, it requires logical thinking, but what is less known is that it will require a good dose of creativity as well.

Before we move on to the next chapter, about variables and data types, let's get some more practice by doing the quiz and exercises first.

Quiz

1. What does `cd` mean in the terminal's language?
    a. Command Directly
    b. Change Directory
    c. Create Directory
    d. Cute Dachshund
2. What does the `pwd` command do in the terminal?
    a. It shows you the folder you're in
    b. It prints all files in the current folder
    c. It runs your Python program
    d. It allows you to change your location using an absolute path
3. Wiesje is trying to speak to the terminal on her macOS laptop – sorry, MacBook. She runs the `dir` command to see which files are in her current folder. Why is this not working?
    a. She hasn't selected a folder first
    b. There might not be any files in the current folder
    c. MacBooks don't have a terminal
    d. She's using a Windows command
4. What does the ~ mean in the terminal's language?
    a. Python
    b. Current location
    c. The home directory
    d. It's purely decorative
5. True or false? You need a modern computer to learn how to code Python.
6. What is an IDE?

Exercises

Let's get some paws-on practice and get familiar with VS Code and the terminal.

1.1 Getting familiar with VS Code

If you've coded along with me (as you should have), you've already created a folder named `python-illustrated` for all the exercises in this book. Well, this is quite a big book with many exercises, so it's probably best to organize them in some way. In order to do this, we're going to create some sub-folders for each chapter.

Steps:

1. If you haven't already, create a folder called `python-illustrated`. If you want some extra practice, delete the folder you created earlier and go through the process again.
2. Create a folder within this `python-illustrated` folder for the exercises for *Chapter 1*. Name it `chatper-1`.
3. Oops, we just introduced a typo! Rename the folder to `chapter-1`.
4. While we're at it, let's create a folder **next to** `chapter-1` for *Chapter 2*. Name it `chapter-2`.
5. Within the `chapter-1` folder, create a file called `exercise1.py`.
6. Did you manage to get the file in the right folder?
7. Open `exercise-1.py` and write this line:

```
print("Hey, I can create folders and files in VS Code!")
```

8. Save your file and run the code to check whether everything is working.
9. Okay, that's enough. Let's close `exercise-1.py` and collapse the `chapter-1` folder.

1.2 A chat with the terminal

Now that we've created a `python-illustrated` folder and some subfolders. Try and see if you can use the terminal to navigate your way around.

Steps:

1. Open the terminal.
2. Check your current location.
3. Find the `python-illustrated` directory and hop in.
4. Navigate to the `chapter-1` folder.
5. List all files in the `chapter-1` directory.
6. Run the code in `exercise-1.py`.
7. Move back up one level in the folder hierarchy and jump into the `chapter-2` folder. Use a command to check whether there are files in this directory.

Bonus challenge: The terminal understands many more commands! Can you go online and browse the internet to find the command that creates a new file? Try and see if you can add a `bonus-challenge.py` file to the `chapter-1` folder. That would be so cool!

Summary

Congratulations on taking your first steps into the world of Python programming! Let's purr over what we've learned in this chapter.

We discussed the importance of setting up your computer to ensure a smooth coding experience. Whether you're on Windows, macOS, Linux, or even using less conventional devices, there's a way to make it work. Remember, it's not about having the fanciest gear but making the most of what you have.

Before we got to installing, we talked about the terminal, turning it from a mysterious hacker's tool into a friendly way to communicate with your computer. You learned how to open it on your system and run basic commands. It's like having a secret handshake with your machine!

Next, we checked whether we had Python installed already. You now know how to check whether Python is already lounging on your system and how to invite it over if it's not. We want to use Python 3.10 or newer for this book.

Right after that, we wrote and ran a simple Python program together. No big deal, just your first step into coding greatness. Even though that worked, life is better with an IDE. We talked about

IDEs in general and focussed on installing and becoming familiar with VS Code. We dipped our paws into its possibilities. Customizing it to your liking is half the fun!

Lastly, we also explored options for when you're on the go or can't install software. This means that you can code anywhere, anytime.

Let's reiterate this too: As we move forward, remember that every expert was once a beginner. Keep being curious, and don't hesitate to explore and play around. After all, coding is as much about creativity as it is about logic.

In the next chapter, we're going to talk about variables and data types. These are the basic building blocks of every language. So, stretch those fingers (and maybe take a catnap), because things are about to get even more interesting.

2

Understanding Variables and Data Types

Before we talk about making your code actually *do* things, we need to talk about variables and data types. Think of variables as little boxes where you can store information, like how I store treasures under the sofa cushions. These things don't do anything. Instead of *doing* something, variables *are* something.

What are variables?

You might wonder, okay, variables are *something*. But what? Variables are like little containers with labels on them. In those containers, you can store a piece of data that you'll need later. You can retrieve the piece of data later, using the label of the container.

Let's say that we want to do a basic calculation, perhaps calculating the surface of a square. How do we calculate that? Well, we grab the length of the side and multiply that by itself. If we have a square with a length of 5 cm, we'll say the surface is 5 * 5. If the length is 100 cm, the surface is 100 * 100.

Where am I going with this? Well, you could say that the formula for calculating the surface is side * side.

And if we want to write that in Python, we could create a variable for *side*. Remember, a variable is a little container with the actual value in it. The label of the container would be `side`, and we can store a value in it. Here's how you'd do that:

```
side = 100
```

On the left, we are specifying the name of the variable.

With the equals sign, we are going to put a value inside the container. We set the value to `100` here, but we could have chosen anything, really.

Then, later in our code, we can use the name of the variable to refer to whatever is inside.

For example, we can print the result of `side` times `side`, like this:

```
print(side * side)
```

The `side` in the `print` is used to look up the container and get the value that's inside the container. And if we want to calculate a square with a different side length, we set it to that value, as in this example:

```
side = 50
```

What happens here is that we overwrite the old value, `100`. After this action, inside the container, we have a value of `50`.

Variables make our code flexible. Without variables, our code would do the exact same thing every time we run it. In some cases, that's actually fine. However, in most cases, we want to have a little bit of flexibility. For example, let's say that we create a little program that will greet a person.

We could write the program like this:

```
print("Hi Wiesje")
```

This little program would only ever greet Wiesje. Here's the output:

```
Hi Wiesje
```

Greeting is a little bit like a program in our brains that works with variables. If I see Wiesje, I'll say *"Hi, Wiesje,"* and if I see my friend Lara, I'll say *"Hi, Lara."* I'm swapping the name for the name of the friend I'm seeing.

If we rewrite it a little, we could make it work with a variable like this:

```
name = "Wiesje"
print("Hi", name)
```

Okay, to be fair, this program would also only ever greet Wiesje. It prints the following:

```
Hi Wiesje
```

This is just like the last one, but this time, using a variable for the name. The reason that it will always print the same is that we coded the value of our variable inside the program. If we want to change the outcome, we'll have to change the program, like this:

```
name = "Lara"
print("Hi", name)
```

We are now writing the values for variables directly in our code. Please note that in real code, when you're a bit further on your learning path, we often don't use the values directly. Often, the values for the variables come from input, for example, the input of the user, but that's something that you'll learn later.

We call these directly coded values, **hardcoded** values. That means that we literally write down the value to put in the container or not even use a container at all. We do this a lot in this book. That is mainly because we have not yet seen how to store user input or get data in our program in different ways.

For now, let me solve that problem like this: I promise you that there will be a way to get data dynamically in your variables later.

But even if you work with hardcoded values, there are advantages. Imagine this piece of code:

```
print("Hi Wiesje")
print("How are you, Wiesje?")
print("It's lovely to talk to you again, Wiesje")
```

Okay, it's a weird piece of code, I'll admit it. But let's say that I now want to adjust this code to talk to another friend of mine, Lara. I would have to adjust the code in **three** places, like this:

```
print("Hi Lara")
print("How are you, Lara?")
print("It's lovely to talk to you again, Lara")
```

If I used a variable, I would only have to adjust it in **one** place, namely, the value of the container, like this:

```
name = "Wiesje"
print("Hi", name)
print("How are you,", name, "?")
print("It's lovely to talk to you again,", name)
```

Or for Lara, I could use this:

```
name = "Lara"
print("Hi", name)
print("How are you,", name, "?")
print("It's lovely to talk to you again,", name)
```

Now that you know what variables are, let's talk about what we should name our variables.

Naming variables

There are a few rules for naming your variables. We have two types of rules: we have Python rules and conventions. The Python rules are non-negotiable; if you break these, your code won't work. The conventions are good practices; however, if you break them, your code will still work.

Let's start with the Python rules. Variables must start with a letter or an underscore. They can't start with a number. The rest of the variable name can have letters, numbers, and underscores. It's important to keep in mind that variable names are case-sensitive. That means that you need to refer to a variable with the exact same casing as you chose at first.

Here are some examples of valid variable names (not all of them follow best practices!):

```
result = 12
Result = 12
_result = 12
result1 = 12
result_1 = 12
result_ONE_1 = 12
```

And here are some examples of invalid variable names:

```
1result
#result
?result
```

The good practices in Python are somewhat simple. For now, you only need to know these two good practices:

- Make sure to have descriptive variable names that mean something.
- Use snake case. This means that your variables should be fully lowercase, and if they contain multiple words, you replace the spaces with underscores instead of omitting them completely.

Here are some examples:

```
age = 4
snake_case = "Good practice"
total_price = 12
```

Many languages use `camelCase`. This is an alternative to `snake_case`. Instead of replacing the spaces with underscores, every new word after the first starts with an uppercase letter, such as `totalPrice`. This is something that's not uncommon to encounter in Python code bases, either. What's best depends on the environment you're in. In general, we use `snake_case` for Python. But if you have to adjust or add code and all the other code is in `camelCase`, it's a situation where it's better to stick to their conventions instead of the general conventions.

Basic data types

If we go back to our containers analogy, we have different types of containers. For example, in the kitchen, there are containers that we use to store leftovers.

We have certain expectations for the content of these containers, for example, that we should be able to reheat it.

And in the kitchen, we also have some containers that are great for liquids (yes, I believe they call these bottles); for these, we have other expectations, such as that we can serve it in a glass.

Okay, back to code.

Let's say we have two variables:

```
number = 42
name = "Zia"
```

What you can't just see from this code is that these are actually stored in different types of containers. And because of that, there are different things you can do with these types of variables. For example, I can do mathematical operations with the `number` variable, but I cannot subtract 7 from the `name` variable.

And that's why all variables have a type. There will be more types later, but for now, we'll discuss the basic types. We will see these three basic types in this chapter:

- Numbers
- Strings
- Booleans

So, with variables, we can do several things. And depending on the type of variable, we can do different things. Sure. But there is something that we can do with all variables: assign them a value.

Variable assignment and reassignment

We've done this already; the equal sign is used for variable assignment. With the equal sign after a variable, we're telling Python: *"Hey Python, this value will be stored in this variable."* And Python will then look at that value and decide the type of container to choose for it. The label is something that we choose (the name of the variable).

We use the = sign to assign a value to a variable:

```
favorite_toy = "ball"
```

At this point, `favorite_toy` holds the `"ball"` value.

Variables are like little boxes where we can store things. But sometimes, we want to change what's inside the box. That's where reassignment comes in! So, if we find a new toy we like better, we can change the value:

```
favorite_toy = "laser pointer"
```

And like magic, `favorite_toy` now holds `"laser pointer"`.

Python is flexible compared to some other languages. In Python, variables can change their type. One moment it's a number, the next it's a string. Python doesn't mind!

```
number = 10
number = "ten"
```

Yes! Python is dynamically typed, which means variables can change type as needed. So what is the type of a variable? As I said, Python determines the type itself. But it's not random.

We can tell what the type of the variable is by looking at the type of the value. We're going to talk about numbers, strings, and booleans in more detail, including how to recognize them. First up, the numbers!

Working with numbers

Let's start with my favorite data type, numbers. Numbers are used for storing all sorts of numeric values. We'll discuss two kinds of numbers:

- `int`
- `float`

The int type

Let's start with the integers. Integers are for the so-called round numbers. This means numbers that don't have a floating point, for example, to store this kind of data:

- How many countries did you visit?
- How many toys are in the basket?
- How many products are in the shopping cart?

These are all questions that will have an `int` answer. That means, you don't say you have visited 2.3 countries. You've visited 2 or 3 countries.

So, here's the code that goes with it:

```
nr_countries_visited = 2
nr_toys_in_basket = 13
nr_products_in_shopping_cart = 5
```

They now all start with `nr`, but that's not required. That's just to leave no confusion about what's stored in the variable. I could imagine that in the `countries_visited`, the actual countries that I did visit are stored (such as Spain and the Netherlands).

So, integers are for round numbers. You can recognize them by just being numbers, without quotes around them. What if we need to talk about halves and more fractions?

We'll use floating points. That's where the `float` type comes in.

The float type

The `float` type is used for floating-point types. This means all the not round numbers, for example, for storing data that answers questions such as the following:

- What's your average grade?
- How many countries have you all visited on average?
- How many liters of water do you use for washing the dishes?

And here's what that code would look like:

```
avg_grad = 85.6
countries_visited_avg = 2.43
liters_water_dishes = 13.0
```

You can recognize floating points easily; they have a number with a floating point. As you can see, even when it's `.0`, it's a floating point.

Operations on numbers

What can we do with numbers? Yes, that's right! Calculations. I know, it's exciting! If you were always bad at math, don't worry. There are lots of Python jobs where it's not the most important thing. And here, we will only discuss the following operations:

- Addition

- Subtraction
- Multiplication
- Division
- Exponentiation
- Modulo
- Integer division

These last two or three of the list might be somewhat new, but I'm sure you can do them.

Before we dive into detail, here are some quick examples to give you an idea of the level:

```
apples = 10
oranges = 5
total_fruits = apples + oranges
```

The value of `total_fruits` will be `15`. Here's another example combining integers and floats:

```
apples = 10
price_per_apple = 0.5
total_cost = apples * price_per_apple
```

Now, `total_cost` will be `10 * 0.5`, which equals `5.0`.

If you want to check the values, just print them!

```
print(total_cost)
```

We'll go through all of it in a little more detail, starting with addition. Let's see whether it adds up.

Addition (+)

Addition is about combining two numbers into a (larger) one. It is like collecting all your favorite toys together. If you have some feathers and some balls of fluffy material, and you want to know how many toys you have in total, you just add them up. Here's how to do that in Python:

```
feathers = 7
fluffy_balls = 3
total_toys = feathers + fluffy_balls
```

The value of `total_toys` will be `10`. And we can also do this with distances. Let's calculate the total walk I take through the house from the couch. Yes, it's in meters. If you'd rather use freedom units (feet and yards), feel free to write a little snippet that converts it!

```
distance_kitchen = 6
distance_sunny_spot_upstairs = 20
total_distance = distance_kitchen + distance_sunny_spot_upstairs
print(total_distance)
```

As you can see, my `total_distance` value will be `26` meters. I do that a few times a day, and that's how I stay fit.

Subtraction (-)

Subtraction is used to find out how far apart two numbers are, or more officially stated, it's about finding the difference. So, for example, we can use it when eating the special cat cookies from a jar. If you start with a certain number of treats and eat an amount, how many are left?

```
cookies_in_jar = 12
cookies_eaten = 5
cookies_left = cookies_in_jar - cookies_eaten
```

See how great these operations are? Now we know that `cookies_left` will be `7`. Almost time for the human to go get some more. And, of course, we could have floating-point subtraction, too:

```
cat_milk_in_bottle = 0.5
milk_drank = 0.25
milk_left = cat_milk_in_bottle - milk_drank
```

While they're at it, they might bring some more milk too, because `milk_left` will be `0.25` liters.

Multiplication (*)

Multiplication is about calculating the product of two or more numbers. To make this more concrete, it's like having multiple packs of crayons, each with the same number of crayons inside, and then wanting to know the total number of crayons:

```
packs = 4
crayons_per_pack = 12
total_crayons = packs * crayons_per_pack
```

And as you can probably figure out, `total_crayons` will be `48`. Floats can also be used for multiplication. Here's an example:

```
price_per_crayon = 0.25
total_price = total_crayons * price_per_crayon
```

The `total_price` value will be `48 * 0.25`, which equals `12.0`. What's important to note is that the total price will be a float. This is because one of the operands (that's what we call the numbers we use to do the calculation with) is a float. Python makes the result of such an operation a float, too.

Division (/)

Division is about sharing an amount into groups of equal size. It's like sharing your candy equally among friends.

Here's an example of sharing:

```
candies = 20
friends = 4
candies_per_friend = candies / friends
```

As you can probably figure out, `candies_per_friend` will be `5.0`. You might wonder: wait, why `5.0` and not `5`? Well, in Python, dividing two numbers gives you a float by default, also when both operands are `int` types, such as in this example.

We've now gone over the most basic mathematical operations. Let's see some slightly more complex ones next.

Exponentiation (**)

Exponentiation is raising something to the power of something else. That may sound difficult, but it's not too bad. We always have a base number and an exponent or power.

Here are some examples:

- 4^2 means 4 * 4. Here, 4 is the base number, and 2 is the exponent.
- 4^3 means 4 * 4 * 4. Here, 4 is the base number, and 3 is the exponent.

- 4^4 means 4 * 4 * 4 * 4. Here, 4 is the base number, and the other 4 is the exponent.
- 4^5 means 4 * 4 * 4 * 4 * 4. Here, 4 is the base number, and 5 is the exponent.

And so on.

In Python, we cannot use superscript (the number hovering right on top of the other number). Instead, we separate the base and the exponent with `**`. Here's how to use it to calculate the surface of our square:

```
side = 10
surface = side ** 2
```

The result of this will be `100`, because 10 * 10 is 100. And we could also do this with floating-point numbers, as in this example:

```
side = 0.6
surface = side ** 2
```

Here, the result will be `0.36`, since 0.6 * 0.6 is 0.36. And similarly, we can use it to calculate the volume as well:

```
side = 3
volume_cube = side ** 3
```

The `volume_cube` value will be `27`, because 3 * 3 * 3 is 27. You can clearly do a lot more complex calculations with the tools we currently have, but this is not a math book. If you understand how to use each, you're good to go when it comes to Python. Let's move on to a slightly less familiar one: the modulo.

Modulo (%)

Modulo gives you the remainder after division. I agree it also would make a great cat name. But in math terms, you can use it, for example, to see how many cookies are left after sharing them equally without breaking any:

```
cookies = 14
friends = 4
leftover_cookies = cookies % friends
```

The value of `leftover_cookies` will be `2`. Since we have four friends, they can each have three whole cookies. This makes the total cookies that we did distribute 12, and that means we have 2 left (14 - 12). With two cookies, we cannot give each friend a whole cookie, so that's why `2` is the remainder. In real life, Wiesje would eat the remaining cookies.

Modulo with floats is a bit trickier, but can be used to find remainders with decimal numbers:

```
distance = 10.5
step_length = 0.8
extra_distance = distance % step_length
```

Now, `extra_distance` will be (approximately) `0.1`. Why approximately? Well, that's a thing. If you run this code, you will get something like this:

```
0.09999999999999942
```

And that very well might not make sense to you because 13 * 0.8 = 10.4. And clearly, we have exactly 0.1 left. Right?

Well yes. But... all programming languages have this problem. It's not Python, it's how computer memory works. And the long story short is this: numbers are stored in binary format (that is 0s and 1s). This gives rounding issues. It's a little bit like how you can't exactly write 1/3 as 0.3333333. No matter how many 3s I'll add, I'll never match the precision of 1/3.

Let's move on to the next one, which is a special type of division, namely, integer division.

Integer division (//)

Integer division divides two numbers and rounds down to the nearest whole number; that's why the name is *integer division*. The result is an integer. It's like filling egg boxes completely and ignoring any leftovers. In that sense, it goes quite well with the modulo. The symbol for integer division is `//`. Here's an example of integer division:

```
eggs = 27
box_capacity = 6
full_boxes = eggs // box_capacity
```

If we have boxes of six eggs, that means we can have four full boxes. So the value will be `4`. And if we want to find out how many eggs we'll have left, we can do the following:

```
eggs_left = eggs % box_capacity
```

Almost done, let's have a look at a shorthand syntax!

Shorthand syntax for operations

We can use all these operators in a slightly different way:

```
total_distance = 0
distance_kitchen = 6
total_distance += distance_kitchen
distance_sunny_spot_upstairs = 20
total_distance += distance_sunny_spot_upstairs
print(total_distance)
```

You can see that we use `+=` here. So, instead of

```
total_distance = total_distance + distance_kitchen
```

We can write the following:

```
total_distance += distance_kitchen
```

Using `+=` is a shorter way of saying that you want to add it to the variable on the left-hand side, and we can do it for all the operators we just discussed. And that's all the basics of numbers that you need to know. Let's move on to the next major data type: text!

Working with text (strings)

Now that we've played with numbers, let's learn about the text type! In programming, text is known as **strings**. This is because text can be considered a string of characters. So, strings are just text – you know, words or sentences. And text is something that you can store, manipulate, and play around with in your code, just like how I love to play with strings in real life, especially when they're attached to feathers.

Strings (str)

So, long story short: strings are sequences of characters enclosed in quotes. You can use either single quotes (' ') or double quotes (" "). Python doesn't mind which one you choose, as long as they match.

Here are two examples:

```
greeting = "Hello humans!"
cat_thoughts = 'Cats are awesome'
```

And here's something you cannot do:

```
not_valid = "Different quotes'
```

If you need to use one type of quote inside your string, you ideally choose the opposite, for example:

```
string_with_double_quotes = 'He said: "How is it going?"'
string_with_single_quote = "How's it going?"
```

But what if you need both? Well, you can put the escape character in front of the quote that you want to be interpreted as a text character and not as the end of your string:

```
escape_char_example1 = "He said: \"How's it going?\""
escape_char_example2 = 'He said: "How\'s it going?"'
```

Can you guess what the escape character is? It is the backslash. Without the backslash in front of the double quote for `escape_char_example1`, Python would interpret that quote as the end of the string, making the rest of the line invalid code. The backslash signals to Python that this is a literal text character without special Python meaning.

Okay, one more question. What if I need a literal backslash in my string? Give it some thought.

Well, we'd escape the escape character. Here it is:

```
backslash = "\\"
```

We can print this value:

```
print(backslash)
```

This will print a single backslash. Without the double backslash (like this: "\"), our code would be invalid, because we'd be escaping the closing quote. So Python would see it as an unfinished string.

Another great use for escape characters is adding new lines inside your string. Just type \n where you want your line break. Alright, time to move on. We can do things with strings as well! Let's talk about it.

Concatenation

We can do some operations with strings as well. **Concatenation** is a fancy word for combining strings together. It's like putting two pieces of yarn end-to-end to make a longer one.

Here's how you do it:

```
first_name = "Wiesje"
last_name = "the Dachshund"
full_name = first_name + " " + last_name
```

And the value of full_name will be the following:

```
Wiesje the Dachshund
```

You can also add more strings, like this:

```
greeting = "Hi, " + full_name + "! How are you?"
```

Now, `greeting` will be the following:

```
Hi, Wiesje the Dachshund! How are you?
```

It's probably quite obvious that we cannot subtract strings. But Python has two funny things that you should know.

You cannot add a number to a string. In many other languages, this would be no problem. But this will give an error:

```
nr = 5
text = "ha"
print(text + nr)
```

There's a way to solve that: you can use a comma instead, and that places a space in between the two values. And we can cast the variable to a different type, something we'll learn about later. Something that you probably think should go wrong (at least what I thought that should go wrong when I first saw it) is multiplying text by a number, as here:

```
nr = 5
text = "ha"
print(text * nr)
```

Instead of giving an error, this will print the following:

```
Hahahahaha
```

Isn't that funny?

String methods

Strings come with special abilities called **methods**. Think of methods as tricks that Python taught strings, and you can now let your strings do it with the right word.

Well, Wiesje might not want to do tricks for me, but Python strings are always doing what I ask them to do. For example, you can make all letters uppercase or lowercase. Here's how:

```
shout = greeting.upper()
whisper = greeting.lower()
```

The value of shout is `"HI, WIESJE THE DACHSHUND! HOW ARE YOU?"`, and whisper is `"hi, wiesje the dachshund! how are you?"`.

Please note, none of this alters the original string. The `greeting` value is still `"Hi, Wiesje the Dachshund! How are you?"`.

Let's talk about another common method. With `len()`, we can find out how many characters are in your string. This is actually not a method on a string. It's a Python method that accepts a string (and a lot of other things that we don't know yet). You'll learn the difference later. For now, you can just remember how to do it:

```
first_name = "Wiesje"
length = len(first_name)
```

Wiesje has six letters. Therefore, the value of `length` will be `6`.

Alright, that's it! Let's move on to a not-so-nuanced type of variable: the booleans.

Boolean values

Booleans are like simple answers to closed questions: either yes or no. They're super helpful when we need our code to make decisions, such as whether it's time for a nap (spoiler: it's always time for a nap). So, whenever there should be more than two options, booleans are not the data type you're looking for.

Booleans represent the concept of truthiness in programming. In Python, they are `True` or `False` (make sure to capitalize the first letter).

Here are some facts about Wiesje right now:

```
is_hungry = True
is_sleepy = False
```

This is how to assign booleans directly. We will do cool things with them in the next chapter. For now, I want to talk about other ways we can get a boolean value.

Comparison operators

Booleans are often the result of comparisons or evaluations, and we do these with the use of comparison operators. Just like `+` and `-` are operators, these are operators too. The `+` and `-` operators result in a number (or string, in the case of concatenation), and the comparison operators result in a boolean.

Here's the Python equivalent of asking, "Are those two numbers the same value?":

```
nr1 = 6
nr2 = 6
same = nr1 == nr2
```

In this case, they're the same. We check whether two variables are the same with the double equal sign, `==`. It turns two values into a boolean: `False` if they are not the same, and `True` if they are the same. So, in this case, the value will be stored in the `same` variable. If they weren't the same, `False` would be stored, as in this example:

```
nr1 = 5
nr2 = 7
same = nr1 == nr2
```

We can also ask Python for the opposite, whether two variables are not the same, like this:

```
nr1 = 5
nr2 = 7
different = nr1 != nr2
```

The != operator will check whether they are not the same. So, here, the `different` variable will hold the `True` value, because `nr1` and `nr2` are not the same. If they were the same, it would hold `False` (because they are not, not the same). We can also see whether a variable is greater than or less than another variable. Here's how to do that:

```
hours_slept = 8
needed_sleep = 12
needs_more_sleep = hours_slept < needed_sleep
```

The `needs_more_sleep` variable will be set to `True`, because `hours_slept` is less than `needed_sleep`.

Here's another example using the greater than operator:

```
temperature = 25
is_hot = temperature > 30
```

We can also check whether something is greater than or equal to, or smaller than or equal to. That is done with `>=` and `<=`, respectively:

```
not_cold = temperature >= 20
not_hot = temperature <= 25
```

We can combine two of these comparison operators with the keyword `and`. In order for that to evaluate to `True`, both of them would have to be true. Here's an example:

```
is_comfortable = temperature >= 20 and temperature <= 25
```

We can also use the `or` operator; in that case, one of them has to be true for the whole thing to be true:

```
is_uncomfortable = temperature <= 20 or temperature >= 25
```

And here's another example, with strings:

```
favorite_food = "tuna"
is_favorite = favorite_food == "tuna"
```

And that's it. No more comments about the type, but I do have a comment about comments in code.

Comments in code

Sometimes, we need to leave ourselves little notes in the code. Maybe to remind us what a piece of code does, or to leave a message for someone else who might read it. In Python, anything after a # symbol is a comment. Python ignores it when running the code. This is just made for the programmers. Here's an example of code with a comment:

```
# This is a comment
# Let's calculate the area of a circle
radius = 5
area = 3.14 * radius ** 2
```

Comments are super helpful for explaining complex code or reminding yourself what you were thinking when you wrote it.

Here's an example combining some of the concepts we've just gone over:

```
# Determine if we have enough treats
treats = 5
cats = 2

# Each cat needs at least 3 treats
enough_treats = treats >= cats * 3  # Evaluates to False

# Comment explaining the calculation
# If enough_treats is True, we have sufficient treats
```

Quiz

1. Which of the following is a valid variable name in Python?

    a. `%dogs_at_home`

    b. `_dogs_at_home`

    c. `#dogs_at_home`

    d. `2_dogs_at_home`

2. True or false? In Python, after you've assigned an integer value to a variable, you can't reassign it to a string.
3. How do you write comments in Python?
4. What is the most conventional way to name variables in Python?
5. Which of the following is a correct example of a variable assignment?

    a. `imke_is_cool = True`

    b. `imke_is_cool == True`

    c. `imke_is_cool != True`

    d. `imke_is_cool : True`

6. Given the following piece of code:

```
x = 5
y = 6
z = x == y
print(z)
```

    Without copying this snippet to VS Code, what do you think will be the output?

    a. `6`

    b. Syntax error

    c. `5`

    d. `False`

7. Debugging is the art of finding and fixing mistakes in code. Wiesje's human has just turned 28, and we want to find out how old she now is in dog years. Wiesje has written the following piece of code, but it's not doing the right thing. Can you see why?

```
name = "Imke"
age = "28"
age_in_dog_years = age * 7
print(name, "is", age_in_dog_years, "years old in dog years")
```

8. What is meant by a hardcoded value?

Exercises

2.1 Creating variables

Create variables using snake case for the following personal information:

- Your name
- Whether you're a cat person
- The number of cookies you've eaten today

Assign values of appropriate data types and print each variable.

2.2 Escape characters in action

You are given the following joke:

Why did Wiesje sit in the shade?

Because she didn't want to be a "hot dog"!

It's so good, it needs to be stored in a variable. Make sure the formatting matches the original when the variable is printed.

2.3 How long will Wiesje's food supply last?

Wiesje is worried about running out of food. There's a bag with 1,500 grams of dry kibble in her cupboard, and she claims she eats 65 grams per day. Write a program that calculates how long Wiesje's current food supply will last. Be sure to use variables, so Wiesje can adjust her actual food intake privately.

Steps:

1. Create variables for Wiesje's food intake per day and the amount of food in her cupboard.
2. Calculate how many full days her food will last, and store the result in a variable. Think about which math operator would be best in this case.
3. Print the result, telling Wiesje how many days her food supply will last.

2.4 Adventure time for Wiesje

As a cat, I'm more of a homebody, but Wiesje loves her adventures. Her humans decided to take her to the woods on every fifth day of the month. However, Wiesje has trouble keeping track of the days. Your task is to help her by writing code that determines whether it's time for an adventure.

Steps:

1. Create a variable to represent the current day of the month (choose any integer between 1 and 31).
2. Use the modulo operator (`%`) to check whether the current day is divisible by 5. If it is, today is an adventure day!
3. Create a boolean variable called `adventure_day` and store the result of whether the current day is divisible by 5. Hint: Use a comparison operator to check whether the result of the modulo is `0`.
4. Print the result in the following format: `"Adventure day? True."` or `"Adventure day? False."`

2.5 Manipulating strings

Create a variable and assign it a string of a fun fact about yourself. I'll go first:

```
fun_fact = "I love cat milk"
```

Now, let's play around with this string!

1. Use Python to find out how many characters are in your fun fact. Print the result.
2. Create another variable that holds your fun fact in all lowercase.
3. Alter the original variable and convert it to all uppercase letters.

Summary

In this chapter, we introduced variables. We learned that variables are like containers: they have labels and hold values, which help keep our code flexible. We learned about naming variables, how they must start with a letter or underscore, and that variable names are case-sensitive. We discussed best practices, such as using descriptive names and the Python convention of using `snake_case` for variable names. Of course, we also learned how to assign a value to a variable using the = sign, as in this example:

```
favorite_toy = "ball"
```

Next, we looked at how different types of data can be assigned to variables: number values (integers and floats), strings, and floats. However, we know these are just some basic data types, and that Python allows many more types.

We also learned that Python is dynamically typed, meaning it doesn't care whether you change the type of a variable when you reassign it to a new value.

With these fundamentals in place, we got to see how number values can be used to perform various operations:

- Addition (+)
- Subtraction (-)
- Multiplication (*)
- Division (/)

- Exponentiation (`**`)
- Modulo (`%`)
- Integer division (`//`)

We practiced storing the results of these operations in variables and even saw how floating-point numbers can cause small rounding errors due to how they're stored in memory.

After we did some basic math, we got to play around with strings! We learned that strings can be enclosed in both single and double quotes. And we dealt with quotes and new lines within these strings using the escape character, \. We saw how we can concatenate strings by simply using the + sign and learned that while we can't add a string to a number, we can multiply a string by a number! Wasn't that fun?

But that's not all we did with strings. We also learned about some string methods, which are special tricks that Python has taught strings. For example, we learned how to convert a string to all caps and made the computer "shout" at Wiesje. I had a blast with this part; I hope you did too!

Then, there was another data type: booleans. A boolean can only have two possible values, `True` or `False`, as in this example:

```
nap_time = True
```

We learned that we can assign boolean values directly, but we also saw more practical examples where we used comparison operators to check whether a value should evaluate to `True` or `False`.

We learned how to use these comparison operators:

- `==` to check whether two values are equal
- `!=` to check whether they are not equal
- `<` and `>` for less than and greater than
- `<=` and `>=` for less than or equal to, and greater than or equal to

With these operators, we started to do some cool things that bring us closer to writing a real app.

Finally, we learned that Python understands that everything after a # symbol is a comment. Comments are like little notes that programmers leave to remind themselves or others about what a piece of code does. As we get to write more complex code in the next chapter, these comments will become even more helpful!

Get this book's PDF version and more

Scan the QR code (or go to `packtpub.com/unlock`). Search for this book by name, confirm the edition, and then follow the steps on the page.

UNLOCK NOW

***Note**: Keep your invoice handy. Purchases made directly from Packt don't require an invoice.*

3

Working with Conditional Statements

We have just learned about variables and data types. So far, these building blocks have the same value throughout our code. But that's a bit boring! How cool would it be if we could have different paths through our code? Well, great news. We have that option!

There are a few types of conditional statements. They allow our programs to make decisions and take different paths based on certain conditions.

So, let's start by talking about the most common conditional statements: `if`, `else`, and `elif`. These are the Python equivalent of making choices!

The if statement

An `if` statement lets your program decide whether to execute a block of code based on a condition. Imagine you're deciding whether you want to chase a laser pointer or take a nap. You probably weigh factors such as how sleepy you are, whether the sun is shining on your favorite spot, or whether the laser pointer is even on. In programming, we use conditional statements to make such decisions. This is what an `if` statement looks like:

```
if condition:
    # Code to execute if condition is True
```

The condition is a statement that evaluates to `True` or `False`. If it evaluates to `True`, it executes the block that comes after. How can we recognize the block? Well, this is where indentation comes in. The block can be recognized by being the same level of indentation. In Python, the code inside the `if` block must be indented. Usually, we use four or two spaces.

Let's see an actual example. Let's say we want to check whether it's time for dinner:

```
hour = 18  # It's 6 PM

if hour == 18:
    print("Time for dinner!")
```

Here, we are checking whether the variable hour is equal to 18. If that is the case, we will see the print executed. In this case, the hour is equal to 18. The condition evaluates to True, and the code inside the if block runs.

So, the output will be the following:

```
Time for dinner!
```

In the previous chapter, we saw the comparison operators. They are commonly used to form conditions. Let's see a bunch of examples to get a good understanding of them.

Comparison operators

In the previous example with the hour, we've already seen a statement that checks whether two values are equal. Here's another one:

```
a = 5
b = 5

if a == b:
    print("a and b are equal")
```

The values of a and b are both 5. That's why this will output the following:

```
a and b are equal
```

We can also check whether two values are not equal, like this:

```
a = 5
b = 3

if a != b:
    print("a and b are not equal")
```

Now, a is 5 and b is 3, which means they're not equal. And the condition will again evaluate to True. This is the output:

```
a and b are not equal
```

You might wonder what this snippet does. Can you guess?

```
a = 5
b = 3

if a == b:
    print("a and b are equal")
```

This will print nothing. Why? Well, `a` and `b` are not equal, so the condition is `False`, and the code block associated with `if` is not executed. So, nothing is printed.

We can also check whether the left value is less than the right value. This is done with the less-than operator. Here's an example:

```
# Weight in kilo
zia_weight = 2.2
wiesje_weight = 2.5

if zia_weight < wiesje_weight:
    print("Wiesje is heavier than Zia.")
```

And since I'm lighter than Wiesje, this will output the following:

```
Wiesje is heavier than Zia.
```

We have a few more examples, one for every comparison operator. The greater-than comparison operator checks whether the left value is greater than the right value:

```
zia_age = 0.8
wiesje_age = 7

if wiesje_age > zia_age:
    print("Wiesje is older than Zia.")
```

And 7 is greater than 0.8, so this will output the following:

```
Wiesje is older than Zia.
```

Similarly, we can also use the greater than or equal to operator. This operator checks whether the left value is greater than or equal to the right value:

```
nap_hours = 5

if nap_hours >= 5:
    print("Had enough sleep")
```

For the "regular" greater than operator, `nap_hours > 5` would have been `False`, because 5 is not greater than 5. For the greater than or equal to operator, it's also `True` when the left value is equal to the right value. And that's why it prints the following:

```
Had enough sleep
```

And, of course, we can also check for less than or equal to. This checks whether the left value is less than or equal to the right value. Let's look at this practical example:

```
fish_in_bowl = 1

if fish_in_bowl <= 1:
    print("There's room for more fish")
```

And since 1 is equal to 1, this outputs the following:

```
There's room for more fish
```

The else atatement

There is more we can do with the `if` conditional statement. Let's look at this example again:

```
zia_age = 0.8
wiesje_age = 7

if wiesje_age > zia_age:
    print("Wiesje is older than Zia.")
```

If I wanted to print `"Zia is older than Wiesje"` in the other scenario, I would have to add a second `if` statement with our current toolbox, like this:

```
zia_age = 0.8
wiesje_age = 7
```

```
if wiesje_age > zia_age:
    print("Wiesje is older than Zia.")
if wiesje_age < zia_age:
    print("Zia is older than Wiesje.")
```

That's a bit inefficient. Even if the first statement is `True`, it will still check the second. When we want to specify what should happen when the `if` condition is not met, we can provide an alternative. That's where the `else` statement comes in.

And here's what it looks like:

```
if condition:
    # Code if condition is True
else:
    # Code if condition is False
```

As you can see, `if` and `else` are both followed by an indented block of code. The `if` statement is followed by a condition, but the `else` statement is not. This is because the `else` block is for all other cases than `if`. Let's check whether it's time for a snack:

```
is_hungry = False

if is_hungry:
    print("Time to eat!")
else:
    print("Maybe later.")
```

You can see here that we use a boolean to check whether we should execute the `if` block. That's also something we can do: directly insert a boolean as a condition. If the value of the boolean is `True`, we'll execute the `if` block; otherwise, we execute the `else` block. In this case, it will print the following:

```
Maybe later.
```

But sometimes, you want to have multiple options, not only one for `if` and one for `else`. That's possible, too. This is done with the `elif` statement.

The elif statement

So, what if we have more than two choices? We are using `elif`, which stands for "else if."

Here's what that syntax looks like:

```
if condition1:
    # Code if condition1 is True
elif condition2:
    # Code if condition2 is True
else:
    # Code if none of the above conditions are True
```

So, let's have Python decide what activity to do based on the weather. Here's the code for it:

```
weather = "rainy"

if weather == "sunny":
    print("Let's go sunbathing!")
elif weather == "rainy":
    print("Better stay inside and nap.")
else:
    print("Let's watch the birds from the window.")
```

This checks the condition of the `if` statement first. That's not `True`. The execution of the code then moves on to the `elif` statement, which is `True`! Python then runs the block that's associated with the following:

```
Better stay inside and nap.
```

The `else` statement is completely skipped, because a match was already found. Much like me, Python is a little lazy and does as little as possible. What do I mean? Well, let's look at this piece of code:

```
weather = "sunny"

if weather == "sunny":
    print("Let's go sunbathing!")
elif weather == "rainy":
    print("Better stay inside and nap.")
else:
    print("Let's watch the birds from the window.")
```

The code will check whether the weather is equal to `"sunny"`. It is. It then runs the code block associated with `if` (in this case, that's printing `"Let's go sunbathing!"`), and it doesn't even look at the `elif` or `else` statements. So, it's possible that the `elif` condition is also `True`, but won't be evaluated because the condition above it was already `True` and executed.

Sometimes, situations can have more options and are a bit more complicated. We can also have multiple `elif` clauses. Let's expand the previous example a little:

```
weather = "cloudy"

if weather == "sunny":
    print("Let's go sunbathing!")
elif weather == "rainy":
    print("Better stay inside and nap.")
```

```
elif weather == "cloudy":
    print("Let's go out for a little and then take a nap.")
else:
    print("Let's watch the birds from the window.")
```

This will output `"Let's go out for a little and then take a nap."`

With `if` statements in your toolbox, you can do a lot more interesting things with your code. The conditions that we want to be checking for can get quite complicated, and you might feel the need to start nesting `if` statements. I'm not a fan, but I'll show you how to do it. Keep reading, because right after that, I'll show you a nicer way to achieve the same.

Nested if statements

You can place an `if` statement inside another `if` or `else` block. For example, let's look at this real case scenario. Let's decide whether to chase a toy:

```
is_awake = True
has_toy = False

if is_awake:
    if has_toy:
        print("Let's play with the toy!")
    else:
        print("Time to find a toy!")
else:
    print("Sleeping... Dreaming of finally catching the red dot.")
```

Can you guess what this code will output? It will print the following:

```
Time to find a toy!
```

And here is why it prints that. The value of `is_awake` is `True`, so we enter the first `if` block. Then, inside that block, we check `has_toy` in the next `if` statement, which is `False`. The `else` statement inside the first `if` runs. And what about the outer `else`? Well, remember, the first `if` was `True`, so that one isn't executed.

This could go many levels deeper, but I'd argue that's a bad thing to do. Writing it might not be too bad, but if we need to go in later and make changes... Reading it will be quite time-consuming, and it will be hard to understand what does what.

So, just to be clear, nesting is not a bad thing per se. Unclear and hard-to-read code is the bad thing here. If you need many layers, you might want to refactor it. And you can! There are multiple ways to do it, and you'd eventually need some building blocks that we haven't seen yet, such as functions and more complex data structures. But logical operators can help as well for simple cases. Let's have a look at a way to flatten our code with logical operators.

Logical operators

We can use logical operators to combine multiple booleans into one boolean value. That might sound more complicated than it is. We'll start with a non-code example. Let's consider Wiesje and the following question: Is Wiesje a blue dachshund? To answer that question, we have two sub-questions:

- Is Wiesje a dachshund?
- Is Wiesje blue?

In order for Wiesje to be a blue dachshund, both of the questions need to be answered with yes (`True`). The first one is yes. Wiesje is a dachshund. The second one, though this book is grayscale and you cannot tell, is no. She is brown. So the answer to the question of whether Wiesje is a blue dachshund is no. This is because one of the properties (blue) is not true.

Logical and operator

Okay, let's move to code and meet the `and` operator:

```
is_dachshund = True
is_blue = False
is_blue_dachshund = is_dachshund and is_blue
```

This last line is evaluating `is_dachshund` and `is_blue`. If both sides of `and` are `True`, it evaluates to `True`. If one or both of them are `False`, it evaluates to `False`. In this case, it evaluates to `False` because `is_blue` is `False`. So, the value of `is_blue_dachshund` is `False`.

And here's another example. Let's say we will go outside if it's sunny and our human is home to open the door:

```
is_sunny = True
is_human_home = True
going_outside = is_sunny and is_human_home
```

The value of `going_outside` will be `True`, because both `is_sunny` and `is_human_home` are `True`. Let's say my human is out buying me treats. Here's how the snippet changes:

```
is_sunny = True
is_human_home = False
going_outside = is_sunny and is_human_home
```

What will be the value of `going_outside` now? It will be `False`, because it's `True` if both `is_sunny` and `is_human_home` are `True`. Since one is not, the combined boolean is `False`.

You can maybe feel it coming, but since the `if` statement requires a boolean value, we can use this operator together with `if` statements as well, like this:

```
is_sunny = True
is_human_home = True
if is_sunny and is_human_home:
    print("Perfect moment for a long nap in the sun!")
```

So, what will this code snippet do? It will print "Perfect moment for a long nap in the sun!" because both is_sunny and is_human_home are True. If one of them were False, it wouldn't output anything. Some situations don't just require action if both sides are True, but already if at least one of them is True. This is where the or operator comes in.

Logical or operator

When at least one condition must be True, we'll use the or operator. Let's start with non-code again.

Let's say we are asking ourselves the question: Is Wiesje blue or a dachshund?

In order for the answer to be yes, she needs to be either blue or a dachshund. So, we are asking ourselves the same sub-questions:

- Is Wiesje a dachshund?
- Is Wiesje blue?

But this time, only one of them needs to be true for the answer to be yes. I agree this is less intuitive, because you might want to answer the question with the one that she is (she is a dachshund).

But technically, if I ask you: *"Is Wiesje a dog or a cat?"*, the answer should be yes.

Also, people will know you're a programmer right away. The non-programmer answer would probably be "*Wiesje is a dog.*"

Let's make this clearer by not doing it with a question. Let's say you go to the doctor, and they say you should call if you get a fever or a headache. In that case, it's more intuitive that only one of the conditions would have to be true, and then you should already call. Here's a code example:

```
is_bored = False
has_toy = True

if is_bored or has_toy:
    print("Time to play!")
```

This code will output the following:

```
Time to play!
```

Even though one of the elements (`is_bored`) is `False`, the overall statement evaluates to `True`, because only one has to be `True`. Since `has_toy` is `True`, the condition `is_bored or has_toy` is `True`; therefore, it will print the output.

If both were `True`, it would also evaluate to `True`. If both were `False`, it would evaluate to `False`. We also have a way of flipping the values around, I kid you not.

The not operator

We can use the `not` operator to invert the boolean value. It's just like normal language. *It is sunny* means that it's sunny. If you put *not* in front of sunny, we will know that it is, well, not sunny. Python can do this, too:

```
is_raining = False

if not is_raining:
    print("Let's go outside!")
```

This will output the following:

```
Let's go outside!
```

So, here's what is happening. The `'not'` in `not is_raining` inverts `False` to `True`. So, the condition is `True`, and therefore the code inside the `if` block runs. That's it for the `if` statement for now. Let's see another relatively new way of making decisions in Python.

The match statement

Many languages have a `switch` statement. This is an alternative to lengthy `if-else` chains. What do I mean by a lengthy `if-else` chain? Well, here is an example:

```
pet_type = "axolotl"

if pet_type == "cat":
    print("A cat goes meow!")
elif pet_type == "dog":
    print("A dog goes woof!")
elif pet_type == "parrot":
    print("A parrot says 'Polly wants a cracker!'")
elif pet_type == "hamster":
    print("A hamster squeaks and loves to run on a wheel.")
elif pet_type == "snake":
    print("A snake goes hiss!")
elif pet_type == "lizard":
    print("A lizard may hiss softly or stay silent.")
elif pet_type == "tarantula":
    print("A tarantula doesn't vocalize, it's scary enough as is.")
else:
    print("I'm not sure what sound this pet makes!")
```

Quite lengthy, huh? This is considered not very pretty. And that's where the new conditional statement comes in. Some languages call this `switch`; in Python, we have something similar, the `match` statement. Here's how to rewrite the previous code with the `match` statement:

```
pet_type = "axolotl"

match pet_type:
    case "cat":
        print("A cat goes meow!")
    case "dog":
        print("A dog goes woof!")
    case "parrot":
        print("A parrot says 'Polly wants a cracker!'")
    case "hamster":
        print("A hamster squeaks and loves to run on a wheel.")
    case "snake":
        print("A snake goes hiss!")
    case "lizard":
        print("A lizard may hiss softly or stay silent.")
    case "tarantula":
        print("A tarantula doesn't vocalize, it's scary enough as is.")
    case _:
        print("I'm not sure what sound this pet makes!")
```

Please note, if you have a slightly older Python 3, this will not work. The `match` statement is part of Python since version 3.10.

So, let's have a look at the syntax. Here's what it roughly looks like:

```
match variable:
    case value1:
        # Code if variable == value1
    case value2:
        # Code if variable == value2
    case _:
        # Code if none of the above match, default case
```

We start with the word `match`, and after that, we have a variable. We then compare this variable to all the values after the cases. When it's equal, it will execute the code block associated with that case. If it matches none, it goes to the default case. This is the case with the underscore. It's comparable to the `else` block.

Here's another example that should be going on in Wiesje's head. As a good dog, she decides what to do based on the command:

```
command = "sit"

match command:
    case "sit":
        print("Wiesje sits down.")
    case "stay":
        print("Wiesje stays put.")
    case "fetch":
        print("Wiesje fetches the ball.")
    case _:
        print("Wiesje tilts her head in confusion.")
```

This code outputs the following:

```
Wiesje sits down.
```

And here's how that works. First, the value of `command` is `"sit"`. So, `case "sit":` matches, so `"Wiesje sits down."` is printed. After that, Python doesn't evaluate the rest of the code.

There's one more thing I'll tell you about the `match` statement for now, and that is that you can specify multiple values for the same case. This is done with the pipe symbol (|), which pretty much means *or*:

```
pet_type = "puppy"
match pet_type:
    case "cat" | "kitten":
        print("A cat goes meow!")
    case "dog" | "puppy":
        print("A dog goes woof!")
```

In this case (pun intended), the code will print `"A dog goes woof!"`. This is because for `puppy` and for `dog`, that case will be triggered.

You will have to be able to read the `match` statement, because colleagues might use it in their code. If you really don't like it, you don't have to use it. You can do everything you can with the `match` statement with the `if` statement as well. Another alternative for the `if` statement, in some cases, is the ternary operator. Let's discuss that one next.

The ternary operator

The ternary operator allows you to write basic `if...else` statements in one line. It might be a bit difficult to read at first. Here's what the syntax looks like:

```
value_if_true if condition else value_if_false
```

So, let's say we decide what to do based on the time:

```
hour = 14  # 2 PM

activity = "Nap time" if hour < 17 else "Play time"

print(activity)
```

Can you guess what this outputs? It prints the following:

```
Nap time
```

Don't worry if you find it difficult. Let me explain. Since `hour < 17` is `True`, `activity` is set to `"Nap time"` because that's the first value. It reads like this:

It is `"Nap time"` if the `hour` variable is smaller than 17, else it is `"Play time"`.

Again, you don't need to write the code like this yourself. At some point in time, you might be more ready for it and write code like this. You'll have to be able to read it, though, since you might encounter this in code.

Common mistakes and how to avoid them

Before you get to do the exercises, let me warn you about some common mistakes. Don't worry if you still make them; let's just hope you'll identify them earlier.

Using = instead of ==

It is so easy to mess up `=` and `==`. Just remember, `=` is for assignment, and `==` is for comparison:

```
a = 5

if a == 5:
    print("a is 5")
```

If you write `if a = 5:`, Python will throw a syntax error, and your code will not complete successfully.

Incorrect indentation

Another common mistake is not having the right level of indentation. Python relies on indentation to define code blocks. Let's say you try something like this:

```
if a == 5:
print("a is 5")
# This will cause an IndentationError
```

This will cause an indentation error. It expects a code block associated with `if`, but since there is no indented block, there is no code block. Hence the indentation error.

Fixing it is easy, just add some space:

```
if a == 5:
    print("a is 5")
```

And now your code can run again.

Forgetting the colon

The last one we'll talk about is the colon, or more specifically, forgetting the colon. Every `if`, `elif`, `else`, `match`, and `case` statement needs a colon at the end.

So, let's say you do this:

```
if a == 5
    print("a is 5")
```

You'll get a syntax error because there is no colon at the end of the line with `if`. The fix is just adding the colon:

```
if a == 5:
    print("a is 5")
```

Quiz

1. What is the correct syntax for an `if` statement in Python?

    a. `if (x == 42){`

    b. `if x == 42 then:`

    c. `if x = 42:`

    d. `if x == 42:`

2. True or false? An `else` block is mandatory in an `if` statement.
3. What is true about the condition inside the `if` statement?

    a. It is evaluated to a boolean value

    b. It needs to evaluate to `True` to prevent errors

    c. It can only be `0` or `1`

    d. The condition in an `if` statement is optional

4. How do you specify multiple values for the same case in a `match` statement?

    a. With the logical `and` operator

    b. With the logical `or` operator

    c. With the pipe symbol (|)

    d. By putting multiple cases on top of each other before the indented block

5. Assuming all programmers think like computers, how would thirsty programmers respond if you asked them whether they'd like coffee or tea?

    a. Syntax error

    b. Coffee

    c. Tea

    d. Yes

6. Given this piece of code:

```
temperature = 25
outfit = "T-shirt" if temperature > 20 else "Sweater"
```

What value will be stored in `outfit`?

   a. `"T-shirt"`
   b. `None`
   c. `"Sweater"`
   d. `25`

7. True or false? The `match` statement only works if you have Python 3.10 or higher.
8. What does the `not` operator do?
9. What is the primary purpose of ternary operators?

   a. They resolve `if/else` statements faster
   b. They allow us to write simple `if/else` statements in a single line
   c. They check for more than one condition
   d. They are a more readable solution for lengthy `if/else` statements

10. Will the code inside the `if` statement run? Yes/No:

```
x = 10

if not x != 10:
    print("Well, this was confusing")
```

Exercises

3.1 Even or odd?

Let's write a program to check whether a number is even or odd.

Steps:

1. Store a number in a variable.
2. Use `if` statements to check whether the number is even or odd (hint: an even number is divisible by 2 without a remainder) and print the result. Run your code a few times, changing the value of the number to check whether it works correctly.

Bonus challenge: Rewrite your `if` statement as a ternary operator.

3.2 Dachshund weight classification

Did you know dachshunds come in three sizes: standard, miniature, and kaninchen (which is German for "rabbit")? Here's what you need to know:

- Standard dachshunds typically weigh 16–32 lbs
- Miniature dachshunds typically weigh 12–16 lbs
- Kaninchen dachshunds typically weigh less than 12 lbs

Wiesje weighs 2.5 kilograms. She wants to find out what kind of dachshund she is. That's why, in this exercise, you'll be writing a program that classifies a dachshund's size based on its weight.

Steps:

1. Store the dachshund's name in a variable.
2. Store the dachshund's weight in kilograms in a variable.
3. Convert weight in kgs to weight in lbs (1 kg is approximately 2.2 lbs).
4. Use `if` statements to classify the dachshund's size.
5. Print the result in the following format:

   "With a weight of [weight in kilograms] kgs, [weight in pounds] lbs, dachshund [name] is classified as: [Standard/Miniature/Kaninchen]"

3.3 Password checker

Ask the user to enter a password and check whether it matches the stored password. We haven't looked at how to get and process user input yet. So don't worry, we'll just hardcode an extra variable and pretend it's user input!

```
stored_password = "whiskers123"
input_password = "whiskers123"
# Assume this is user input
# Your code here
```

Bonus challenge: add a username and check whether both the username and password are correct!

3.4 Grading system

Let's write a program that converts a percentile score (0–100%) to a letter grade (F–A).

Things you should know:

- A score between 90 and 100% is an A
- A score between 80 and 89% is a B
- A score between 70 and 79% is a C
- A score between 60 and 69% is a D
- A score lower than 60% is an F

Steps:

1. Create a variable for the score (a number between 0 and 100).
2. Use `if-elif-else` to determine the grade.
3. Let your program announce the grade by printing something like: `"Your grade is: B"`

3.5 Fun activities for humans per weekday

You know how humans can be. Always working, and when they finally do have free time, they do not know how to spend it well. To be honest, I think they could just nap more, but apparently, humans thrive when they're a bit more active. That's why, in this exercise, you'll create a program that matches each day of the week to a fun activity.

Steps:

1. Create a variable that holds the "input" day of the week.
2. Think of seven fun activities for humans in their free time, one for each day of the week.
3. Use a `match` statement to link each day of the week to one of your recommended activities and add a backup plan in case someone enters a non-existent or misspelled weekday.
4. Print the result, for example, `"On [weekday], you should: [activity]."`

Summary

In this chapter, we learned how to work with conditional statements, which are ways to let Python make decisions based on specified conditions.

A condition is a statement that evaluates to a boolean value: either `True` or `False`. We also learned about the correct syntax for conditional statements and that the code block must be indented correctly for it to work. The comparison operators we studied in the previous chapter came in handy when we played around with different conditional statements. To specify what should happen if an `if` condition is not met, we practiced using the `else` statement:

```
bites = True
is_cute = True

if not bites and is_cute:
    print("You want to pet that dog")
else:
    print("Do not pet that dog")
```

For scenarios with more than two possibilities, we discovered the `elif` statements and the `match` statement, which help simplify lengthy `if-else` chains.

Let's not forget about the logical operators. We used the following:

- The `and` operator, to check whether two conditions were both true
- The `or` operator, to check whether at least one of two conditions was true
- The `not` operator, for when the boolean value needs to be inverted

True, it can be *not not* confusing, but I'm sure you'll get the hang of it with practice.

After that, we saw what a ternary statement looks like. It's just a concise way to write simple `if-else` conditions in one line. They might seem tricky at first, but you'll soon see how they save a lot of space in your code when you need to make a lot of simple `if-else` decisions.

All clear?

```
all_clear = True
message = "Next chapter!" if all_clear else "More revision needed."
print(message)
```

4

Using Lists, Tuples, and Dictionaries

In the previous chapters, we learned how to store individual pieces of data using variables and how we can use variables to make decisions. But imagine trying to keep track of every single treat, toy, or bird you've ever seen using separate variables. It would be like having a separate bowl for each piece of kibble. Yes, I agree, that's not very efficient!

Luckily, Python offers us tools to handle collections of data. These are lists, dictionaries, and tuples. We call those data types as well, but they are special kinds of data types called collections. They are like containers where you can store multiple values, each with its own special abilities and characteristics. Think of them as different types of boxes, each suited for a particular kind of content.

For example, storing the kibble in the basket that we use to store all my toys is not great for the kibble. And storing all the toys in the container for the kibble won't allow me to take them out myself—again, not great. Each box and data structure serves a purpose.

In this chapter, we'll explore these data structures in detail. We'll learn how to create them, manipulate them, and decide when to use each one. So, grab your favorite snack (or toy), and let's talk about collections!

Lists

The first type of collection we'll discuss is lists. A list is probably the most straightforward data type. It's an ordered collection of items that can be changed. It's like having a basket where you can toss in your toys, snacks, or anything else you fancy. The items in a list can be of different types. You may wonder what types can be on the list? Well, any type! They could, for example, be numbers, strings, or even other lists! Let's see how to make them.

Creating lists

We create a list in a similar way to creating another variable. We specify a name followed by an equal sign and then the value. The value is the part where it's a little different. To create an empty list, you simply use square brackets [] without any items inside.

```
# An empty list
my_first_list = []
```

This creates a list called `my_first_list` that currently holds no items. Soon I'll tell you how to add items, but let's first see how we can create a list with items from the start.

List with items

Creating a list with items is not rocket science either. You can create a list with items by placing them inside square brackets, separated by commas.

```
# A list of cat toys
cat_toys = ["feather", "ball", "laser pointer", "scratching post"]
```

Let's go over what is happening here. We define a `cat_toys` variable, and in it we store a list. The square brackets [] define the list. Inside the list, there are items. These items are separated by commas (,). There are four items on this list. The items are enclosed in quotes `" "` because they are strings.

Accessing list items

So great, we've created a list. It would be even cooler if we could get the values out of the list. The great news is, we can! Lists are ordered. This means each item has a number associated with it. This number is called the index. When we assign list elements such as index, we start counting from 0. So the index of the first element in the list is 0, the index of the second element in the list is 1, and so on. You can access items using their index. Python is a bit special; it allows both a positive and a negative index. Let's start with the first one, the positive index.

Accessing by positive index

As mentioned, the first element in the list is the element at index 0. To get an element out of a list, we use the name of the list followed by square brackets with the index in it, like so:

```
cat_toys = ["feather", "ball", "laser pointer", "scratching post"]
first_toy = cat_toys[0]
print("First toy:", first_toy)
```

This will output the following:

```
First toy: feather
```

The variable name is `cat_toys`. With `[0]` after it, we access the item at index 0, which is `"feather"`. Next, we store it in `first_toy` and print it. We could also have printed it directly without first storing it, like this:

```
cat_toys = ["feather", "ball", "laser pointer", "scratching post"]
print("First toy:", cat_toys[0])
```

This is how to access elements by their positive index. Here's how to print all the elements:

```
cat_toys = ["feather", "ball", "laser pointer", "scratching post"]
print("First toy:", cat_toys[0])
print("Second toy:", cat_toys[1])
print("Third toy:", cat_toys[2])
print("Fourth toy:", cat_toys[3])
```

If we try to print an element that doesn't exist, we get an error. So, we can not access elements with an index that is higher than the length of the list minus one. The minus one is to correct for the first index being 0. In this case, the length of our list is 4. So, the maximum index is 3.

We can also do something slightly more complex: access the elements by their negative index.

Accessing by negative index

This might sound crazier than it is. When we use negative indices, we are simply accessing items starting from the end of the list. So when we say -1, we just mean the index of the last element. -2? The index of the second-to-last element, and so on. Here's an overview for the following list:

```
cat_toys = ["feather", "ball", "laser pointer", "scratching post"]
```

Element	Positive index	Negative index
feather	0	-4
ball	1	-3
laser pointer	2	-2
scratching post	3	-1

So, if we want to get the last toy, we just put -1 as the index, like this:

```
cat_toys = ["feather", "ball", "laser pointer", "scratching post"]
last_toy = cat_toys[-1]
print("Last toy:", last_toy)
```

This will output the following:

```
Last toy: scratching post
```

With `cat_toys[-1]`, we access the last item in the list. As you can see in the preceding table, the negative indices count backward. So, -1 is the last item, -2 is the second last, and so on. If we go to -5, we get an error because that element is not in the list. So far, we've created lists and accessed the elements, but we can also change lists after creating them. That's exactly what's next on our list!

Modifying lists

We can change lists. The programming way of putting that is saying that lists are **mutable**. It means that you can change them after creation. We can add items, remove items, and even change existing items in a list. Let's first see how to add.

Adding items

To add items to a list, lists have built-in methods. Remember what methods are? Those are the tricks that Python taught a certain type. We have also seen methods for strings. Just like strings can have methods, lists can have methods too. We can use these methods to let our lists do special things with the right word.

The `append()` method adds an item to the end of a list. We simply pass the element that we want to add to the list between the parentheses `()`, and that's it.

```
cat_toys = ["feather", "ball", "laser pointer", "scratching post"]
cat_toys.append("cardboard box")
print("Updated toys:", cat_toys)
```

This will output the following:

```
Updated toys: ['feather', 'ball', 'laser pointer', 'scratching post',
'cardboard box']
```

The `cat_toys.append("cardboard box")` adds `"cardboard box"` to the end of the list. Then we print the updated list, and you can see it has been added.

Another method to add elements is the insert method. While `append()` adds them to the end of the list, the `insert()` method adds an item at a specific index. This is why we need to put two things between the parentheses: the index that we want to insert it at and the element that we want to insert.

It won't remove the current element at that position; instead, it shifts all the elements one position to the right. Here's an example:

```
cat_toys.insert(1, "mouse toy")
print("After inserting at index 1:", cat_toys)
```

This will output the following:

```
After inserting at index 1: ['feather', 'mouse toy', 'ball', 'laser
pointer', 'scratching post', 'cardboard box']
```

With `cat_toys.insert(1, "mouse toy")`, we insert `"mouse toy"` at index 1. As you can see, `"ball"` moves to index 2. Not just ball, all items from index 1 onwards are shifted one position to the right. This is what the new table with indices looks like:

Element	Positive index	Negative index
feather	0	-6
mouse toy	1	-5
ball	2	-4
laser pointer	3	-3
scratching post	4	-2
cardboard box	5	-1

We have seen how to add items to a list. It might be no surprise that there are also ways of removing items from a list.

Removing items

There are different ways to remove elements from a list. The first one we'll talk about is what we call remove by value. The `remove()` method removes the first occurrence of the specified value. Let's say that we want to remove the ball from our `cat_toys` list. Here's how to do it:

```
cat_toys = ["feather", "mouse toy", "ball", "laser pointer", "scratching
post", "cardboard box"]
cat_toys.remove("ball")
print("After removing 'ball':", cat_toys)
```

This is what this code will output:

```
After removing 'ball': ['feather', 'mouse toy', 'laser pointer',
'scratching post', 'cardboard box']
```

The `cat_toys.remove("ball")` removes the first occurrence of `"ball"`. If `"ball"` is not found, it raises a `ValueError`. In this case, it is found and removed. If there were more occurrences of `"ball"` in our list, those would stay in there. The elements that came after `"ball"` have lowered their index by one (shift to the left). There are no gaps between the numbers in the indices.

We can also remove by index. We don't do this with the `remove()` method, but with the `pop()` method. This method removes the item at the specified index. If no index is specified, it removes the last item.

```
cat_toys.pop(2)
print("After popping index 2:", cat_toys)
```

This will output the following:

```
After popping index 2: ['feather', 'mouse toy', 'scratching post',
'cardboard box']
```

The `cat_toys.pop(2)` removes the item at index 2 (which is sadly `"laser pointer"`). The list is updated accordingly, meaning that the elements after the removed element shift one position to the left.

If we want to remove all the elements from the list, we can do that in one go as well. The `clear()` method removes all items from the list.

So, let's say we run the following:

```
cat_toys.clear()
print("After clearing:", cat_toys)
```

It will output this:

```
After clearing: []
```

The `cat_toys.clear()` empties the list. As you can see, the `cat_toys` list is now empty (`[]`). Heartbreaking.

Changing items

We can use the index to overwrite what is on an item in the list. Take this example:

```
cat_toys = ["feather", "mouse toy", "ball", "laser pointer", "scratching
post", "cardboard box"]
cat_toys[0] = "cat wand"
print("After changing:", cat_toys)
```

This is what this code will output:

```
After removing 'ball': ['cat wand', 'mouse toy', 'ball', 'laser pointer',
'scratching post', 'cardboard box']
```

As you can see, the value has changed to `"cat wand"` with `cat_toys[0] = "cat wand"`. And that's it for modifying a list. Let's see some other cool things we can do!

This book may visually wrap long lines of code over multiple lines, we're dealing with limited page width here. It's important to know that in actual code, that line is still one line in your IDE. If you were to put an enter there, it would break your code. If you're ever unsure, you can check out the code snippets on GitHub.

More list actions

We have seen how to modify lists and how to access variables. There are a few special things we can do with lists. Let's talk about a somewhat difficult one first: slicing!

Slicing lists

Slicing allows you to get a subset of the list. This does not alter the original list but returns a new list. The syntax for it is a little bit special. We use the square brackets again, but this time we specify two indices: one that we want to start our subset with, and the one that will be the end. This last one is not included. So, slicing syntax is like this: `list_name[start:stop]`

Here, you can see it in action:

```
# Reset the list after clearing it
cat_toys = ["feather", "mouse toy", "ball", "laser pointer", "scratching
post"]
```

```
favorite_toys = cat_toys[1:4]
print("Favorite toys:", favorite_toys)
```

This will output the following:

```
Favorite toys: ['mouse toy', 'ball', 'laser pointer']
```

The cat_toys[1:4] gets items from index 1 up to, but not including, index 4. This means that we do include the elements at index 1, 2, and 3. The original cat_toys list is not modified and still contains the whole list. So, we have to store the subset in its own list. In this code, we called favorite_toys. When we print it, you can see that the elements from positions 1, 2, and 3 are now in the list. Of course, in this new favorite_toys list, the indices are simply 0, 1, and 2. This is what we call slicing.

List length

Sometimes size matters. For lists, it's often useful to know the size. With the `len()` function, we can find out how many items we have in our list. A function is similar to a method; it's a trick that we can do. It's also different. A method, we use on a variable:

```
variable_name.method()
```

A function exists independently of a variable, and we can call it anywhere, like this:

```
function_name(some_argument)
```

Here's the `len()` function in action:

```
cat_toys = ["feather", "mouse toy", "ball", "laser pointer", "scratching
post"]
number_of_toys = len(cat_toys)
print("I have", number_of_toys, "toys.")
```

This will output the following:

```
I have 5 toys.
```

The `len(cat_toys)` results in `5`, the number of items in the list. We store that result in the `number_of_toys` variable. After that, we print the result. This can come in handy for different reasons – for example, if you want to know the maximum index that you can access. That would be the length minus one.

Another useful thing to do is check whether a certain item appears in a list. Let's see how to do that next.

Checking item existence using in

If you need to check whether an item appears in a list, you can check this using the `in` keyword. Here's how to do it:

```
cat_toys = ["feather", "mouse toy", "ball", "laser pointer", "scratching
post"]
item_exists = "laser pointer" in cat_toys
```

This is going to store the `True` value in `item_exists`. We can also use this directly in an `if` statement:

```
if "laser pointer" in cat_toys:
    print("Time to play with the laser pointer!")
else:
    print("No laser pointer found.")
```

This will output the following:

```
Time to play with the laser pointer!
```

The `"laser pointer" in cat_toys` returns `True` because `"laser pointer"` is in the list. Since it's `True`, the code block associated with the `if` is executed and the `else` is skipped. Remember when I told you we get an error if we try to remove something by value that isn't there?

Well, that would be a great use case:

```
cat_toys = ["feather", "mouse toy", "ball", "laser pointer", "scratching
post", "cardboard box"]

if "cardboard box" in cat_toys:
    print("Oh no, she's throwing away my box!")
    cat_toys.remove("cardboard box")
else:
    print("No box to throw away.")
```

This will remove the box only if it's in the list. In this case, it is, so it will be thrown away. If it's not, and you try to remove it, you'll get an error. This check avoids that! And that's it for what you need to know about lists. Let's move on to the next collection: tuples.

Tuples

A tuple is similar to a list. There is one important difference: after you create a tuple, it cannot be modified. We call that: **immutability**. A tuple is immutable and cannot be changed after creation. It's like your date of birth; you can't change it, no matter how badly you might want to be younger!

Let's see how we can create tuples!

Creating tuples

Again, let's start by creating an empty tuple. It's like creating a list, but we replace the square brackets with parentheses, like this:

```
my_first_tuple = ()
```

This is an empty tuple. It's immutable, so we can't place items in there. It's likely that we'd want to create a tuple with items. Again, this is similar to creating a list with items! We can create a tuple by placing items inside parentheses `()`, separated by commas.

```
# A tuple of coordinates
position = (10, 20)
```

Just like lists, tuples can have items with different data types in them, like this:

```
# A tuple with mixed data types
cat_info = ("Zia", 1, "grey")
```

Let me tell you something important about tuples with only one item. If you have a tuple with a single item, you must include a comma; otherwise, Python interprets it as a simple value in parentheses.

```
# Not a tuple, just a string
not_a_tuple = ("only item")

# Correct way to create a single-item tuple
single_item_tuple = ("only item",)
```

So, without the comma, `("only item")` is just a string in parentheses. With the comma, `("only item",)` is recognized as a tuple. In case you're wondering, the length of this tuple with a single element is one.

You can actually also create a tuple if you leave out the parentheses. As your teacher, I must say I'm not a fan because it could create confusion about the type:

```
still_a_tuple = "Zia", 1, "grey"
```

So, the type of `still_a_tuple` is tuple. Just like lists, we can access the separate items in a tuple.

Accessing tuple items

After having seen lists, accessing the items of a tuple is trivial. You can access tuple items using their indices, just like lists. Here's an example:

```
cat_info = ("Zia", 1, "grey")

name = cat_info[0]
age = cat_info[1]
color = cat_info[2]

print("Name:", name)
print("Age:", age)
print("Color:", color)
```

This will output the following:

```
Name: Zia
Age: 1
Color: grey
```

In this code, we access each item using its index. It's just like we did for lists. The indexing starts at 0 and we use square brackets around the index. Let's talk about something that's not the same as with lists. Trying to change the tuple.

Immutability

So, tuples are immutable, and that means they cannot be changed after creation. What happens if we try that anyway? Well, attempting to modify a tuple results in an error.

```
cat_info = ("Zia", 1, "grey")

cat_info[1] = 4
```

Here's the output:

```
Error: 'tuple' object does not support item assignment
```

We get an error because we try to change the age to 4. Tuples cannot be modified, so Python raises a `TypeError`. This means that if you need to be able to change the values, don't use a tuple but go for a list. That brings us to a valid point, but when would you need to use tuples?

Why use tuples?

We choose a tuple when we want to make sure that our data remains constant. Since they are immutable, we know this for sure. This makes them great for keys in dictionaries, which is another concept we will look at soon. Another reason, and this is only relevant for large datasets, is that tuples can be more efficient in terms of memory and speed. For the simple code we've seen so far, that's not relevant yet.

Tuple unpacking

Since tuples are not mutable, there's less to discuss! We can use the `len()` function just like we did for lists. But before we move on to the next collection, let's unpack something that we haven't seen yet: unpacking. We can assign each item in a tuple to a variable in a single statement.

```
cat_info = ("Zia", 1, "grey")
name, age, color = cat_info
```

Here, we are creating three variables on this second line. The first item in the tuple, `"Zia"`, will go to `name`. The second item in the tuple, `1`, will go to `age`. And the third item in the tuple, `"grey"`, will go to `color`. To put this in Python terms: `name, age, color = cat_info` unpacks the tuple into variables.

So, is this something that's unique to tuples? No, we can actually also do this with lists. This would work the same way:

```
cat_info = ["Zia", 1, "grey"]
name, age, color = cat_info
```

That's it for tuples. Let's move on to a collection type that's quite different: dictionaries!

Dictionaries: key-value pairs

In English, a dictionary is a big book with words and their meanings. In Python, a dictionary is a collection of key-value pairs. It's a little like a real-life dictionary where you look up a word (key) to get its definition (value). In programming, it's similar but not limited to words and their definitions. Dictionaries allow you to store and retrieve data based on unique keys.

Creating dictionaries

Let's start by creating an empty dictionary. This is similar to the tuple and the list. But this time, we are going to use curly brackets. These are the ones that are used for the dictionary.

```
my_first_dict = {}
```

We can add values to this empty dictionary after creating the empty dictionary, but for now, it might be more interesting to create a dictionary with items. The items of a dictionary are key-value pairs. We can add multiple key-value pairs separated by commas.

The keys and values are separated by colons, like this:

```
cat_attributes = {
    "name": "Zia",
    "age": 1,
    "color": "grey",
    "favorite_food": "tuna"
}
```

In here, each key-value pair is in the form `"key": value`. The keys are usually strings, but they can be any immutable type. That kind of requires me to explain immutable a bit better to you. Please don't worry if you don't fully grasp this yet. We've just seen that tuples are immutable. If you try to change them, you get an error. With that in mind, you might think that a number is mutable, for example:

```
number = 3
number = 4
```

It would make sense to think that the 3 has changed into a 4. But it actually has not. The value that is stored in the variable number has indeed changed from 3 to 4. However, in the Python memory, the box with the three is still there and unchanged; the number is now just pointing to a different memory box that holds the value 4.

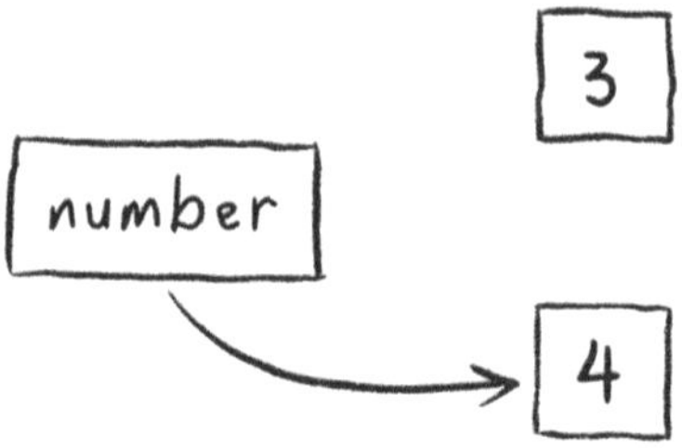

If this is too much, don't worry. For now, just know that these are very common types for keys:

- Strings
- Tuples
- Numbers

The values in the key-value pairs can be of any data type. We cannot use indices to access the items in the dictionary. So, let's talk about how we can access values.

Accessing values

In order to access the values in a dictionary, we'll be using their keys. To be more precise, we can do this by putting their key between square brackets `[]`. You can see this here:

```
cat_attributes = {
    "name": "Zia",
    "age": 1,
    "color": "grey",
    "favorite_food": "tuna"
}

cat_name = cat_attributes["name"]
print("My name is", cat_name)
```

This will print the following:

```
My name is Zia
```

So, what's happening? The `cat_attributes["name"]` retrieves the value associated with the `"name"` key. That is the value `"Zia"`. We store this in `cat_name`. So, the string `"Zia"` will be in the `cat_name` variable. We then use that to print it.

You might wonder what happens if you try to access a key that doesn't exist. Well, that's a problem, and that's why Python raises a `KeyError`.

```
cat_attributes = {
    "name": "Zia",
    "age": 1,
    "color": "grey",
    "favorite_food": "tuna"
}

breed = cat_attributes["breed"]
```

This will show the following in the console:

```
KeyError: 'breed'
```

Since `"breed"` is not a key in the dictionary, the preceding `KeyError` is raised. If you don't want to get an error when the key is not there, you can use the `get()` method instead.

The `get()` method returns `None` or a default value if the key is not found. `None` is a special value in Python. In some other languages, this is `null`. It is used to indicate that there is a variable, but that it's not holding a value.

Here's how we can use get:

```
cat_attributes = {
    "name": "Zia",
    "age": 1,
    "color": "grey",
    "favorite_food": "tuna"
}

breed = cat_attributes.get("breed")
print("Breed:", breed)
```

This will output the following:

```
Breed: None
```

When we did this with the square brackets, we got an error. With the `get()` method, we don't get an error; we simply get `None` back. This indicates that there is no value.

We can also specify a default value to get back instead of `None`. Here's how that's done:

```
breed = cat_attributes.get("breed", "Unknown")
print("Breed:", breed)
```

This time, it will output the following:

```
Breed: Unknown
```

The `cat_attributes.get("breed", "Unknown")` tries to get the value for `"breed"`. But still, the `"breed"` key doesn't exist. This time, we specified what to give back if it doesn't exist, so it returns the default value `"Unknown"`.

That's how to access the values in the dictionaries. Let's talk about how we can modify dictionaries.

Modifying dictionaries

With modifying, we don't only mean adding and updating entries, but also removing entries. Let's start with adding and updating entries.

Adding or updating entries

We can add new key-value pairs or update existing ones. Funnily enough, it's done in the same way.

Here is how to add a new key-value pair:

```
cat_attributes["hobby"] = "napping"
```

Since the hobby key is not there yet, it will be added. If we use a key that already exists, it will update the value. Here's an example:

```
cat_attributes["age"] = 2

print("Updated attributes:", cat_attributes)
```

This will output both the updates:

```
Updated attributes: {'name': 'Zia', 'age': 2, 'color': 'grey', 'favorite_
food': 'tuna', 'hobby': 'napping'}
```

As you can see, the `cat_attributes["hobby"] = "napping"` has added a new key, `"hobby"`, with the `"napping"` value. After that, the `cat_attributes["age"] = 2` updated the value of the already existing key, `"age"`.

That's how to change values and add key-value pairs. Let's see the different ways of removing entries from a dictionary.

Removing entries

At this point, it probably won't surprise you that there are different ways to delete. The different ways of deleting have small differences. Let's start with deleting by using the `del` statement. The `del` statement removes a key-value pair, like this:

```
del cat_attributes["favorite_food"]
print("After deletion:", cat_attributes)
```

This will output the following:

```
After deletion: {'name': 'Zia', 'age': 2, 'color': 'grey', 'hobby':
'napping'}
```

The `'favorite_food': 'tuna'` is no longer present in the output. This is because the `del cat_attributes["favorite_food"]` removes the `"favorite_food"` key and its associated value. If we try to delete a key this way that doesn't exist, we get another `KeyError`.

```
del cat_attributes["breed"]
```

This will give an error:

```
KeyError: 'breed'
```

If we don't want that. We can use the `pop()` method instead. The `pop()` method removes the specified key and returns the value of the removed key. Here's how we can use it:

```
hobby = cat_attributes.pop("hobby")
print("Removed hobby:", hobby)
print("After popping 'hobby':", cat_attributes)
```

This will output the following:

```
Removed hobby: napping
After popping 'hobby': {'name': 'Zia', 'age': 2, 'color': 'grey'}
```

The `cat_attributes.pop("hobby")` removes `"hobby"` and gives its value back. We store the returned value in `hobby`. We don't have to store it in a variable; that's only relevant if we want to use the removed value.

So, what if we try to pop `breed`?

```
breed = cat_attributes.pop("breed")
```

We still get the `KeyError`! Why? Well, it has to give something back, and it's not giving back anything. If we don't want the `KeyError`, we'll have to specify a default value, like this:

```
breed = cat_attributes.pop("breed", "Not specified")
```

This will store `"Not specified"` in `breed`. No errors this time. Let's talk about a few more methods that are useful to know when working with dictionaries.

Dictionary methods

Dictionaries are a very different data type compared to lists or tuples, because they contain key-data pairs instead of just values. That's why we have several different methods that are special for dictionaries. Let's go over them.

Getting all keys

First, it is possible that we want to get all the keys from the dictionary, without their values. For this, we can use the `keys()` method. This method gives us a view object of all the keys, which we then can turn into a list with the built-in `list()` function.

```
cat_attributes = {
    "name": "Zia",
    "age": 1,
    "color": "grey",
}
keys = cat_attributes.keys()
print("Keys:", list(keys))
```

This will output all the keys after turning them into a list:

```
Keys: ['name', 'age', 'color']
```

So, to go over what's happening here. The `cat_attributes.keys()` returns a view object. This is a data type that we haven't covered and won't worry about for now. Instead, we convert it to a list for display purposes using the built-in `list()` function.

Getting all values

Just like getting all the keys, we can get all the values. The `values()` method returns a view object of all the values. It works in a very similar way:

```
cat_attributes = {
    "name": "Zia",
    "age": 1,
    "color": "grey",
}

values = cat_attributes.values()
print("Values:", list(values))
```

This will output the values instead of the keys:

```
Values: ['Zia', 1, 'grey']
```

Similar to `keys()`, we use `values()` and convert it to a list. Sometimes we want to get both. Well, that's possible too!

Getting all key-value pairs

With the `items()` method, we get a view object of all the key-value pairs. Here's what that looks like in Python:

```
cat_attributes = {
    "name": "Zia",
    "age": 1,
    "color": "grey",
}
items = cat_attributes.items()
print("Items:", list(items))
```

The output might be more interesting:

```
Items: [('name', 'Zia'), ('age', 1), ('color', 'grey')]
```

The `cat_attributes.items()` returns tuples of key-value pairs. We turn this into a list of key-value pairs with the `list()` function. So, what we see in the output is a list, and the items in the list are tuples. This `items()` method is useful for viewing all key-value pairs at once.

Checking for key existence

We can use the `in` keyword to check if a key exists, much like checking for an item in a list.

Here's a code snippet that uses that:

```
cat_attributes = {
    "name": "Zia",
    "age": 1,
    "color": "grey",
}

if "age" in cat_attributes:
    print("I know my age!")
else:
    print("Age is unknown.")
```

This code outputs the following:

```
I know my age!
```

The `"age" in cat_attributes` results in `True` if `"age"` is a key in that dictionary. We print a message based on the result. In this case, it is `True`, so it prints `"I know my age!"`.

That's it for dictionaries! Let's talk a little bit about when to use each of them and how to combine them.

Choosing between lists, dictionaries, and tuples

So, we've explored lists, dictionaries, and tuples. You might wonder when to use each one. This depends heavily on the situation, and sometimes there's not one correct answer. In that case, I'd recommend using a list. Let's review each of them and give some examples.

Lists

The collection list is ordered, mutable, and allowed to contain duplicates. Ordered means that items have a specific position in the list, and the list keeps track of that order. You can still change the order later. For example by inserting items at specific positions. You can use lists when you have an ordered collection of items that may change over time. Some examples of lists could be storing favorite songs, a shopping list, to-do items, and more!

Tuples

Tuples are ordered, immutable, and allowed to contain duplicates. The time to use them is when you have an ordered collection of items that should not change. When is that? Well, for example, if you want to store fixed coordinates, fixed dates, fixed configurations, or need to use a collection as a key for a dictionary.

Dictionaries

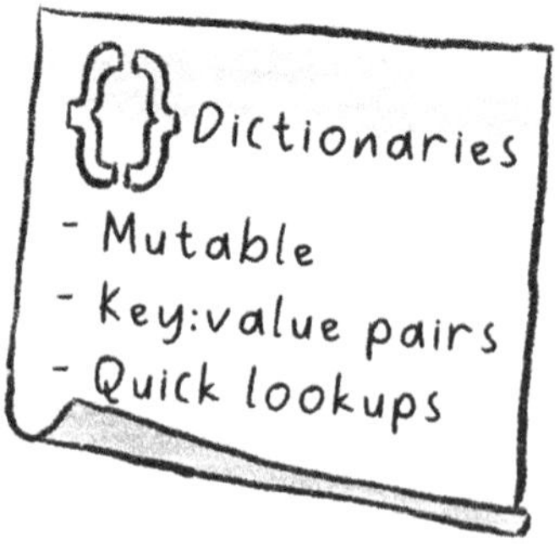

So, what about dictionaries? Well, these are ordered (they use the insertion order), mutable, and their keys must be unique. Dictionaries are more complex data types that are great when you need to associate keys with values for quick lookups. Some examples of that could be phonebooks, user profiles, and configuration properties.

You should choose the data structure that best fits the needs of your data and how you plan to interact with it. Sometimes, that would be a combination of different data types.

Combining different data types

I already mentioned that the values in lists, tuples, and dictionaries could be anything. The keys of the dictionaries have limitations, but the values do not. Let's make a somewhat more complicated data structure. Let's start with this dictionary (we could have started with a list or a tuple as well):

```
cat_attributes = {
    "name": "Zia",
    "age": 1,
    "color": "grey",
    "favorite_food": "tuna"
}
```

Let's say I want to create a dictionary just like this one, but with my hobbies included. Since I have multiple hobbies and not a single hobby, I'd like to make that new value of the key-value pair a list, like this:

```
cat_attributes = {
    "name": "Zia",
    "age": 1,
    "color": "grey",
    "favorite_food": "tuna",
    "hobbies": ["napping", "programming", "playing"]
}
```

As you can see, we now have a key, `"hobbies"`, holding a value that is a list, and that list contains three strings. We probably know how to get and print all the hobbies, like this:

```
print(cat_attributes["hobbies"])
```

This will output the list of hobbies:

```
['napping', 'programming', 'playing']
```

But what if we only wanted to print 'programming'? Well, in order to get an item from a list, we use the index, and `cat_attributes["hobbies"]` is a list. So, `cat_attributes` is a dictionary, but because we select the list by appending `["hobbies"]`, we are now operating on a list. So, we can just append square brackets and the index, like this:

```
print(cat_attributes["hobbies"][1])
```

This will print the following:

```
programming
```

We could even make it more complex! I'm going to add my friends to the `cat_attributes` dictionary. So, clearly, friends should be a list, because we have multiple friends.

But what should each friend be? If it's just a list of strings with the names, that is a somewhat shallow representation of my friends. My friends have many properties, just like myself. So, let's start by adding an empty list for friends:

```
cat_attributes = {
    "name": "Zia",
    "age": 1,
    "color": "grey",
    "favorite_food": "tuna",
    "hobbies": ["napping", "programming", "playing"],
    "friends": [],

}
```

Right now, there are no friends specified. This would mean I have no friends. Luckily, that's not true! Let's start by adding my best friend, Wiesje, and for now, only give her a key-value pair with her name and age.

```
cat_attributes = {
    "name": "Zia",
    "age": 1,
    "color": "grey",
    "favorite_food": "tuna",
    "hobbies": ["napping", "programming", "playing"],
    "friends": [{"name": "Wiesje", "age": 7}]
}
```

I'm building this up slowly and trying my best not to overwhelm you here. Right now, we have a list of friends, with one friend specified. This friend has two key-value pairs. What if I wanted to print the name of the friend? Well, first, I would need to select the friends key. Then I would need to get the first item in the list, and then I would need to get the key name of the first item in the list. Let me show you:

```
print(cat_attributes["friends"][0]["name"])
```

This will print the following:

```
Wiesje
```

We could give my friend Wiesje a list of hobbies as well. Before I do that, I want to show the same code with a different level of indentation:

```
cat_attributes = {
    "name": "Zia",
    "age": 1,
    "color": "grey",
    "favorite_food": "tuna",
    "hobbies": ["napping", "programming", "playing"],
    "friends": [
        {
            "name": "Wiesje",
            "age": 7
        }
    ]
}
```

This contains the same information. If this were all the information I had, I'd actually prefer the previous indentation for the previous amount of data. This prepares you better for what is to come, though. It's easier to identify that there is only one friend at this moment. Let's go ahead and add some hobbies for our friend Wiesje:

```
cat_attributes = {
    "name": "Zia",
    "age": 1,
    "color": "grey",
    "favorite_food": "tuna",
    "hobbies": ["napping", "programming", "playing"],
    "friends": [
        {
            "name": "Wiesje",
            "age": 7,
            "hobbies": ["napping", "visiting the forest"]
        }
    ]
}
```

Let's say we want to print Wiesje's second hobby. Here's how to do that:

```
print(cat_attributes["friends"][0]["hobbies"][1])
```

This will print the following:

```
visiting the forest
```

Can you keep up? This is quite challenging! Let me talk you through it. First, we grab our dictionary, `cat_attributes`. Then, we select our list of friends with `["friends"]`, and grab the first friend on the list using `[0]`. Now that we have this friend dictionary, I want to get the list of hobbies, and that is done with `["hobbies"]`. On that list, I want the second element, hence the `[1]`.

This could go on endlessly! We can add multiple friends, like this:

```
cat_attributes = {
    "name": "Zia",
    "age": 1,
    "color": "grey",
    "favorite_food": "tuna",
    "hobbies": ["napping", "programming", "playing"],
    "friends": [
        {
            "name": "Wiesje",
            "age": 7,
            "hobbies": ["napping", "visiting the forest"]
        },
```

```
        {
            "name": "Muchu",
            "age": 0,
            "hobbies": [
                "napping in the couch",
                "chasing anything",
                "exploring new things"
            ]
        }
    ]
}
```

Now, I have two friends! My second friend, Muchu, is on my list of friends as well. It's important to have a comma between the two dictionaries in the friends list. List items are separated by commas, even if they are big list items! You might wonder about the spacing I'm using for her hobbies. This is only because it didn't fit on one line. It doesn't change anything. Let's say I want to print her hobby `"napping in the couch"`. This is not a grammatical error, by the way; she literally crawls inside the couch from underneath. If she crawls under the couch and you later check under the couch, she won't be there, as she is now inside the couch.

Anyway, let's get Muchu's name and her hobby:

```
print(cat_attributes["friends"][1]["name"], "loves",
cat_attributes["friends"][1]["hobbies"][0])
```

This prints the following:

```
Muchu loves napping in the couch
```

First, we get her name. In order to get to her name, we need to access the friends key-value pair with `["friends"]`. The first one in the list is Wiesje, the second is Muchu; that's why we use `[1]`. This gives us the dictionary with her data, and we then select the value for her name using `["name"]`.

To get Muchu's first hobby, we again select the correct friend from the list of friends with `cat_attributes["friends"][1]`. Then we get the list of hobbies using `["hobbies"]`. Since it's the first hobby, we use `[0]`.

Selecting things in combined data types is always a step-by-step process. It looks overwhelming, but just take it one step at a time and try to keep track of the type of object you have. If you're not sure, just print it mid-steps:

```
print(cat_attributes["friends"][1])
```

That would print the following:

```
{'name': 'Muchu', 'age': 0, 'hobbies': ['napping in the couch', 'chasing anything', 'exploring new things']}
```

As you can see, we have a dictionary representing our friend Muchu here. Alright, that's it for complex data types. I could go on and on about this, but instead, let's see some common mistakes and how we can avoid making them.

Common mistakes and how to avoid them

Before we wrap up the chapter, let's go over some common pitfalls when working with collections. Again, it's not about avoiding mistakes as much. We all make mistakes, but being able to identify them and fix them is a great skill. That takes a lot of practice, so please be patient with yourself.

IndexError with lists and tuples

I have talked about this one already. If you try to access an index that doesn't exist on a tuple or a list, you'll get an `IndexError`.

```
some_numbers = [1, 2, 3]
print(some_numbers[3])  # Giving IndexError: list index out of range
```

The list has indices 0, 1, and 2. That's why `some_numbers[3]` is out of range. Before accessing an index, we can check if it's in a valid range using `len(some_numbers)` to check the list's length.

```
index = 3
if index < len(some_numbers):
    print(some_numbers[index])
else:
    print("Index out of range.")
```

Since we are out of range, it will print the following:

```
Index out of range.
```

It will check if we can access the index; if not, it will print a message, instead of trying to do something that's not possible that would result in an error. We have a similar issue with dictionaries; let's see how to tackle that.

KeyError with dictionaries

With dictionaries, we can get an error if we try to access a key that doesn't exist.

```
friends_ages = {"Zia": 1, "Wiesje": 7, "Muchu": 0}
print(friends_ages["Szara"])  # KeyError: 'Szara'
```

This will give an error, because `"Szara"` is not a key in `friends_ages`. To solve this, we can check if the key exists using `in` or use the `get()` method with a default value.

Here's the checking:

```
key = "Szara"
if key in friends_ages:
    print(friends_ages[key])
else:
    print("Key not found.")
```

This will avoid the error and simply print `"Key not found."` An alternative way of avoiding the method is using the `get()` method with a default value.

```
key = "Szara"
value = friends_ages.get(key, "Key not found.")
print(value)
```

Because there is no `Szara` key, this will return the value `"Key not found."`

When to use `get()` with a default value and when to use `in` depends on the situation. You don't always want to have a default value. For example, if the default value were a whole friend dictionary, I might try to continue to access elements on the friend that is returned, even though it's a default dummy value. Chances are that the default value might not have that property you're trying to retrieve next, and your code might break.

In that case, the first approach, with `in`, will probably be more suitable as it allows for multiple solutions. Very often, there is not one right solution, and both approaches can be applied in multiple situations. At that point, it's a matter of preference!

Quiz

1. Consider this list of dog names.

```
dog_names = ["Chewie", "Frits", "Wiesje", "Doesie", "Takkie",
"Timo","Bobby"]
```

Which of the following options removes "Wiesje" from the list?

   a. `dog_names.pop("Wiesje")`
   b. `dog_names.pop(3)`
   c. `dog_names.del(3)`
   d. `dog_names.remove("Wiesje")`

2. What method allows you to add items at a specific index of a list?

   a. `append()`
   b. `insert()`
   c. `slice()`
   d. `add()`

3. What is the type of the following variable?

```
mystery_variable = ("Hey there")
```

   a. Tuple
   b. List
   c. Object
   d. String

4. What is **not** allowed in a tuple?

   a. Accessing by index
   b. Nested data
   c. Changing an element directly in the tuple
   d. Duplicate items

5. This is a dictionary of human attributes:

```
human_attributes = {
    "name": "Imke",
    "age": 28,
    "pet": {"name": "Wiesje", "age": 7, "species": "dog"},
```

```
    "hobbies": ["crochet", "skating", "sewing"]
}
```

How would you change the hobby "crochet" to "knitting" in the "hobbies" of human_attributes?

a. `human_attributes["hobbies"][0] = "knitting"`
b. `human_attributes["hobbies"]["crochet"] = "knitting"`
c. `human_attributes["hobbies"].insert(1, "knitting")`
d. `human_attributes.hobbies[0] = "knitting"`

6. What is the correct way to check if a key exists in a dictionary?

   a. `key in dictionary`
   b. `key.exists()`
   c. `dictionary.contains(key)`
   d. `key.isin(dictionary)`

7. True or false? Using the `get()` method when you're trying to access dictionary keys only prevents errors if you specify a default value.
8. What will be the output?

```
grocery_list = ["apples", "cucumber", "peanut butter", "bread",
"coffee", "chocolate"]

print(grocery_list[2:-2])
```

   a. `SyntaxError`
   b. `['peanut butter', 'bread']`
   c. `['apples', 'cucumber', 'peanut butter']`
   d. `['cucumber', 'peanut butter', 'bread']`

9. How can you find the number of items in a list?

   a. `len(list_name)`
   b. `list_name.length()`
   c. `length(list_name)`
   d. `count(list_name)`

10. What is happening in the preceding code snippet?

```
menu = ["nachos", "enchiladas", "churros"]
appetizer, main_course, dessert = menu
```

a. The list menu is being modified to contain the `appetizer`, `main_course` and `dessert` variables

b. The `menu` list is being converted to a dictionary to hold key-value pairs

c. The values of the `menu` list are being unpacked and assigned to separate variables

d. The `menu` list is being sorted alphabetically

Exercises

4.1 Favorite animals

Create a list of your favorite animals and print the list.

Print how many favorite animals you have – for example:

```
I have 5 favorite animals.
```

Grab the first item in your list and print a sentence like the following, but with your first favorite animal:

```
The dachshund is my first favorite animal.
```

Now, grab the last animal on your list and print something like this:

```
The axolotl is the last favorite animal on my list.
```

4.2 Favorite nap spots

Here's a list of my favorite nap spots. We're going to play around with it.

```
fav_nap_spots = ["window", "cardboard box", "human's lap", "luxurious cat
bed"]
```

- On second thoughts, I don't like `"luxurious cat bed"`. Your first task is to remove it from the list.
- Now, add `"keyboard"` to the `fav_nap_spots` list. It's my absolute favorite, so it should be the very first item on the list.
- I also like napping in the sun. Add `"sunbeam on the floor"` as the third item on the list.
- Wiesje can't know, but I kind of like her bed too. Add `"Wiesje's bed"` at the end of the list.
- Wait, how many favorite nap spots do I have in my list now? Print the length of the list.
- Check if I already added `"human bed"` to my list, and add it to the end of the list if I didn't. Use an `if` statement.

- Okay, let's make another list of my top three favorite spots. Use slicing to do this and print the result.

Bonus challenge: Wait a minute, the cardboard box did not make it to my top three! Swap `"cardboard box"` with `"window"` on the original list to make sure it ends up in my top three. Grab the items by their indices.

4.3 Phone book

It's time to put your dictionary skills to the test! Here are your tasks:

- Create a `contacts` dictionary with a few names (as keys) and phone numbers (as values).
- Add a new contact to `contacts` without altering the dictionary directly.
- Check if the contact `"Maaike"` exists in `contacts`. If not, add her with a made-up phone number.
- Delete one of your contacts from the dictionary; use a method that will not cause an error if the contact does not exist.
- Print all the names in the dictionary.

4.4 Combining data types for a library database

Imagine your local library asks you to organize its book catalog in a Python dictionary. In this exercise, we are going to focus on structuring and choosing the right data types.

This is the information we need to store about each book:

- Title
- Author's name, birth year, and nationality
- Page count
- Availability
- Which library member has currently borrowed it
- Publication year
- Genres
- Rating (1-5)

Here are some book titles to get you started. Feel free to add some books you personally love.

Title: Jane Eyre
Author: Charlotte Brontë, 1816, British
Page count: 659
Publication year: 1847
Genres: Victorian fiction, Bildungsroman, Historical
Rating: 4.6
Available: yes

Title: Python Illustrated
Authors: Zia van Putten, 2023, Dutch - Maaike van Putten, 1991, Dutch - Imke van Putten, 1997, Dutch
Page count: 432
Publication year: 2026
Genres: Informative, Education
Rating: 5
Available: no
Borrowed by: Jacob

Title: If Cats Disappeared From The World
Author: Genki Kawamura
Page count: 144
Publication year: 2012
Genres: Literary Fiction, Magical Realism, Philosophical Fiction
Rating: 4.2
Available: no
Borrowed by: Wiesje

If you would like a hint to get started with this exercise, make sure the titles are the top-level keys of your library dictionary.

When you've created the full dictionary, here are some tasks:

- Print a list of all book titles the library owns.
- Check if "Romance" is a genre of "Python Illustrated" and print the answer.

- Print the nationality of the author of *Jane Eyre*.
- Wiesje brought back the book she borrowed. Update the values of *If Cats Disappeared From The World* accordingly.
- Check whether *Python Illustrated* is available and print who borrowed it if it isn't. The output could look like:

```
Python Illustrated is currently not available and borrowed by: Jacob
```

Summary

In this chapter, we learned how to handle collections of data with lists, tuples, and dictionaries, new kinds of containers for storing multiple values. Let's go over them once more, so we surely understand them before we move on to the next chapter.

We first looked at lists. Lists are ordered collections that can be changed. You can create and recognize lists using square brackets [ ]. For example, this is how you'd create an empty list:

```
my_list = []
```

Usually, lists would have items in them. We learned how to access these items by both positive and negative indices. An important thing to remember is that lists (tuples too, by the way) are 0-indexed, meaning that the first element of a list is at index 0.

After accessing list items in multiple ways, we practiced modifying lists: adding items at the end with the `append()` method, placing a new item at a specific index with `insert()`, and removing items with `pop()` and `remove()`. Remember the difference between those two? Anyway, after that, we saw that you can simply overwrite items by using the index, or clear the whole thing using `clear()`, if you'd like. Wiesje got hungry for pizza when she read about slicing lists. We took a good look at how slicing gives you a subset of a list. The syntax was a bit weird, but in the end, we all understood how `cat_toys[1:4]` returned a new list with the items from index 1 up to but not including index 4. Before moving on to tuples, we studied how to use the `in` keyword to check for existence in a list.

Tuples are pretty similar to lists, but their content cannot be modified. Call it immutable, call it stubborn, the content of a tuple will not change. Of course, we looked at the syntax:

```
example_tuple = ()
```

Tuples cannot be changed, so instead of looking at cool modifying methods, we looked at tuple unpacking, a fascinating way to create multiple variables—something that doesn't just work with tuples, but with lists as well, for your information.

Then, we looked at another exciting data type: dictionaries! Dictionaries are special because they are collections of key-value pairs. We use curly brackets `{}` to create them, and keys and values are separated by colons. An example of a dictionary could look like this:

```
cat_attributes = {
    "name": "Zia",
    "age": 1,
    "color": "grey",
    "favorite_food": "tuna"
}
```

To access values in dictionaries, we used keys, which explains why each key needs to be unique. After trying to access a non-existent key, we got a `KeyError`. Luckily, we got to use the `get()` method to work around that.

That was not all we did with dictionaries. We added and updated entries as well. For example, with `cat_attributes["hobby"] = "napping"`, we would add the `"hobby"` key if it didn't exist or update it if it already did. For removal, we used the `del` statement and the `pop()` method, the latter allowing us to add a default value to prevent a `KeyError`.

You might have thought we were done after this, but we weren't. Besides accessing specific values in dictionaries, there are ways to get all keys, values, or key-value pairs. We learned how to use the `keys()`, `values()`, and `items()` methods to do this and how to use the built-in `list()` function to convert the returned so-called view object to a list.

We went full inception with combining different data types. Essentially, you can have a tuple in a dictionary in a list inside another tuple. Mind-boggling, right? But I'm sure you get the idea. By now, you probably know how to access that tuple nested in the list, inside the dictionary, wrapped in that other tuple.

Lastly, we studied some common mistakes and, more importantly, how to avoid them. To prevent an `IndexError` when accessing list items, we found out that applying the `len()` function combined with an `if` statement can protect us from accidentally trying to access a non-existent index. Similarly, we used the `in` keyword with an `if` statement to prevent key errors when we were trying to access keys in dictionaries that didn't exist. We also prevented key errors with the `get()` method, but then we did have to declare a default value.

Get this book's PDF version and more

Scan the QR code (or go to `packtpub.com/unlock`). Search for this book by name, confirm the edition, and then follow the steps on the page.

UNLOCK NOW

Note: *Keep your invoice handy. Purchases made directly from Packt don't require an invoice.*

5

Iterating with Loops

In the previous chapters, we've learned how to store data and make decisions in our code. But what happens when we need to perform the same action multiple times? Imagine I want to count and register all the birds outside the window, but there are too many to count and enter into my administration system manually. Repeating the same code over and over isn't efficient or practical.

This is where loops come in! Loops make it possible to run a block of code multiple times without copying and pasting it. In this chapter, we'll explore the magic of loops in Python. First, I'll show you the challenges of repetitive code. After that, we'll learn about `while` loops. Once we understand that construct, we'll gradually build it up to `for` loops to iterate over collections, and we'll see how we can work with `for` loops and `range`.

Let's wait no longer, and let's get looping!

The problem with repetitive code

Whenever you feel the need to copy and paste your code, there's a better way, and sometimes that better way is loops. Suppose we want to print `"I love Python!"` five times.

Without loops, we'd have to write the following:

```
print("I love Python!")
print("I love Python!")
print("I love Python!")
print("I love Python!")
print("I love Python!")
```

And this would output the following:

```
I love Python!
I love Python!
I love Python!
I love Python!
I love Python!
```

In order to get this output, we had to write the same line of code five times. Five times might not be too bad, but this is not efficient and makes our code longer and harder to maintain. It is also easy to make mistakes when doing the same thing over and over; we can make a typo and ruin a line.

And then, even worse, imagine we start to hate Python, and we want to change our messages accordingly. We need to change all the messages for every line we've written. Not very efficient.

At this moment, we're only repeating it five times. But imagine if we wanted to print it 10,000 times! We'd spend all day copying and pasting. We might actually start to hate Python at that point.

The great news is, there is a better way! This is where loops come in.

Introducing loops

With loops, we don't need to repeat our code like we've seen before, because loops are constructs that are meant to repeat a block of code multiple times. We primarily use two types of loops:

- `while` loops
- `for` loops

In practice, I find myself using `for` loops the most. However, let's start by exploring the `while` loop since that might be easier for learning.

The while loop

A `while` loop executes a block of code as long as a given condition is `True`. It's like me when I am chasing a laser pointer (I keep running after it while it's moving), or Wiesje chasing her tail (she keeps chasing it as long as she believes it's following her). Here's what the syntax of a `while` loop looks like:

```
while condition:
    # Code to execute repeatedly
```

And again, indentation matters! The code inside the loop must be indented. Let's print `"I love Python!"` five times using a `while` loop:

```
count = 0

while count < 5:
    print("I love Python!")
    count += 1
```

This will output the following:

```
I love Python!
I love Python!
I love Python!
I love Python!
I love Python!
```

Let's go over what is happening. We initialize `count` to `0`. The `count < 5` condition checks whether `count` is less than `5`; if that condition evaluates to `True`, the code block associated with the loop is executed. Next, let's talk about what is inside the loop. We print the message, and we increment `count` by 1 using `count += 1`. The loop repeats until the `count` variable is no longer less than `5`. Without this increment, we'd be stuck in an infinite loop, but more about that later.

If we wanted to update this code so that it runs 10,000 times, we simply change `5` in the condition to `10000`, and we're good to go.

Before we move on to a more complicated example, let's make sure the flow is clear. We have five iterations of this loop. Here's what is happening in each of these iterations.

1. First iteration:
   - `count = 0`
   - The `0 < 5` condition is `True`
   - Print `"I love Python!"`
   - `count` becomes `1`
2. Second iteration:
   - `count = 1`
   - The `1 < 5` condition is `True`
   - Print `"I love Python!"`
   - `count` becomes `2`
3. Third iteration:
   - `count = 2`
   - The `2 < 5` condition is `True`
   - Print `"I love Python!"`
   - `count` becomes `3`
4. Fourth iteration:
   - `count = 3`
   - The `3 < 5` condition is `True`
   - Print `"I love Python!"`
   - `count` becomes `4`
5. Fifth iteration:
   - `count = 4`
   - The `4 < 5` condition is `True`
   - Print `"I love Python!"`
   - `count` becomes `5`
6. Exit loop:
   - `count = 5`
   - The `5 < 5` condition is `False`
   - Loop stops

Fun fact, we could have written this iteration description with a Python script. Here's how:

```
count = 0

while count < 5:
    print("Iteration", count + 1)
    print("count =", count)
    print("Condition", count, "< 5 is", count < 5)
    print("Print, 'I love Python!'")
    count += 1
    print("count becomes", count)
    print("------------")

print("count =", count)
print("Loop stops")
```

This will output pretty much the description of what happens every loop! We have extended the block that is repeated. And you can see that we have code that is being executed after the loop. That is the code that is indented at the same level as the `while` loop itself. Here is what it will output:

```
Iteration 1
count = 0
Condition 0 < 5 is True
Print, 'I love Python!'
count becomes 1
------------
Iteration 2
count = 1
Condition 1 < 5 is True
Print, 'I love Python!'
count becomes 2
------------
Iteration 3
count = 2
Condition 2 < 5 is True
Print, 'I love Python!'
count becomes 3
------------
```

```
Iteration 4
count = 3
Condition 3 < 5 is True
Print, 'I love Python!'
count becomes 4
------------
Iteration 5
count = 4
Condition 4 < 5 is True
Print, 'I love Python!'
count becomes 5
------------
count = 5
Loop stops
```

Let's say the red dot won't randomly disappear. Will I stop chasing it? No, of course not. I'd be stuck in an infinite loop, a little bit like this:

```
red_dot = True
while red_dot:
    print("Chasing the red dot")
```

And of course, I love the red dot. But this would be bad; I'd be stuck trying to catch it. That's why we need to avoid infinite loops.

Avoiding infinite loops

So, an infinite loop occurs when the condition always remains `True`. We need to avoid this, because it will freeze our program. Here's an example of an honest mistake that would lead to an infinite loop:

```
count = 0

while count < 5:
    print("This will print forever!")
    # Missing count increment
```

Since we never increment `count`, it remains `0`. And that's why the `count < 5` condition is always `True`. The result is that the loop never stops, and we're stuck in an infinite loop.

We can avoid it by making sure that the loop's condition will eventually become `False`. This typically means that we need to update variables inside the loop that affect the condition, or that we break out of the loop (which is something we'll see later).

It can happen that you get stuck in an infinite loop and that you need to kill the program. There are different options, depending on how you are running the loop. If you are running it with the **Play** button in VS Code, you can press the **Stop** button.

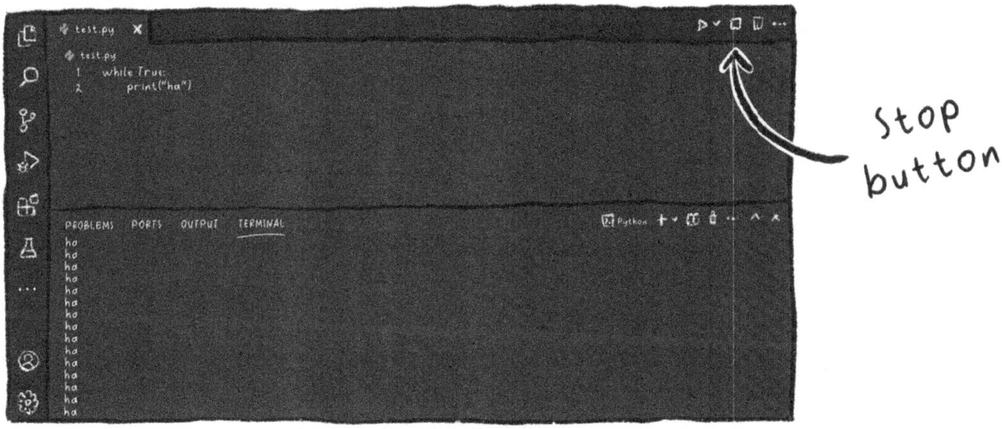

If you are running it in the command line, or don't have the **Stop** button for some reason, you can press *Ctrl* + *C* to force the program to stop (don't press the + button, press *Ctrl* and *C* as if you are copying something while the command line is in focus (click on it)).

Using while loops in practical examples

Before we continue to the `for` loop, let's see some more practical examples using the `while` loop. For example, we can create a countdown from 5 to 1:

```
number = 5

while number > 0:
    print("Countdown:", number)
    number -= 1

print("Blast off!")
```

And here's what it will output:

```
Countdown: 5
Countdown: 4
Countdown: 3
Countdown: 2
Countdown: 1
Blast off!
```

This time, we don't start at 0; we start with `number = 5`. The loop continues while `number > 0`. In our code block, we decrement `number` by `1` each time, and after the loop (same indentation as the `while` loop), we print `"Blast off!"`.

Now, let's see something even cooler. First, we'll need to introduce a new built-in feature: input. This is a little bit like a reversed print. Print is printing output to the console. The `input()` function, on the other hand, enables us to get text from the console. Here's a basic example:

```
name = input("What is your name? ")
print("Hello", name)
```

This code will pause when we run it. It prints the following:

```
What is your name?
```

Then, it waits for input. You can click in the console and start typing your name. After that, press *Enter*. What you've typed will be stored in the variable name as text, and it will then be used for the message that comes after.

If you are running this with the **Play** button in VS Code, this might not work when we work with the `input()` function. For some reason, it doesn't allow me to type if I try that. To get around that, I need to run it on the command line with the Python command. The exact Python command might differ based on your computer. Remember the command for Python you used to check the version? That's the one you'll use, followed by the name of the file (if you are in the folder). In VS Code, you can right-click on the folder of your file and choose **Open in integrated terminal**. Then, in there, I'd type the following:

```
python3 name_of_my_file.py
```

It then starts running the program. You can then proceed to type in the console.

Okay, now that we've seen `input()`, let's write a different example.

```
secret_word = "python123"
attempt = ""

while attempt != secret_word:
    attempt = input("Guess the word: ")

print("You've guessed it!")
```

The loop continues until the user enters the correct word. As long as the guessed word is not equal to `secret_word`, the loop will run again. Each time, it prompts the user to enter the word. Once it's guessed correctly, the user will leave the loop. And that's it for the `while` loop, let's move on to the next loop: `for`.

Introducing the for loop

While `while` loops are great, there's another loop that's often more convenient: the `for` loop.

A for loop iterates over a sequence (such as a list, tuple, or range) and executes a block of code for each item in the sequence. Here's what the syntax looks like:

```
for variable in sequence:
    # Code to execute for each item
```

The variable identifier is a temporary name that will be given to the item that we're currently iterating over. This variable takes the value of each item in the sequence one at a time. The for loop runs until all items have been processed.

Let's say I am checking and inspecting each toy in my toy basket one by one. Here's what that could look like:

```
basket_toys = ["feather", "ball", "laser pointer"]
for toy in basket_toys:
    print("Checking and inspecting:", toy)
```

I could have called toy something else, such as x. It would work the same way. However, I think the name toy is more descriptive:

```
basket_toys = ["feather", "ball", "laser pointer"]
for x in basket_toys:
    print("Checking and inspecting:", x)
```

Both will print the same thing:

```
Checking and inspecting: feather
Checking and inspecting: ball
Checking and inspecting: laser pointer
```

We don't necessarily need to have a collection; we'll see more of those later. Let's first see another common usage, combining for loops with the range function.

Using range() with for loops

First things first, what is this range function? The range function generates a sequence of numbers. This happens to be very useful with for loops.

Here's an example of a basic usage:

```
for i in range(5):
    print(i)
```

And here's what it will output:

```
0
1
2
3
4
```

Let's go over what's happening here. The `range(5)` function generates numbers from `0` to `4`, so please note that it's what we call an exclusive range.

This means that the number `5` is excluded from the sequence. And then we have an iteration for each item in the sequence (`0, 1, 2, 3, 4`). In each iteration, `i` takes the value of the next number in the sequence. So in the first iteration, `i` is `0`. In the second iteration, `i` is `2`, and in the last iteration, `i` is `4`.

We can also use the `for` loop to print `"I love Python!"` five times. Here's how to do it:

```
for count in range(5):
    print("I love Python!")
```

This will output the following:

```
I love Python!
I love Python!
I love Python!
I love Python!
I love Python!
```

Again, the loop runs five times. We are not using `count` inside the loop right now; we are just using this as a counter. Please note that we don't need to do any increment like we had to in the `while` loop, because we are working with a sequence with a certain length. For every element in the sequence, we do an iteration, and in each iteration, we print the message.

We can do some more things with `range()` that can be useful for using with `for` loops. So, let's see how we can customize `range()` a little.

First of all, we can specify custom start and ending points. Right now, the ranges start at `0`, but we can make them start at any point. Let's say that we want to start at `1` instead. Here's how to do it:

```
for i in range(1, 6):
    print("Number:", i)
```

And this is the output:

```
Number: 1
Number: 2
Number: 3
Number: 4
Number: 5
```

So, we do start at the first number. The `range(start, stop)` function generates numbers from `start to stop - 1`. That's why here, `range(1, 6)` generates `1 to 5`.

Another thing that can come in handy is that we can adjust the step size of the sequence. Let's say we want to only get even numbers. We can! Here's an example:

```
for i in range(2, 10, 2):
    print(i)
```

Here's what it will output:

```
2
4
6
8
```

This time, the first argument of the `range()` function is where we start, the second one is where we stop, and the third is the size of the step. Here's what it looks like:

```
range(start, stop, step)
```

We use `step` to determine the increment. And that's why, in this case, `range(2, 10, 2)` generates numbers from `2` to `9`, stepping by `2`. The number `9` won't actually be generated, because of the stepping by `2`, it stops at `8`.

One last thing I'd like to point out is that we can use a negative step size as well. Here's how we can do a countdown with the `for` loop:

```
for number in range(5, 0, -1):
    print("Countdown:", number)

print("Blast off!")
```

And here's the output:

```
Countdown: 5
Countdown: 4
Countdown: 3
Countdown: 2
Countdown: 1
Blast off!
```

This is a different use of `range()`. The start is higher than the end, and in order for this to generate a sequence, the `step` size will have to be negative. In this case, we use `range(5, 0, -1)` to count down from `5` to `1`. The step size is `-1`, so it decrements by 1 each time. And that's it for looping with the range function. Let's get back to looping over collections. This is a feature that I find myself using a lot.

Looping over collections

Now, let's revisit loops (*Chapter 4*) and see how we can use loops to process collections such as lists and dictionaries.

Looping through a list

We have already seen how to loop over a list. Suppose that we have a list of cat toys:

```
cat_toys = ["feather", "ball", "laser pointer", "scratching post"]
```

We can loop over them with a `for` loop, just like we've seen before. This time, we don't need `range()` to create a sequence. In fact, we already have one! The `cat_toys` value is a sequence:

```
print("Listing all my toys:")
for toy in cat_toys:
    print("-", toy)
```

And here's what it will output:

```
Listing all my toys:
- feather
- ball
- laser pointer
- scratching post
```

So, the loop iterates over each item in `cat_toys`. In each iteration, `toy` holds the current item. In the execution block for the `for` loop, we print each toy.

And that's how to loop over the items in a list. Easy, right? In a very similar way, we can loop over the items in a tuple.

Looping through a tuple

Tuples can also be iterated over. Here's a basic example:

```
coordinates = (10, 20, 30)

print("Coordinates:")
for coordinate in coordinates:
    print(coordinate)
```

And this will output the following:

```
Coordinates:
10
20
30
```

We loop over each item in the `coordinates` tuple, and then we print each coordinate. Looping through a list and a tuple is the same. Looping over a dictionary is a little different, though. Let's have a look.

Looping through a dictionary

For looping over a dictionary, we'll first need one. So, let's suppose we have a dictionary of cat attributes:

```
cat_attributes = {
    "name": "Zia",
    "age": 1,
    "color": "grey",
    "favorite_food": "tuna"
}
```

We can loop over the keys like this:

```
print("Cat attributes:")
for key in cat_attributes:
    print("-", key)
```

And this will output the following:

```
Cat attributes:
- name
- age
- color
- favorite_food
```

So, by default, looping over a dictionary iterates over its keys. We can, of course, use the keys to get access to the values, like this:

```
print("Cat attributes:")
for key in cat_attributes:
    print("-", key, ":", cat_attributes[key])
```

And this will output the following:

```
- name : Zia
- age : 1
- color : grey
- favorite_food : tuna
```

We can also loop over the values exclusively by using the `values()` method on the dictionary:

```
print("Cat attribute values:")
for value in cat_attributes.values():
    print("-", value)
```

And this will output the following:

```
Cat attribute values:
- Zia
- 3
- grey
- tuna
```

Here, `cat_attributes.values()` returns the values in the dictionary as a sequence. We then loop over the values and print them.

In addition, there is also a method to enable us to loop over the key-value pairs. This is very different from the other ones. This time, we get the key and the value back, so we'll need to work with two variables in the loop, like this:

```
print("Cat attributes and values:")
for key, value in cat_attributes.items():
    print(f"- {key}: {value}")
```

And here's what it will output:

```
Cat attributes and values:
- name: Zia
- age: 3
- color: grey
- favorite_food: tuna
```

Okay, okay, Wiesje. Yes, I'm using something new here: `f"`. We also have not seen this method of printing. It's not related to looping; it's just a way of being allowed to use variables in a string directly when we print them. The letter `f` inside the print is for *format*. In the string that follows, we can use variables between curly brackets (`{}`). Those are then recognized as variables, and the values are printed.

Back to the loop and the `items()` method. The `cat_attributes.items()` returns pairs of keys and values. Remember unpacking? That was the one where we store the items on the right in separate variables on the left. This is what we are doing here. We unpack the pair into `key` and `value`, and then print both.

Nested loops

Sometimes, we need to loop inside the loop. Luckily, that's possible; loops can be nested inside other loops. This is useful when working with multi-dimensional data, such as lists that are stored in a list.

Let's create a simple multiplication table from 1 to 3. Here's how we can do that with a nested loop:

```
for i in range(1, 4):
    for j in range(1, 4):
        product = i * j
        print(f"{i} x {j} = {product}")
    print("---")
```

And this is what will be output:

```
1 x 1 = 1
1 x 2 = 2
1 x 3 = 3
---
2 x 1 = 2
2 x 2 = 4
2 x 3 = 6
---
3 x 1 = 3
3 x 2 = 6
3 x 3 = 9
---
```

So there's a lot happening here! First, the outer loop (with `i`) runs from `1` to `3`. Next, the inner loop (`j`) also runs from `1` to `3`. In terms of flow, it goes like this: for each `i`, we loop through all `j`. And in that inner loop, we calculate the product and print it. Then, we move on to the next `i`, and loop through all of `j` again. And that's how we get the multiplication table!

Let's say we have a nested list; we can also iterate over that in a similar way:

```
list_of_lists = [
    ["Wiesje", "Pino", "Hedgehog"],
    ["Zia", "Python", "Writing"],
    ["Muchu", "Napping"]
]

for inner_list in list_of_lists:
    for item in inner_list:
        print(item)
```

Here, we have a list containing lists, conveniently called `list_of_lists`. First, we loop over all the lists in `list_of_lists`. We call the item `inner_list`. This is to make clear to ourselves that it's still a list. Then, we loop over the items in `inner_list`, storing them temporarily in `item` and printing them.

And that's it for nested loops; it can go much crazier with extra layers. However, it's always important to keep readability in mind. Let's go to the last new concept of this chapter, ways to control the execution of the loop from within the code block of the loop itself.

Loop control statements

Sometimes, you need more control over your loops. We can do this with the `break` and `continue` statements. Let's do `break` first.

The break statement

The word `break` is a keyword in Python that can be used inside a loop. The `break` statement exits the loop immediately. Here's a silly example to demonstrate how this works:

```
for number in range(1, 10):
    if number == 5:
        print("Number 5 found! Exiting loop.")
        break
    print("Current number:", number)
print("The loop has ended.")
```

And here is what it prints:

```
Current number: 1
Current number: 2
Current number: 3
Current number: 4
Number 5 found! Exiting loop.
The loop has ended.
```

Let's talk about the flow. The loop runs from 1 to 9. When `number` equals `5`, we print a message and break out of the loop. After the loop, it outputs `"The loop has ended."`

This is a bit of a silly example, of course, we can also have different situations. The next one would be less silly:

```
while True:
    text = input("Do you want to stop? " )
    if(text == "yes"):
        break
```

This code snippet keeps asking whether you want to stop. Once the user enters `yes`, it will stop. If that's never entered, it will keep going forever. So, we sort of create an infinite loop on purpose with `while True:`, then there's a way to get out by entering `yes` as input. And that's it for the `break` statement, let's continue with... `continue`.

The continue statement

Using the `break` statement will stop the loop altogether. The `continue` statement is related, but different. Instead of stopping the loop completely, the `continue` statement skips the current iteration and moves to the next one:

```
for number in range(1, 6):
    if number == 3:
        print("Skipping number...")
        continue
    print("Current number:", number)
```

This will output the following:

```
Current number: 1
Current number: 2
Skipping number...
Current number: 4
Current number: 5
```

When the `number` variable is `3`, we continue to the next iteration (but before we do that, we print a message). The `print` statement after `continue` (the one that prints the current number) is skipped for that iteration.

Before we wrap up this chapter on loops, let's see some common mistakes and how we can avoid them.

For else

Yes, `for else`, not `or else`. (Also, not `if else` or `else if`.)

A feature quite unique to Python is that loops can have `else` statements. But here's the thing that surprised me when I learned about it: the `else` block runs when the loop completes normally, not when the condition is never `True`. It's not an "otherwise" *else*, but more an "and then" *else*.

Here's what the syntax looks like:

```
for variable in sequence:
    # Code to execute for each item
else:
    # Code to execute when loop completes normally
```

Let's see this in action. Imagine I'm looking for my favorite feather toy in my basket:

```
toys = ["all", "mouse", "string"]

for toy in toys:
    print("Checking:", toy)
    if toy == "feather":
        print("Found my feather! Time to play!")
        break # that skips the whole loop, including else
else:
    print("No feather found. I guess I'll nap instead.")
```

This will output the following:

```
Checking: ball
Checking: mouse
Checking: string
No feather found. I guess I'll nap instead.
```

The `else` block runs because the loop finished checking all toys without finding the feather. But watch what happens when the feather is actually there:

```
toys = ["ball", "feather", "string"]

for toy in toys:
    print("Checking:", toy)
    if toy == "feather":
        print("Found my feather! Time to play!")
        break
else:
    print("No feather found. I guess I'll nap instead.")
```

This outputs the following:

```
Checking: ball
Checking: feather
Found my feather! Time to play!
```

Notice that `"No feather found. I guess I'll nap instead."` doesn't print this time! That's because when we use `break` to exit the loop early, the `else` block is skipped as well, since it belongs to the loop. The `else` block only runs when the loop completes all its iterations without being interrupted by `break`.

And before you ask, yes, `while` loops can also have `else` statements, and they work exactly the same way as with `for` loops. The `else` block runs when the loop completes normally, and by that, I mean when the condition becomes `False` naturally. But the `else` block gets skipped if you exit the loop early with `break`.

Common mistakes and how to avoid them

Infinite while loops

The first one is getting stuck in infinite loops. As we have seen, this can happen when you use a `while` loop where the exit condition is never met:

```
i = 0
while i < 5:
    print(i)
    # Missing increment
```

This can easily be avoided by making sure that any variables affecting the condition are updated within the loop. Always double-check your conditions and increments to avoid this problem. But there's another way to get an infinite loop. Let's talk about a thing to be very, very careful about: modifying your list within a loop.

Modifying a list while looping over it

Things can get tricky quite easily when we start to modify lists while we loop over them. Changing a list while iterating over it can lead to unexpected behavior. For example, can you guess what this will do?

```
toys = ["ball", "hedgehog"]

for item in toys:
    toys.append("new toy")
    print(toys)
```

If you try to run this, you can see that the list that is printed is ever-growing. It's another infinite loop! And every time we iterate, we get a new toy. Not all infinite loops are bad, so it seems! Here's the first part of the output:

```
['ball', 'feather', 'new toy']
```

```
['ball', 'feather', 'new toy', 'new toy']
['ball', 'feather', 'new toy', 'new toy', 'new toy']
['ball', 'feather', 'new toy', 'new toy', 'new toy', 'new toy']
['ball', 'feather', 'new toy', 'new toy', 'new toy', 'new toy', 'new toy']
```

And this goes on forever and ever!

Just like adding in a loop, removing in a loop is dangerous, too. It won't necessarily crash your program, but it can be unpredictable in what it does. For example, what will this print?

```
numbers = [1, 2, 3, 4, 5]

for num in numbers:
    if num % 2 == 0:
        numbers.remove(num)

print(numbers)
```

Only the odd numbers can stay:

```
[1, 3, 5]
```

It's not happening here, but removing items while looping can skip elements, as here:

```
numbers = [1, 2, 2, 3, 4, 4, 5]

for num in numbers:
    if num == 2:
        numbers.remove(num)
print(numbers)
```

What do you think this code does? At first glance, you might think it removes all the 2s. But does it, though? Here's the output:

```
[1, 2, 3, 4, 4, 5]
```

Wait?! A 2! Let me explain why this is happening. We start with a list with two 2s. In the first iteration, the loop sees `num = 1`. It's not `2`, so it does nothing. In the second iteration, the loop sees `num = 2` (the first `2`). It removes it. The list becomes `[1, 2, 3, 4, 4, 5]`. Now, the loop moves on to the next index (which points to the item after the removed element). However, the second `2` has now shifted into the place of the removed `2`, so the loop effectively skips over it. By the time the loop finishes, it has removed only one of the `2`s, ending up with the preceding output.

That is why it is typically safer to loop over a copy of the list to make sure we are not iterating less than we thought, if you need to do something like this. You can make a copy by adding `[:]` after the list, like this:

```
numbers = [1, 2, 2, 3, 4, 4, 5]
for num in numbers[:]:
```

```
    if num == 2:
        numbers.remove(num)

print(numbers)
```

Here, `[:]` copies the list, and that is the one we are iterating over; that's why this one will output the list with all the 2s removed.

Off-by-one errors

Lastly, a very common error in coding in general is off-by-one errors, and these are easy to create with loops. For example, misunderstanding the start and stop points in loops can happen to the best of us, especially with `range()`. Make sure that we understand the step size and that the range is exclusive. For example, it might not be very intuitive to see that `4` is not printed here:

```
for i in range(0, 4, 2):
    print(i)
```

This will output the following:

```
0
2
```

The sequence here is `[0, 2]`. Remember that `range(start, stop, step)` goes up to but does not include `stop`.

Quiz

1. What is the `while` loop for?

    a. Executing a block of code when we call the magic word

    b. Repeating a block of code while a certain condition is `True`

    c. Easily iterating over sequences and executing a block of code for each item in the sequence

    d. Generating a sequence of numbers

2. What kind of loop would be the first choice if we want to iterate over a list?

3. What sequence will be produced by `range(2, 10, 2)`?

    a. `2, 10, 2`

    b. `2, 4, 6, 8, 10`

    c. `4, 6, 8`

    d. `2, 4, 6, 8`

4. How many times will the following loop run?

```
for i in range(1, 7, 2):
    print(i)
```

    a. 2 times

    b. 3 times

    c. 6 times

    d. 7 times

5. What happens if the condition in a loop is `False` upon the first iteration?

    a. Python throws an error

    b. The executable code block in the loop runs once

    c. The code block associated with the loop just doesn't run at all

    d. The loop runs infinitely

6. True or false? You can stop a loop early with the `break` statement.

7. What does the `values()` method do?

    a. It returns all values in a dictionary as a sequence

    b. It prints all values in a list or tuple separately

    c. It gets the value of a specific key in a dictionary

    d. It loops over dictionaries

8. What does `list[:]` do in Python?

   a. It reverses the order of a list

   b. It exits loops

   c. It creates a copy of a list

   d. It iterates over a list

9. True or false? A `for` loop can only be used with a `range()` function.

Exercises

5.1 Summing numbers

We can use Python to do lengthy calculations for us. Imagine we need to calculate *1+2+3+4+5+6+...*. If we had to do that from the top of our heads, it would take quite some time. Of course, there's a smart and exciting mathematical way to solve such a problem, but I'll keep a lid on that. You're going to write a program that calculates the sum of all numbers from 1 to 10 using a `for` loop, and print the result.

5.2 Greeting a list of friends

Given a list of names, print each name with a greeting:

```
names = ["Zia", "Wiesje", "Muchu"]
```

5.3 Infinite squirrel chasing?

Wiesje loves to chase squirrels; if she had infinite energy (and never got distracted), she probably would like to do it forever. Let's recreate this scenario in Python.

Create an infinite loop that prints `"Wiesje chases the squirrel!"` over and over again.

Let's stop that loop and rewrite our code. Wiesje can get tired and does not chase squirrels infinitely. Create a variable to track Wiesje's energy level. Modify the loop so that Wiesje only chases the squirrel while she has energy. With each loop iteration, Wiesje loses energy. When she runs out of energy, print the following:

```
Wiesje is too tired and gives up.
```

Bonus challenge: Wiesje will never catch a squirrel, but let's imagine she could! Add a variable to track the squirrel's energy level. Each time Wiesje chases, the squirrel also gets tired. If the squirrel runs out of energy before Wiesje does, print the following:

```
Wiesje caught the squirrel!
```

Now, think about what happens if both Wiesje and the squirrel get too tired to continue at the same time. What should the program do in that case?

Play around with the program and see whether your code is working as expected with different energy levels.

5.4 Team up for game night

It's game night, and we need a program to divide all the friends who want to play into two teams. Let's start with a list of six friends:

```
friends = ["Max", "Louise", "Jacob", "Sam", "Farah", "Selim"]
```

Your task is to split them into two teams:

- Team A contains friends with even indices
- Team B contains friends with odd indices

Once you've created the two teams, print the results like this:

```
Team A:
Max
Jacob
Farah

Team B:
Louise
Sam
Selim
```

If you already figured out how to do this, go ahead! Here are the steps to take if you need a little guidance:

1. Create two empty lists for `team_a` and `team_b`.
2. Use a `for` loop to iterate over a range that has the length of the `friends` list.
3. Use an `if` statement in the `for` loop to add names with even indices to `team_a` and names with odd indices to `team_b`.
4. Loop over each team to print all of the names per team, one name per line.

5.5 Factorial calculation

I know, I promised you all this wasn't going to be a math book. However, I think we can all have a bit of fun with factorials here! What's a factorial? Well, it's a number multiplied by all the positive numbers that come before it. Here's what you need to know:

- A factorial is a number multiplied by all the whole numbers less than it, down to 1. For example, for a 5 factorial, or 5!, you calculate *5 * 4 * 3 * 2 * 1 = 120.*
- The factorial of 0 is 1. Why, you may ask? The answer to that question is quite fascinating, but I should contain myself and stick to Python here.
- Factorial operations only work on non-negative integers.
- Factorials can get big quickly, so keep that in mind.

In this exercise, you'll write a program that calculates the factorial of a number in a variable. After your program has calculated the factorial, you print the result: `5! = 120`.

Here are the steps I'd recommend:

1. Create a variable to hold the number you're calculating the factorial of.
2. Create another variable for the actual factorial. Assign it a value of `1`. (Why? Because multiplying by 1 doesn't change the result.)
3. Write a `for` loop to multiply the `factorial` variable by every number from `1` to the number you're calculating the factorial of. Use the `range()` function to generate the sequence of numbers and update the `factorial` variable inside the loop.
4. Print the result in the format `5! = 120`.
5. Play around by assigning different numbers to the initial number variable to see what happens.
6. I'm sure you can refactor your code to handle negative numbers. If the initial number variable holds a negative value, we cannot calculate a factorial. Print a message such as `"Factorials are only defined for non-negative integers."` and prevent the program from running.

5.6 Secret pet gym

I probably shouldn't disclose all my secrets in one book, but besides being a secret programmer, I'm also a secret gym rat. Wiesje likes to come with me. That's why we'll be building a small app to look at our workouts in this exercise! Spoiler alert: Wiesje didn't exactly crush hers today, but she did manage to eat four protein bars.

Her definition of "gains," I guess. I've tracked today's workouts of the secret gym members in the following dictionary. The weights are in kilograms, by the way; did I mention I'm Dutch?

```
workouts = {
    "Zia": {
        "bench_press": {"weight": 5, "sets": 3, "reps": 10},
        "bicep_curls": {"weight": 2, "sets": 3, "reps": 10},
        "box_jumps": {"weight": 0, "sets": 2, "reps": 10},
        "deadlifts": {"weight": 10, "sets": 2, "reps": 1},
        "kettle_bell_swings": {"weight": 2, "sets": 3, "reps": 10},
        "lateral_raises": {"weight": 1, "sets": 3, "reps": 10},
        "stair_climber": {"minutes": 10}
    },
    "Wiesje": {
        "bench_press": {"weight": 5, "sets": 1, "reps": 1},
        "leg_extension": {"weight": 1, "sets": 2, "reps": 5},
        "planking": {"minutes": 5},
        "zoomies": {"minutes": 2}
    }
}
```

Here's what I want you to do:

- Remember how to loop over key-value pairs? Print all of the exercises for each gym member.
- Calculate the total weight lifted by Zia and Wiesje separately and print the results. Don't worry if you're confused by gym terms. Here's how you calculate the total weight lifted in an exercise: *weight * sets * reps*. Note that we do not lift weights in each exercise of our workout. How would you work around that?

Here's what your output should look like:

```
Zia's workout:
- bench_press: weight 5kg, 3 sets of 10 reps
- bicep_curls: weight 2kg, 3 sets of 10 reps
- box_jumps: weight 0kg, 2 sets of 10 reps
- deadlifts: weight 10kg, 2 sets of 1 reps
- kettle_bell_swings: weight 2kg, 3 sets of 10 reps
- lateral_raises: weight 1kg, 3 sets of 10 reps
- stair_climber: 10 minutes
```

```
Wiesje's workout:
- bench_press: weight 5kg, 1 sets of 1 reps
- leg_extension: weight 1kg, 2 sets of 5 reps
- planking: 5 minutes
- zoomies: 2 minutes

Total weight lifted by Zia: 320kg
Total weight lifted by Wiesje: 15kg
```

Summary

In this chapter, we got a little closer to writing actual programs when we learned how to use loops. Loops make it possible to run a block of code multiple times, without having to repeat the same code over and over.

We first looked at the `while` loop. A `while` loop executes a block of code as long as a certain condition is `True`. Pretty simple, but you do have to watch out for accidental infinite loops. This is what happens when the condition remains `True` forever, and the code block just keeps getting executed. Just make sure your condition eventually evaluates to `False`, and you'll be fine. Oh, of course, we also studied the correct syntax of the `while` loop:

```
while condition_is_true:
    # Code to execute repeatedly
```

Things got even more exciting when I got to tell you what the `for` loop is for. A `for` loop iterates over a sequence and executes a block of code for each item in the sequence. Sequence? We mean a list or a tuple, for example. This is what the syntax looks like:

```
for variable in sequence:
    # Code to execute for each item
```

We learned that the `variable` identifier can be anything, but that it is wise to give it a descriptive name.

After looping over a fun list of toys, things got a little more mathy with the `range()` function, which generates a sequence of numbers and works great with for loops. It can be used in many ways. Depending on the number of arguments you pass in, `range()` can define start points, end points, and even the step size of a sequence. Here is a quick reminder:

```
range(start, stop, step)
```

And this is what `range` in combination with a `for` loop could look like:

```
for i in range(4):
    print("You've got this!")
```

It's probably more than clear to you how many times this loop will cheer you on: `(i = 0, 1, 2, 3)`. Okay, so we had already looped over sequences such as lists, tuples, and ranges. But looping through dictionaries was a little bit different. There are keys and values, and we practiced how to iterate over each. By default, looping through a dictionary iterates over its keys. Obviously, we could use those keys to access the values, but we also discovered the `values()` method to exclusively loop over the values. To loop over key-value pairs, we used two variables in the loop along with the `items()` method.

We had seen `if` statements inside `if` statements and lists inside lists, so it was only natural to explore nested loops next. They're great for handling multi-dimensional data. This got pretty complex, and we all needed a break. The word `break` is a keyword in Python that stops a loop completely. The `continue` statement is similar to `break`, but instead of stopping the entire loop, it just skips the rest of the current iteration and moves on to the next one.

As usual, we wrapped up the chapter by looking at some common mistakes and how to avoid them. We had already touched upon infinite loops earlier: they can be avoided by checking your conditions and increments. Besides that, you need to be careful when modifying lists while looping over them. It can lead to unexpected behavior. It's safer to loop over a copy of your list. We did this by adding `[:]` after the list in the loop. The last common mistake we discussed was off-by-one errors. They are common with loops, especially when using `range()`, so remember that the `stop` value is exclusive.

6

Writing Functions and Using Built-In Functions

We've done a lot already! We've learned how to store data in variables, make decisions, and even loop over our code. But imagine having blocks of code that you want to reuse throughout your program, or even across multiple programs. Without a more structured approach, you'll find yourself copy-pasting those blocks everywhere. Copy and paste should always be an indicator that there's a better way to do it. That's where functions come in. Functions allow us to bundle code into a single place and call on that code whenever we need it. It's like having your own little magic spells in Python. Once you define them, you can cast them any time you like.

Understanding functions

Whenever you find yourself writing the same or very similar lines of code multiple times at different places in your code, a function can prevent that. By wrapping code in a function, you can call it with just one line. This means that you'll have less duplicate code. And that's great! Imagine if, at some point, we'd have to change that chunk of code that appears multiple times in multiple places across our code... Yup, we'd have to change it in all those places! It's easy to miss one and a lot of work.

That's why functions also bring organization. Instead of scattering logic throughout your file, you can place each piece of logic in a function with a descriptive name. Then, if you need to change it, you do so in one place (the function itself), and the change applies everywhere the function is called.

We have already used functions! Python has built-in functions itself as well, to mention just a few of them:

- `print`
- `input`
- `range`

We have used `print()` to write messages to the console and `input()` to get the user input. This is something we do a lot! If functions didn't exist, we'd have to write complex logic for that ourselves all the time. Luckily, functions do exist. There are a lot of built-in functions, and we'll get to them. Let's first talk about how we can write our own functions.

Writing functions

We can think of a function as a magic spell that groups separate lines of code. Instead of rewriting the incantation each time, you name your spell, define it once, and then call it at will. The more spells (functions) you have in your code, the more readable and easy to maintain your program becomes, because it can do complex tasks with a single invocation of the right function (ideally with a very descriptive name).

We declare a function with the keyword `def`, followed by the function name, a pair of parentheses, and a colon. Inside the parentheses, we can optionally have parameters; we'll see these soon. Here's a simple example without parameters:

```
def greet():
    print("Hello humans!")
```

We used `def` to say, *"I'm defining a function."* The name of the function is `greet`. And inside the function body (which is indented), we placed a `print` statement. As it stands, this function just prints a message when called. However, if we run this code, you'll see nothing in the output.

Why? Because we haven't called the function yet. Calling the function means that we invoke the function and that the lines of code in the function are being executed.

How do you call this function? Well, easy:

```
greet()
```

You use the name of the functions, followed by the parentheses. Now our output will be this:

```
Hello humans!
```

Let's see how we can spice it up with parameters.

Parameters versus arguments

We just had an example function with nothing between our parentheses in the function definition. We can put parameters in there; these are a little bit like variables that we can only use inside the function. We provide the values for these parameters when we call the function. These values that we specify when calling the function are called arguments.

So, a parameter is like a placeholder in your function definition, and an argument is the actual value you pass into that placeholder when you call the function. Here's a function with a parameter:

```
def greet_by_name(name):
    print("Hello", name)
```

In this definition, `name` is the parameter. Let me show you how to call this function:

```
greet_by_name("Zia")
greet_by_name("Wiesje")
```

I'm calling the function twice here. The output will be the following:

```
Hello Zia
Hello Wiesje
```

When we call `greet_by_name("Zia")`, `"Zia"` is the argument. For that specific time we call it, inside the function, wherever we see `name`, it refers to `"Zia"`. If we later call `greet_by_name("Wiesje")`, then during that call, `name` will refer to `"Wiesje"`. That's why we get the output that's specified above!

We can also create functions with multiple parameters. Here's an example:

```
def feed_pet(pet_name, food):
    print("Feeding", pet_name, "some delicious", food)
```

You can see that we can add multiple parameters by just splitting them with a comma. Calling them is similar:

```
feed_pet("Zia", "tuna")
feed_pet("Wiesje", "kibble")
```

Again, we are calling the function twice, with different arguments. This will output the following:

```
Feeding Zia some delicious tuna
Feeding Wiesje some delicious kibble
```

When Python sees `feed_pet("Zia", "tuna")`, it assigns `"Zia"` to `pet_name` and `"tuna"` to `food`, then executes the code inside the function. The same goes for the second function call. We can call functions as often as we like. By using parameters, we can use the same function to do different things.

So far, we've only seen functions with one single line. That's not very common. Let's have a look at a function that has more lines, takes some input, makes a decision based on that input, and even contains a little loop. Here's an example:

```
def interactive_feeding():
    print("Welcome to the pet feeding station!")
    print("Type 'quit' when you're done feeding your pets.")

    while True:
        pet_name = input("What's your pet's name? ")

        if pet_name.lower() == "quit":
            print("All done feeding pets! Bye!")
            break

        species = input("What species is your pet? (e.g. cat, dog): ")
        food = input("What food do you want to give them? ")

        # A small decision based on the species input
```

```
        if species.lower() == "cat":
            print(pet_name, "arches their back and sniffs the", food)
        elif species.lower() == "dog":
            print(pet_name, "wags their tail at the sight of", food)
        else:
            print(pet_name, "looks curious about the", food)

        # Finally, we print a message about feeding
        print("Feeding", pet_name, "some delicious", food, "now!\n")
```

Let's break down what's happening here. We define `interactive_feeding()`, so the code inside this function won't run until we call it. Inside the function, we first print a welcome message and instructions to type `'quit'` when done.

Inside the `while True:` loop, we ask the user for a pet name. If the user types `'quit'`, we break out of the loop (ending the function). Otherwise, we ask for the pet's species and the food we want to feed them. We make a small decision based on the species. If it's `"cat"`, we do one thing; if it's `"dog"`, we do something else; otherwise, we give a default behavior.

Finally, we print a line about feeding them, including the pet's name and food. Then we loop back to ask for another pet name again. To actually run this function, we still have to call it in our code:

```
interactive_feeding()
```

If you run your program and call `interactive_feeding()`, you'll see Python repeatedly ask for a pet name, species, and food, printing different lines depending on the user's input. Once you type `'quit'`, it stops. This is a bigger, more realistic example of a function that does several things: it takes input, makes decisions, and even uses a loop. It's in fact so big that you might split it up. But we'll get to that later.

We need to deal with one very big concept first, and that's having functions give back a result. This is done with return values.

Return values

Sometimes, you don't just want to display a message. You might want your function to produce a piece of data. That's where the `return` statement comes in.

When Python reaches a `return` statement inside a function, it exits that function immediately and sends the specified value back to where the function was called. Let's see an example that calculates the area of a rectangle:

```
def area_of_rectangle(length, width):
    area = length * width
    return area

result = area_of_rectangle(5, 3) # Store 15 in result
print("Area is:", result)
```

When we call `area_of_rectangle(5, 3)`, Python executes the function body, calculates `5 * 3`, then returns `15`. We store that `15` in `result` and then print it.

We can have multiple `return` statements if we want to handle different conditions inside one function. The moment Python hits a return, it stops the function. That can be handy if we need to exit early in some scenarios as well.

If a function doesn't include a `return` statement, Python returns a special value called `None`. Here's an example:

```
def return_nothing():
    print("Hi")

val = return_nothing()
print(val)
```

This code will first print `Hi`, and then `None`. This `None` indicates the function didn't return any meaningful value. You might not need to return anything in many functions – for instance, if your function just prints a message or updates something behind the scenes.

Let's grab the long function we had before and split it up into two functions. We'll refactor (re-organize) our earlier `interactive_feeding()` code into two smaller functions, with one of them returning a piece of data instead of just printing. This way, each function has a clearer job. One function will collect the user's input and return it, and another function will use that data.

```
def get_pet_info():
    pet_name = input("What's your pet's name? ")

    if pet_name.lower() == "quit":
        return None
    species = input("What species is your pet? (e.g. cat, dog): ")
    food = input("What food do you want to give them? ")

    return (pet_name, species, food)

def feed_pet(pet_name, species, food):
    if species.lower() == "cat":
        print(pet_name, "arches their back and sniffs the", food)
    elif species.lower() == "dog":
        print(pet_name, "wags their tail excitedly at the sight of", food)
    else:
        print(pet_name, "looks curious about the", food)

    print("Feeding", pet_name, "some delicious", food, "now!\n")

def interactive_feeding():
    print("Welcome to the pet feeding station!")
    print("Type 'quit' when you're done feeding your pets.")

    while True:
        pet_data = get_pet_info()

        if pet_data is None:  # user typed 'quit' for the pet's name
            print("All done feeding pets! Bye!")
            break

        pet_name, species, food = pet_data
        feed_pet(pet_name, species, food)
```

```
# Call the main function to start the feeding loop
interactive_feeding()
```

This might be a lot to take in – don't worry, I'll walk you through it. First, `get_pet_info()` asks the user for a pet's name, species, and food. If the user enters `'quit'` for the pet name, it returns `None` to signal that we're done. Otherwise, it returns a tuple `(pet_name, species, food)`.

The `feed_pet(pet_name, species, food)` function takes that data and handles the logic of reacting and printing. Notice how it doesn't ask the user any questions. It just uses the data passed into it.

Then we have `interactive_feeding()`. This function loops indefinitely, repeatedly calling `get_pet_info()` and `feed_pet`. If `get_pet_info()` ever returns `None`, we know the user wants to stop, so we break out of the loop. Otherwise, we unpack the returned tuple and call `feed_pet`.

With this setup, our code is more modular. Each function has a clearer job:

- `get_pet_info()`: Collects and returns data
- `feed_pet()`: Uses data to perform a task
- `interactive_feeding()`: Coordinates the loop and manages when to quit

Importantly, in `get_pet_info()`, we're using a return value. If we don't want to feed any pets, we indicate that by returning `None`. Our calling function can check that and respond accordingly. This highlights how `return` statements let us pass information (or signals) back to the code that's using the function.

If you got this all at once, good for you! If not, go over it line by line again and see whether it makes sense. Once you're ready, let's zoom in on function parameters for a bit.

Function parameters in detail

So far, we've seen regular parameters. But there are a few different flavors! We have several ways to define parameters in Python, depending on how flexible or strict you want your function to be. We won't look at all the details, but I want to make sure you've heard of them. Let's talk about the first one, default parameters.

Default parameters

A default parameter means you can omit that argument when calling the function, and Python will assume a default value. Here's a greeting function with a default greeting:

```
def greet_friend(name, greeting="Hello"):
    print(greeting, name)


greet_friend("Zia")            # Uses default: "Hello Zia"
greet_friend("Wiesje", "Hi")   # Uses "Hi Wiesje"
```

If you call `greet_friend("Zia")`, the default greeting `"Hello"` is used becau se we don't provide an argument for the last parameter. This is a nice way to offer optional arguments without forcing the caller to always provide them. Of course, not all situations make this possible, since we don't always have a logical default value.

Keyword arguments

Normally, arguments are positional: the first argument goes into the first parameter, the second argument goes into the second parameter, and so on. But we also have keyword arguments. This is where you explicitly name which parameter to match the argument with:

```
def describe_pet(pet_name, species, age):
    print(f"{pet_name} is a {species} who is {age} years old.")


describe_pet(species="dachshund", pet_name="Wiesje", age=7)
```

Here, the order doesn't matter because we label each argument with its corresponding parameter. That can make your code more readable, especially if the function has many parameters. How we are using it now is not making the code more readable. It's better to stick to the position, but I suppose it suits the purpose of explaining keyword arguments.

Variable-length arguments

Sometimes we don't know how many arguments might be passed to the function. In that case, we can use `*args` or `**kwargs`. When you use `*args`, Python collects extra positional arguments into a tuple. If you use `**kwargs`, it collects extra keyword arguments into a dictionary. It might sound more difficult than it is. Hopefully, this example clarifies it:

```
def show_off(*args, **kwargs):
    print("Positional args:", args)
    print("Keyword args:", kwargs)

show_off("Zia", "Wiesje", toy="feather wand", snack="tuna")
```

This outputs the following:

```
Positional args: ('Zia', 'Wiesje')
Keyword args: {'toy': 'feather wand', 'snack': 'tuna'}
```

Here, `("Zia", "Wiesje")` goes into `args`, and `{"toy": "feather wand", "snack": "tuna"}` goes into `kwargs`. This is helpful when you want a function to handle an unpredictable number of arguments. Examples of that could be a flexible printing function or a function that processes commands.

That's all that is in scope for the parameters. Let's talk about scope.

Scope of variables

By scope, we mean the part of the code where we can refer to variables or functions by their name. We have two scopes in Python: the local scope and the global scope.

Local scope

Variables inside a function are local by default. This means that they're created when the function is called and destroyed when the function exits. This applies not only to variables created inside the function, but also to parameters – for instance:

```
def feed_cat():
    food = "tuna"
    print("Feeding cat with", food)

feed_cat()
print(food)
```

The second `print` statement will raise a `NameError` because food only exists inside `feed_cat` and we are referring to it in the global scope. Let's talk about what that is.

Global scope

Variables outside of functions and other code blocks are global. So, anything that's defined on the very left (not indented) is part of the global scope. Here's an example:

```
favority_toy = "ball"
```

You can access `favority_toy` everywhere in your file – inside a function and outside functions.

That's why it would work like this:

```
food = "kibble"

def feed_cat():
    print("Feeding cat with", food)

feed_cat()
print(food)
```

This will now use the global scope variable in the local scope of the `feed_cat` function. This will output the following:

```
Feeding cat with kibble
kibble
```

The global scope variable has the value `"kibble"` , and that's why it prints that. That's a bad situation, of course, because as a sophisticated cat, I quite fancy the nice food and not the plain dry kibble. I can make it extra funky, though, and fix this situation. What do you think this does?

```
food = "kibble"

def feed_cat():
    food = "tuna"
    print("Feeding cat with", food)

feed_cat()
print(food)
```

Let's see if you managed to figure out what it does correctly. It's a trick question, so don't worry! It will print the following:

```
Feeding cat with tuna
kibble
```

This is because we now have a variable named `food` in the global scope and the local (function) scope. As you can see, when we call the function, it makes a local variable `food` that is set to `"tuna"`. That is printed inside the function. After the function, we print `food` again. This is the global scope `food`, and hence it is printing `"kibble"`. If we didn't have the `food` variable in the global scope, trying to print it would give us an error because the function scope is not accessible outside.

The global keyword (and why to use it sparingly)

If we need to access something from the outer scope inside a function, we need to specify that we want to access the global scope. We can use the global variable inside a function to do this. This is useful if you want to modify a global variable from within a function. We can use the `global` keyword for that. However, this is usually discouraged because it can lead to confusing code:

```
food = "kibble"

def feed_cat():
    global food
    food = "tuna"
    print("Feeding cat with", food)

feed_cat()
print(food)
```

This will now print the following:

```
Feeding cat with tuna
tuna
```

While this works to change the variable in the global scope, it's often better to pass variables as parameters and return updated values if needed. That would look like this:

```
food = "kibble"

def feed_cat(food):
    food = "tuna"
    print("Feeding cat with", food)
    return food

food = feed_cat(food)
print(food)
```

Here, we are now accessing the global variable by passing it in with `feed_cat(food)`. However, if we overwrite it, it will create a new string variable and store it in the local scope, and not overwrite the value stored in the global variable `food`. So, in order to do that, we `return food` from the function and store it with `food = feed_cat(food)`. This overwrites the old value of the global variable. I agree that the passing in of arguments is not particularly useful in this example; it's just meant to explain the mechanism to you.

Built-in functions overview

I already mentioned that we can write our own functions, but we also often use the many built-in functions that Python comes with. This is predefined functionality that we can call right away. Having these functions built in is great, because this is all about basic functionality that we'll often need when we write our programs. We've already seen a few, including `print`. Let's see a few others.

Common Python built-ins for data types

There are a few functions you should know about the data types:

- `type`
- `int`
- `float`
- `str`

The `type()` function tells you the data type of a variable. The `int()`, `float()`, and `str()` functions help convert between data types. You can see them in action here:

```
items = ["feather", "laser pointer", "ball"]
count = len(items)
type_count = type(count)
print("Count:", count)
print("Type of count:", type_count)
count_text = str(count)
type_count_text = type(count_text)
print("Count:", count_text)
print("Type of count:", type_count_text)
```

If you run this code, you'll see the following:

```
Count: 3
Type of count: <class 'int'>
Count: 3
Type of count: <class 'str'>
```

The first time, the type of count is an integer. We then use the `str()` function to turn it into a string: `count_text = str(count)`. This doesn't change the type of the original count itself, but creates a new value with that type. The `float()` and `int()` functions work in the same way, but they give an error if you try to convert something to a number that cannot be converted (for example, the text "hi").

Exploring the standard library

Beyond the built-in functions, Python has a huge standard library that you can import whenever you need specialized functions. They're not available unless you import them first. Here are just a few highlights of the library; there are incredibly many, and it would be impossible to discuss them all (as the number keeps growing). If you know how to use them, the sky's the limit, and you can continue to explore them as you go. Before we get going with importing, let's talk about modules very briefly first.

Creating modules

So far, we've been writing all the code in one file. And so far, that has been totally fine as we're just starting out. But as our programs get longer, we'll notice that we start scrolling through our files a lot. The files get too long and would benefit from better code organization. Let's fix that by creating a module.

In Python, a module is just a fancy word for a file that contains Python code. That means we have been writing modules already! But we have not yet benefited from creating multiple ones and organizing our code better. When we create a module, we can import it into other Python files (yes, other modules) and use its contents without rewriting anything.

Let's make a module together. First, create a new file and call it `catspells.py`. Then add this code to it:

```
def summon_snack():
    print("Snack summoned! Tuna arrives on a silver plate.")


def meow_times(n):
    for i in range(n):
        print(i, ": Meow!")
```

That's it! We've made a module. Two small functions, ready to be used elsewhere. Let's see how to use it elsewhere.

Working with modules

Now let's use that module in another file. Create a new file called `main.py` and add this:

```
import catspells


catspells.summon_snack()
catspells.meow_times(3)
```

When you run `main.py`, Python will look at `catspells.py`, read it, and give us access to the functions and variables inside.

You'll see this output:

```
Snack summoned! Tuna arrives on a silver plate.
```

```
0 : Meow!
1 : Meow!
2 : Meow!
```

That's how easy it is to use code from other files (yes, how easy it is to use code from modules). Sometimes, other files can be really big, and we might want to import only specific parts of a module. Well, we can, and here's how:

```
from catspells import summon_snack

summon_snack()
```

As you can see, we don't need to call it with `catspells.summon_snack` this time. When we import the function like this, we can call it directly. One last thing I want to mention here is that we can give our imported modules a nickname:

```
import catspells as cs

cs.meow_times(2)
```

Now, instead of `catspells`, say that we call it `cs`. Then we can use it with the nickname instead of the full `catspells` name. This can be a must-have if you need to avoid naming conflicts, but more often it's a convention, and we just prefer to type two letters instead of a whole word.

Now that we've seen how to create our own modules, let's see how we can use the built-in modules. For that, let's start with my favorite, the `math` module!

The math module

The `math` module provides trigonometric, logarithmic, and other mathematical functions. Here's how you can calculate the square root:

```
import math

x = math.sqrt(25)
print("Square root of 25 is", x)
```

If you run this, you'll get the following:

```
Square root of 25 is 5.0
```

In order to use the `sqrt()` function, we need to specify where it can be found: in the `math` module. We do that here: `math.sqrt(25)`. We also specify the number we want to get the square root of (25 in this case). The function returns the result, and we store that in `x`.

This is how all the modules work; we can import them and use functions from them.

But that's only one of the many functions in the `math` module. Here are a few more quick examples.

We can raise something to the power of something else, like this:

```
math.pow(base, exponent)
```

This raises the `base` to the power of `exponent`, returning a float. For example, `math.pow(2, 3)` gives `8.0`.

```
y = math.pow(2, 3)
print("2 to the power of 3 is", y)  # 8.0
```

Just like that, we can also use the factorial, like this:

```
math.factorial(x)
```

Returns x! (x factorial). For example, 5 factorial is 120.

```
print(math.factorial(5))  # 120
```

We also have `math.sin(x)`, `math.cos(x)`, and `math.tan(x)`. These functions provide the sine, cosine, and tangent of an angle. Note that x is in radians. We can do something like this, for example:

```
angle_in_radians = math.radians(90)  # convert 90 degrees to radians
print(math.sin(angle_in_radians))    # 1.0 (approximately)
```

Don't worry if you don't get the math; that's not the point. We can also compute the natural logarithm of x (base e), like this:

```
math.log(x)
```

But if you need a base-10 logarithm, you can call `math.log10(x)`.

```
print(math.log(10))    # ~2.302585 (natural log of 10)
print(math.log10(10))  # 1.0 (log base 10 of 10)
```

The last couple I'll mention are `math.ceil(x)` and `math.floor(x)`. These round `x` up or down to the nearest integer.

```
print(math.ceil(3.2))   # 4, rounding up (the ceiling)
print(math.floor(3.8))  # 3, rounding down (the floor)
```

The `math` module doesn't only have functions; it also has a few constants – for example, `math.pi` and `math.e`:

```
print("Pi is about", math.pi)
print("e is about", math.e)
```

As you can see, the `math` module contains a wide range of mathematical tools to help you out. If you want even more, Python also has `cmath` for complex numbers, `decimal` for precise decimal arithmetic, and more specialized libraries such as NumPy for advanced numerical computations. There are so many available! You don't even need to be good at math to get complex calculations done.

Let's see how we can use the `random` module next.

The random module

The `random` module helps you shuffle lists, pick random items, or generate random numbers. Here's how to generate a random number:

```
import random

roll = random.randint(1, 6)
print("Dice roll:", roll)
```

Now you have a `random` integer between 1 and 6 (like a dice throw). I can't tell you what it will print exactly, because... it's random! The `random.randint(a, b)` gives you an integer from `a` to `b` inclusive. But there are many other functions to explore, such as `random.random()`. This one gives you a random float in the range zero to 1.

```
val = random.random()
print("A random float between 0 and 1:", val)
```

Or, another personal favorite of mine, you can get a random element from a list with `random.choice(sequence)`. This one picks and returns one random element from a sequence (such as a list).

```
pets = ["Zia", "Wiesje", "Axolotl King"]
```

```
chosen_pet = random.choice(pets)
print("Your random pet is:", chosen_pet)
```

I can't tell you what it prints because it's random, but it will print one of the items from the list. This next one is nice too! The `random.shuffle(sequence)` function changes the order of the items in a list randomly. All the items get to stay, though.

```
toys = ["ball", "laser pointer", "feather wand"]
random.shuffle(toys)
print("Shuffled toys:", toys)
```

The last one I'll mention is `random.sample(sequence, k)`. This one returns a new list containing `k` distinct elements from the sequence. It's great for sampling without replacement.

```
sample_toys = random.sample(toys, 2)
print("Randomly chosen toys:", sample_toys)
```

That's it for `random`! With the `random` module, you can create small games, shuffle decks of cards, randomize quiz questions, or pick a random winner from a list of participants. It's also commonly used in simulations and statistical sampling. It makes the things we can do a lot more interesting since the outcome becomes unpredictable to some extent.

Let's talk about the last module here, the `datetime` module.

The datetime module

When you need to work with dates and times, `datetime` is your friend.

```
from datetime import datetime

now = datetime.now()
print("Right now:", now)
```

You get an object describing the current date and time, plus you can manipulate or format it however you like. That prints something like:

```
Right now: 2025-01-24 22:32:47.731533
```

We can break this datetime object down:

```
current_time = datetime.now()
print("Year:", current_time.year)
print("Month:", current_time.month)
print("Day:", current_time.day)
print("Hour:", current_time.hour)
print("Minute:", current_time.minute)
print("Second:", current_time.second)
```

This will output:

```
Year: 2025
Month: 1
Day: 24
Hour: 22
Minute: 32
Second: 47
```

There's more to `datetime` than just current timestamps. We have other classes like `date`, `time`, `timedelta`, and more. I won't go into detail about all of these, but `timedelta` helps you do math with dates, like adding or subtracting days. And since I love math... Let's do it:

```
from datetime import datetime, timedelta

future_date = datetime.now() + timedelta(days=5)
print("Five days from now:", future_date)
```

This will output something like:

```
Five days from now: 2025-01-29 22:45:11.166744
```

There's more that you can do with this of course, but this should get you introduced to my friend `datetime`!

Let's talk about the last topic of this chapter, documentation and docstrings. They are great for our future-selves and other people to understand what our function is supposed to do.

Documentation and docstrings

Documentation is a description of what your code is for. This is a must-have for applications that you're writing. Documentation has to be written in a clear manner. Writing documentation helps everyone (including future you) understand what your function does, and that saves time! Also, it helps with debugging. We can do this with docstrings.

Writing good docstrings

A docstring is a string, surrounded by `"""`, which is placed right inside your function definition. This special docstring describes the function's purpose, parameters, and return value –for instance:

```
def area_of_circle(radius):
    # start of the docstring
    """
    Returns the area of a circle with a given radius.
    Uses the formula pi * r^2.
    """
    # end of the docstring
    import math
    return math.pi * radius * radius
```

If someone reads the function or uses it in an IDE, they'll see the docstring. This tells them what the function returns and what parameters are required. How can you use this? Well, editors will show it when you hover over the function. Here's how to create docstrings on our previous example:

```
def get_pet_info():
    """
    Asks the user for pet information and returns it as (pet_name,
species, food).
    If the user types 'quit' for pet_name, returns None to signal we're
done.
    """
    pet_name = input("What's your pet's name? ")
    if pet_name.lower() == "quit":
        return None
    species = input("What species is your pet? (e.g. cat, dog): ")
    food = input("What food do you want to give them? ")

    return (pet_name, species, food)
```

```
def feed_pet(pet_name, species, food):
    """
    Decides how a pet reacts based on its species and prints a feeding
message.
    """
    if species.lower() == "cat":
        print(pet_name, "arches their back and sniffs the", food)
    elif species.lower() == "dog":
        print(pet_name, "wags their tail excitedly at the sight of", food)
    else:
        print(pet_name, "looks curious about the", food)
    print("Feeding", pet_name, "some delicious", food, "now!\n")

def interactive_feeding():
    """
    Loops, gathering pet info and feeding them until user quits.
    """
    print("Welcome to the pet feeding station!")
    print("Type 'quit' when you're done feeding your pets.")

    while True:
        pet_data = get_pet_info()

        if pet_data is None:  # user typed 'quit' for the pet's name
            print("All done feeding pets! Bye!")
            break

        pet_name, species, food = pet_data
        feed_pet(pet_name, species, food)

# Call the main function to start the feeding loop
interactive_feeding()
```

This helps everybody understand what the functions do. This will prevent modifications that lead to errors, and it's easier to tell whether it's behaving as expected because, this way, you know the intended behavior.

Quiz

1. What keyword is used to declare a function?
    a. `fun`
    b. `def`
    c. `function`
    d. `decl`
2. What are `nr1` and `nr2` called in the following code?

```
def add_two_nrs(nr1, nr2):
    pass
```

    a. Arguments
    b. Libraries
    c. Parameters
    d. Keywords
3. What will the following code snippet output?

```
number = 7


def sneaky_quiz_question():
    if number > 5:
        print("Hello world")
    return True
```

    a. `Hello world, True`
    b. `Hello world`
    c. `True`
    d. Nothing
4. Why might you use keyword arguments `(keyword=value)` when calling a function?
    a. To make the function more flexible and able to handle varying inputs
    b. To provide default values for parameters
    c. For clarity and to allow changing argument order
    d. To force the function to return a value

5. If a function doesn't explicitly use `return`, what does it return by default?

    a. Undefined

    b. An empty string

    c. `None`

    d. It raises an error

6. True or false? A `return` statement exits a function immediately.

7. What is the `global` keyword used for?

    a. Declaring variables in the global scope that can be used inside a function

    b. Exporting variables from one file to another

    c. Accessing and modifying global variables inside functions

    d. Checking for loose equality between values

8. What is the purpose of `**kwargs` in Python functions?

    a. To collect extra keyword arguments into a dictionary

    b. To collect extra positional arguments into a list

    c. To collect all extra arguments into a tuple

    d. To define default arguments for a function

9. Why is the following piece of code not working?

```
from datetime import datetime

yesterday = datetime.now() + timedelta(days=-1)

print("Yesterday:", yesterday)
```

    a. There are no arguments passed into `datetime.now()`

    b. `timedelta` was never imported

    c. There was no function declared

    d. `timedelta` can't take negative values

10. What are docstrings for?

    a. When you want a multi-line string without using `\n` for new lines

    b. Writing comments in code

    c. Storing extra arguments that were passed into a function

    d. Describing a function's purpose

Exercises

6.1 Temperature conversion

In this exercise, you're going to create a function that converts temperatures from Celsius to Fahrenheit and the other way around! By default, the function should assume the input temperature is in Celsius and convert it to Fahrenheit. Think of a clever way to switch conversion modes when necessary and include a docstring.

Here are the temperature conversion formulas you'll need in this exercise:

- Celsius to Fahrenheit: Fahrenheit = (9/5 * Celsius) + 32
- Fahrenheit to Celsius: Celsius = 5/9 * (Fahrenheit – 32)

Test your function by calling it multiple times to make sure it all works correctly.

6.2 Tricky treat tracker

One of my students – no names will be mentioned – wrote the following functions to keep track of her remaining treats. She created one function to print the number of treats left and another to update the treat counter when she eats some. However, something isn't working as expected. The number of remaining treats doesn't seem to update. Here's your task: Figure out why this happens and fix the code so that the program correctly keeps track of the treats.

```
remaining_treats = 200

def print_treats_left():
    print(f"You have {remaining_treats} treats left.")

def eat_treats(remaining_treats, eaten_treats):
    print(f"Ate {eaten_treats} treats.")
    remaining_treats = remaining_treats - eaten_treats

print_treats_left()
eat_treats(remaining_treats, 50)
print_treats_left()
```

This outputs the following:

```
You have 200 treats left.
Ate 50 treats.
You have 200 treats left.
```

6.3 Packing lunch boxes

We're writing a function to pack lunchboxes. The `pack_lunchbox` function will accept an unknown number of keyword arguments, since we don't pack the same amount and categories of drinks and snacks every day. The function will simply print what's inside the lunchbox, clearly showing each category. Here's an example:

```
You packed your lunchbox:
Main: sandwich
Snack: chips
Drink: water
```

To make it a little bit more challenging, I'm asking you to print a reminder if no value was passed into the function with the label "snack". Here's an example:

```
Better pack a snack!
```

Pack your "lunchbox" a few times to see whether your function is working as it should.

6.4 Sorting hat

Now that you know all about functions, the magic spells of Python, it's safe to say that you're a wizard. Your next challenge is to create a function that mimics Hogwarts' legendary sorting hat. This function should randomly assign a Hogwarts house (Gryffindor, Slytherin, Hufflepuff, or Ravenclaw) to a student when called.

A possible output of your program could be the following:

```
You belong in... Gryffindor!
```

Here are the suggested steps:

1. Define a function: `sorting_hat()`
2. Declare a collection that holds the houses: Gryffindor, Slytherin, Hufflepuff, and Ravenclaw.
3. Select a random house from the houses using a function from the `random` module and store the result in a variable.
4. Print the sorting hat's decision!

Bonus challenge: Add some suspense! Python's `time` module has a cool function that can pause your program for a number of seconds: `time.sleep(seconds)`. That's just what you need to add a dramatic touch to your sorting hat function. Can you figure out how to use `time.sleep`? Let's adjust the function so it outputs something like the following:

```
The sorting hat is thinking...
```

Dramatic two-second pause:

```
You belong in Slytherin!
```

6.5 Dachshund fetch simulator

Dachshunds are smart, funny, and... very stubborn. In this exercise, you will create a function that simulates playing fetch with a dachshund.

Here's what you're going to do:

1. Write a `fetch()` function that takes two parameters: the dachshund's name and the object you want it to fetch.
2. For starters, make the function print a message such as the following:

```
"Wiesje fetched the newspaper!"
```

3. However, we all know this is highly unrealistic. Dachshunds have their own will, are easily distracted, and often refuse to fetch. Modify your function so that it randomly chooses a response instead of always saying the dachshund fetched the item. Create a list of possible responses.

Here's some inspiration:

- "Wiesje fetched the ball!"
- "Wiesje ignored you."
- "Wiesje went after the sock, but never brought it to you."
- "Wiesje got distracted!"
- "Wiesje goes after the toy, but halfway there, decides to take a nap."

4. Use a built-in function from the `random` module to select a random response from the list.
5. Call your function multiple times to see how stubborn your dachshund is!

6.6 Shopping cart checkout tool

When shopping, you often buy multiple items at different prices. In this exercise, you'll create a program that acts as a simple checkout tool. It will do the following:

- Ask the user how many items they bought
- Ask for the price of each item
- Calculate the total cost
- Display the final total in a clear way

By the end, your program will look something like this:

```
How many items are you buying? 2
Enter price of item 1: 4.57
Enter price of item 2: 10
Total: €14.57
```

Here are the suggested steps:

1. Define a function called `checkout`.
2. Inside this function, use the built-in `input()` function to ask the user how many items they're buying and convert their answer to an integer using the `int()` function.
3. Create a `total` variable and set it to `0` for now. Think about the scope of variables and place it wisely.
4. Use a `for` loop to ask the user to enter the price of each item they bought and add this to the total. Do not forget to convert the user input to the right data type.
5. Print the total.
6. Call the `checkout` function and check it out!

6.7 Rock-paper-scissors against the computer

In this exercise, you'll create a rock-paper-scissors game where you play against the computer. The game will ask the player to choose one of three options: rock, paper, or scissors. The computer will randomly pick one of the options as well. After that, the program will compare the choices to determine who won this round. The game will keep track of the score, and when either the computer or the player reaches 5 wins, the winner will be announced, and the game will stop. You can then interact with the console to restart the game.

There are multiple ways to program such a game, but here are the steps I'd recommend for now:

1. Define a function for the main game. Declare a collection for the options the players can choose from (rock, paper, or scissors) and variables that can keep track of both the computer's and the player's score.
2. Make sure the game runs while nobody has reached 5 wins yet. As long as that's the case, ask the player to enter rock, paper, scissors. Of course, store their response in a variable. Think of a smart way to deal with players accidentally entering invalid choices or capitalized answers.
3. Next, let the computer randomly pick one of the options.
4. Print both the computer's and the player's choice.
5. You probably know the rules of rock-paper-scissors. Write an extra function that handles the logic of determining the winner of a round. Return the result.
6. Print who won this round and update the winner's score.
7. At some point, either the computer or the player will have won five times and come out as the winner of the game. The winner is announced, and the player is asked whether they'd like a rematch. If they do, the game starts again.
8. Check whether everything is working properly. Can you beat the machine?

Summary

That was *Chapter 6* already! Time for a little recap. In this chapter, we discovered the magic spells in Python: functions. Functions are snippets of code that you can run by calling their name. Calling a function can also be called invoking a function. This comes in handy when we want to reuse blocks of code throughout programs. Without functions, there would be a lot of duplicate code. They make your code base more readable and easier to maintain.

A function is declared with the keyword `def`, followed by the function name and parentheses. You could pass parameters into these parentheses if you feel like your function needs them, but some functions work just fine without them. Parameters are placeholders for values you pass in when you call the function. Look at this simple example where we passed in the parameter name:

```
def praise_dog(name):
    print(f"{name} is a good dog!")
```

The code inside a function will not run unless you call the function. To call a function, simply use its name followed by parentheses, and pass in the arguments, which are the values that replace the placeholders – easy:

```
praise_dog("Wiesje")
```

Functions usually get a bit more complicated than this. They can contain all sorts of logic and even call other functions.

We studied quite a few interesting things around parameters and arguments. If you use default parameters, Python will use the default value if you don't provide an argument when calling the function.

Usually, arguments are positional. Which argument goes into which parameter is based on the order they are passed in. However, with keyword arguments, you explicitly specify which parameter the argument should match with by naming it in the function call.

When you don't know how many arguments might be passed to a function, you can use `*args` for extra positional arguments (collected in a tuple) and `**kwargs` for extra keyword arguments (collected in a dictionary). This makes your function more flexible and able to handle varying inputs.

Sometimes, you want your function to produce a piece of data. This is when we use the `return` statement. The `return` statement exits the function immediately, and gives back the value to where the function was called. For example, you could store the result of a calculation in a variable.

We also learned about scope in this chapter. Scope refers to the part of the code where variables or functions are available. By default, a variable created inside a function is only available within that function. This is called the local scope. Variables and functions declared outside of any function are accessible throughout the entire program: in the global scope. Sometimes, you might need to modify a global variable inside a function. This can be done with the `global` keyword or by returning the modified value from the function and reassigning it to the global variable outside the function.

We learned how to define our own functions, but we had already been using functions from the start. Python comes with lots of built-in functions, which saves us the trouble of writing complex code ourselves. Some examples of built-in functions we have been using already are `print()` and `input()`, but there are more! For example, for converting or checking data types. Python has a huge standard library with even more functions. We looked at modules for tasks such as calculations, generating random numbers, and working with dates and times. All of that was just the beginning. Python libraries offer so much more! Just remember, you need to import a library before you can use its functions.

At the end of this chapter, we covered the subject of documentation and docstrings. Docstrings are special strings placed inside a function to describe what it does. To write a docstring, simply place a triple-quoted (`"""`) string directly below the function definition. A well-written docstring clearly describes the function's purpose, making your code easier to understand and maintain.

Now that we all understand functions, the fun of programming in Python can really begin! Get ready for the next chapter: handling files.

Get this book's PDF version and more

Scan the QR code (or go to `packtpub.com/unlock`). Search for this book by name, confirm the edition, and then follow the steps on the page.

UNLOCK NOW

***Note:** Keep your invoice handy. Purchases made directly from Packt don't require an invoice.*

7

Handling Files and Exceptions

So far, we've talked a lot about storing information in variables, lists, dictionaries, and tuples. However, all of that stored data disappears once our Python program stops running. Imagine if every time you closed your code, you lost all the progress on your cat toy inventory, or the results of all the hard work that goes into tracking bird sightings. Not ideal to say the least.

That's where this chapter comes in. We'll learn how we can make programs that are going to alter files, for example, writing the cat toy inventory to a file. That way, we can see the results of our efforts later, and if we want, we can load it again the next time the program runs.

When handling files, it's important to also deal with problems related to handling files. What if a file that you rely on turns out to be missing or inaccessible, for example? This would give an error if we don't deal with it. And a problem like this is something that you don't always have control over from a developer perspective. If someone moved or locked the file, your code can't possibly know that beforehand. That's why we need to specify protocols for what to do when that happens. We'll talk about that later in the chapter.

Different types of files to handle

There are many ways to store data in files. There are also many ways to make distinctions between them. Let's say that the two main categories are text files and binary files. Text files are human-readable and typically contain text-based data. These might be `.txt` files, `.csv` files, `.json` files, or even code files such as `.py` itself—things you as (supposedly) a non-computer can read and understand.

Binary files, on the other hand, might be images, audio, or other non-textual data. We don't usually open them in a regular text editor. You might have done that accidentally sometimes, and if you did that, you probably could not make a lot of sense of what was displayed on the screen.

A few formats are especially common in Python. We'll explore the following files:

- Plain text files
- CSV files (useful for tabular data)
- JSON files (useful for storing structured data)

You'll also occasionally deal with images, PDFs, or other binary formats, but the basics remain the same: open the file, read or write its contents, then close it. We won't cover handling binary formats in this chapter. Let's start with the first step of reading and writing to files: opening and closing them.

Opening and closing files

Imagine you want to write a summary of this book, digitally. To do that, your first step would be to open a file before you can start writing. Python is just like that. In order to interact with a file in our code, we have to open the file first. And then when we are done with the file, we should close it again.

There is a very big difference between opening files in, for example, Word and opening files with Python. When we open a file in Python, we need to specify the actions we want to do with the file. It's a little bit like telling the customs office why you are visiting.

Specifying this action is done with an opening *mode*. The operating system may allow you to read from it, or to write to it, or both, depending on the opening mode you choose. We'll see those soon. Before we dive into opening files, let's first talk about the most common error beginners encounter when trying to work with files: getting the file location wrong.

File path considerations

If we want to open a file, we need to specify the location. Files live in directories (folders). Specifying the correct path so they can be found can be a tricky part of w orking with files.

We have two kinds of paths: absolute and relative. An absolute path starts at the root of your hard drive. A relative path starts wherever your Python program is running.

For example, on Windows, an absolute path might look like `C:\Users\Zia\Documents\cat_data.txt`, while on Linux or macOS, an absolute path might be `/home/zia/Documents/cat_data.txt`. If it doesn't start with `C:` (or another letter, depending on the drive name) on Windows, or with a forward slash (/) on Linux or macOS, it's not an absolute path.

Working with absolute paths is safe when running the code on your computer, because you specify the exact location and nothing can go wrong. However, if you transport it to another computer, it often fails because the path where the file is stored changes. Even if Wiesje and I had the same structure on our computer, we'd still have two different paths:

- **Mine**: `/home/zia/Documents/cat_data.txt`
- **Hers**: `/home/wiesje/Documents/cat_data.txt`

So, if I have the absolute path and I want to transport the Python file to another computer, it's a recipe for errors. Or at least, it would require customization of the code for the new system, and that's not recommended. It's better to use relative paths.

Relative paths let you write something such as `data.txt`. This works if `data.txt` is in the same folder as your Python file. Please bear in mind that if you are running Python from the terminal, you need to be in the same folder as your Python file when you run the Python file; otherwise, the relative path won't work.

If all the data is in a folder called `data` in your Python project, you could use a relative path like this: `data/data.txt`. This is looking for a folder, `data`, and then the `data.txt` file inside there, from wherever the program is running. This is safer, because it works when both Wiesje and I have our Python file in this location:

- **Mine**: `/home/zia/Documents/main.py`
- **Hers**: `/home/wiesje/Documents/main.py`

We'll assume we also have this file:

- **Mine**: `/home/zia/Documents/data/data.txt`
- **Hers**: `/home/wiesje/Documents/data/data.txt`

Even though the absolute paths are different, the relative paths will work. And that should prevent some errors with running code on different machines!

One last thing to note here: paths on Windows and Linux work differently. Linux uses forward slashes and Windows uses backslashes (or backward slashes). In order to make sure it is working, we can use Python's `os.path` module. This helps us deal with paths in a more platform-independent way:

```
import os

folder = "some_folder"
filename = "data.txt"

path = os.path.join(folder, filename)
print("Full path is:", path)
```

This produces a path sticking to the conventions of the operating system. On Windows, this might produce `some_folder\data.txt`. On macOS or Linux, it might produce `some_folder/data.txt`. That's a big help for writing code that runs anywhere.

Okay, having said that, let's talk about basic file handling now.

Basic file handling

Let's start by opening files. Here's how you might open a file in Python:

```
file_object = open("filename.txt", "r")
# Do something with file_object
file_object.close()
```

In this code, `"filename.txt"` is the file's name. Here, the file that we're reading is in the same folder as our `.py` file, which is reading the file. In order for this to work, you'll need to run the file from that folder directly. It might not work if you have it in a nested folder in VS Code and use the code runner button. You have options for solving that problem: opening that specific folder directly, moving it to the root of the project, specifying the path, or running it in the terminal should fix that problem. (Only one of these is required.)

`"r"` is the opening mode. This indicates we want to read the file. I'm omitting the middle part for now (the part where the comment is), but you can imagine that we can do things in between, such as actually reading the file. Then, when we are done, we eventually call `file_object.close()` to let Python (and our operating system) know we're done with the file.

Different read modes

If we want to read data as text, we use `"r"`. If we want to read binary data (such as an image), we might use `"rb"`. That tells Python that we're reading binary rather than text data. When you open a file in `"r"` mode and it doesn't exist, Python will complain by giving `FileNotFoundError`.

Different write modes

To write to a file, you use modes such as `"w"` for write or `"a"` for append. `"w"` will overwrite the file if it already exists. This is great if you want to create a fresh file from scratch, but it is terrible if you were hoping to keep that file. So, be mindful about choosing `"w"`. The `"a"` option will append data to the end of the file, which is handy for adding new lines. This can be used to add to a log without wiping out what's already there.

Here's an example of using `"w"` mode:

```
file_object = open("filename.txt", "w")
# Do something with file_object
file_object.close()
```

As you can see, it looks just like using `"r"`. There is a difference, though: if the file doesn't exist, it won't give an error. Instead, it will simply create it because we're in write mode.

The with statement

The previous way of opening works, but often, it's more convenient to use a `with` statement to open your file. The `with` statement automatically closes the file once you exit the indented block. That means even if something goes wrong, the file still gets closed:

```
with open("filename.txt", "r") as file:
    content = file.read()
    print(content)
```

In the preceding example, we again open the `filename.txt` file in reading mode. We store it in a `file` variable. Inside the indented code block, we can refer to `file`. In this case, we're using a read method; we'll get to that soon. When we're done reading (which happens as soon as we exit the indented block), Python closes the file automatically.

Opening files like this is considered best practice because it saves us from having to remember to call `close()` manually. And that prevents tricky "leftover open file" errors.

Reading files

Alright, onto the exciting part! Let's see how we can actually do something with these opened files. Once we have a file open in reading mode, we need to decide how we want to read the contents. Python offers a few different ways of reading that we can choose from.

read() versus readline() versus readlines()

- `read()` slurps up the entire file's content as a single string. If the file is large, that might be a lot of data to swallow at once. If it's too large (larger than the RAM that the Python program gets to use), the execution will become slow or crash.
- `readline()` reads a single line each time it's called. If you call it in a loop, you can process the file line by line without loading everything into memory at once. This is safer to use as it won't crash because of the file being too big to swallow at once.
- `readlines()` gives us a way of reading all lines at once. We'll get back a list containing all of those lines. That can be convenient if you don't mind having them all in memory. Again, we'll have to be careful that it fits in the available memory.

For a file with 1,000 lines, `readlines()` is probably fine. For a file with millions and millions of lines, you might have to choose reading line by line with `readline()`, to avoid using too much memory.

Using read() to read a file

Let's see how we can read the data in a file. Let's assume we're using the following file:

```
Wiesje, you act so grumpy, yet your Python code is bright;
Behind that bark and moody face is a heart filled with light.
Love,
Zia
```

I have stored this text in a file called `poem_for_wiesje.txt`.

Since I know for sure it's only a few lines, I can read it with the `read()` method:

```
with open("poem_for_wiesje.txt", "r") as file:
    content = file.read()
    print(content)
```

This will open the file, read the content, and store it in a variable called `content`. After that, it prints the entire content to the screen.

We could also have done this with `readline()` or `readlines()`. Let's see those methods as well.

readline() to read the file one line at a time

If you have a possibly larger file or you want to process each line as soon as you read it, `readline()` lets you read a single line each time it's called. It also moves the cursor of where it is reading to the next line, so the second time you call it, the second line (assuming there is one) is read. This way requires a few more lines of code. Here's how you can do it:

```
with open("poem_for_wiesje.txt", "r") as file:
    while True:
        line = file.readline()
        if not line:  # no more lines to read
            break
        print("Line read:", line.strip())
```

Here, we are again opening the file. Then, we need to start a loop, and we'll break out of that loop once we have finished reading all the lines in the file. First, we read a line from the file. After reading the line, we check whether there was indeed a line to read. If that's not the case, we snap out of the loop. Otherwise, we proceed to print the line we've just read. `strip()` is just to remove any trailing newline or spaces, making it cleaner when printing.

This is a better way for larger files, because it's more memory efficient. It only has one line of the file in memory at a time. It also allows for real-time processing as you read each line. That said, there are some cons. This doesn't allow us to randomly access lines in the file, and we can't jump back and forth as a result. If that's what we need, `readlines()` might actually be what we're looking for.

readlines() to get all lines as a list

With `readlines()`, we get a list of all lines in the file. Here's how to use it:

```
with open("poem_for_wiesje.txt", "r") as file:
    lines = file.readlines()
    for index, line in enumerate(lines):
        print(f"Line {index+1}:", line.strip())
```

Here, we are again opening the file in read mode. Then, we are reading the whole file at once with the `readlines()` method. We store the list in `lines`. This is very helpful if we want each line in a list and don't mind storing them all in memory. Once we have a list, we can easily iterate over or slice the list. In this case, we use the `enumerate()` function.

This function adds a counter to each item in a list, and that way, we can print line numbers in front of each line. That's why you see `index, line`, instead of one name. Remember, we can only use `readlines()` when the file is of a manageable size.

There's another way to loop over the lines in a file. Let's see that next.

Iterating over a file object

There's another way to read the lines: we can iterate over the file object in a `for` loop. This gives you each line one at a time, without loading the whole file at once. As a bonus, the syntax is a little friendlier than the `readline()` syntax:

```
with open("poem_for_wiesje.txt", "r") as file:
    for line in file:
        print("Read line:", line.strip())
```

With these three lines of code, we read each line in the file, one by one, until it reaches the end of the file.

And that's how to read files. Time to move on to writing!

Writing to files

Writing is, in a way, more exciting, and it's not too different from reading. I remember learning how to write to a file in my first programming language; finally, my changes persisted after ending the program! How cool is that?

An important warning here first! Do not overwrite files (especially important ones), unless they are backed up first and you are sure that's what you want. Once you overwrite a file, the original content will be gone. Alright, now that I have given that warning, let's write to a file!

Just like when we start reading from a file, we start by opening the file, but this time i n write mode, using "w", "a", or "wb" for binary. After that, we call the writing methods.

The simplest approach is to use `write()`:

```
with open("log.txt", "w") as file:
    file.write("Zia loved her new toy!\n")
    file.write("Wiesje remained unimpressed...\n")
```

After these lines, our `log.txt` file contains those two lines of text. If the file existed before, it's wiped clean (yes, empty) at the very moment we opened it with "w". If we want to add lines to an existing file without erasing it, we should use "a" as the opening mode instead. This "a" stands for *append*, and it will allow us to add to the end of the file. Here's how that looks:

```
with open("log.txt", "a") as file:
    file.write("Adding one more line...\n")
```

As you can see, appending works the same as writing. It just starts with "a" as the chosen mode. Appending is commonly used for logs, and for any other scenario where you want to build up a file over time.

Working with different file formats

So far, we've only seen how to read and write plain text files. These text files are nice, but many files have special formats, and that requires a slightly different approach. CSV and JSON are two such formats that are extremely common. Writing and reading these files are done differently. In order to do this, we'll have to use built-in modules that make reading and writing them simpler.

Let's start by seeing how this is done for CSV files.

CSV files

CSV stands for **comma-separated values.** It's a text-based format that's easy to open in spreadsheets such as Excel, but also easy to parse programmatically. Let's see an example of a CSV file:

```
name,species,age,favorite_food
Zia,cat,1,tuna
Wiesje,dog,7,kibble
Axel,axolotl,2,worms
```

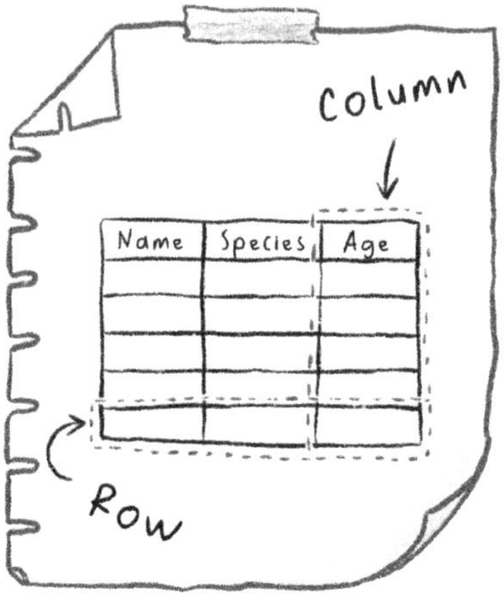

The first line in this file represents the column names. For example, the last column is the favorite food of a pet. The next rows are the pet records, where every value represents the column in order. So, for example, Wiesje's favorite food is kibble.

With Python's `csv` module, we can handle comma-delimited text (the splitting of lines by commas). Here's how we can write to a file named `pets.csv`. Please bear in mind that this is not related to the preceding file; this is a new file (and even if it were the same file, we'd be overwriting it since we're opening it in write mode anyway). Here's how to write to a CSV file:

```
import csv

with open("pets.csv", "w", newline="") as file:
    writer = csv.writer(file)
    writer.writerow(["Name", "Species", "Age"])
    writer.writerow(["Zia", "Cat", "1"])
    writer.writerow(["Wiesje", "Dog", "7"])
```

Here, we are opening a file, `pets.csv`. If it doesn't exist yet, it will be created as we're using `"w"` as the open mode. We specify that the newline character is empty. This lets the `csv` module handle the endings of the lines (which is sufficient in most cases when working with `csv`). Then, we create a special writer using our opened file.

This writer has a method, `writerow`, that we can use to add new rows. As you can see, we are passing in lists to specify the different columns. The first row is again representing the column headers, and the next rows are the data that is in there. We can append in a similar way. We'll just have to choose a different opening mode:

```
import csv
with open("pets.csv", "a", newline="") as file:
    writer = csv.writer(file)
    writer.writerow(["Muchu","cat",0])
```

When reading CSV files, we do something similar:

```
import csv
with open("pets.csv", "r") as file:
    reader = csv.reader(file)
    for row in reader:
        print(row)
```

Here, we open the file in reading mode, and this time we use the `csv` module to create a reader. We can then iterate over the rows in the reader with a `for` loop. We print every row. Every row is a list. Here's the exact output:

```
['Name', 'Species', 'Age']
['Zia', 'Cat', '1']
['Wiesje', 'Dog', '7']
['Muchu', 'cat', '0']
```

As you can see, every row is a list. In order to get the column of a list, we'll have to specify the list index. For example, this will only print the names:

```
import csv
with open("pets.csv", "r") as file:
    reader = csv.reader(file)
    for row in reader:
        print(row[0])
```

Here's the output:

```
Name
Zia
Wiesje
Muchu
```

That's how to deal with reading and writing CSV files. Let's see JSON files next.

JSON files

JSON is a somewhat more complex format than CSV. **JSON** stands for **JavaScript Object Notation**. This sort of means it represents objects using the syntax of JavaScript. It also happens to be very similar to the dictionary syntax. The JSON format represents data as dictionaries and lists in text form. It's very handy for configurations or any scenario where we want some sort of structured data.

Here's an example of a simple JSON object:

```
{
  "name": "Zia",
  "species": "cat",
  "age": 1,
  "favorite_foods": ["tuna", "chicken"]
}
```

Please note that around the object, we have two curly brackets. Inside the object, we have key-value pairs. The keys are on the left-hand side, while the values are on the right-hand side. The values can be strings, such as `"Zia"`, which is the value associated with the `"name"` key. But values can also be numbers, booleans, or null values, as well as more complex structures, such as lists. The `favorite_foods` key has a list as a value. Values can even be objects as well. That can't be seen in the preceding JSON, but here's an example of an object in another object:

```
{
  "name": "Zia",
  "species": "cat",
  "age": 1,
  "favorite_foods": ["tuna", "chicken"],
  "best_friend": {
  "name": "Wiesje",
  "species": "dog",
  "age": 7,
  "favorite_foods": ["kibble", "cheese"]
  }
}
```

Here, we have a `best_friend` key. The type of `best_friend` is object, as we can tell by the curly braces around it (remember, JSON syntax is very similar to dictionaries). Inside `best_friend`, we have other sets of key-value pairs, including another `favorite_foods` key, which in its turn is a list.

Often, JSON objects are more complex. For example, I'm currently working with a big JSON file that holds all the translations to different languages for all the labels on a website. That is so big that it would take the rest of the book to cover it. Also, I don't think my client would like it if I shared their data. So, let's see a smaller example of a more nested structure:

```
{
  "pets": [
    {
      "name": "Zia",
      "species": "cat",
      "age": 1,
      "favorite_foods": ["tuna", "chicken"]
    },
    {
      "name": "Wiesje",
      "species": "dog",
      "age": 7,
      "favorite_foods": ["kibble", "cheese"]
    },
    {
      "name": "Axel",
      "species": "axolotl",
      "age": 2,
      "favorite_foods": ["earthworms", "pellets"]
    }
  ]
}
```

Question: Is this JSON representing an overall list or an overall object? Try not to look at the next line, but look at the JSON structure.

The outer brackets are curly, and that's how you can tell it's an object. If they were square, it would have been a list. These are the only two options for the JSON data structure: it's either one object (so not multiple, comma-separated) or a list. There always has to be one root. In this case, the outer object only contains one key-value pair, and that is the `pets` key with a list as the value.

Inside that list, we have three objects: one representing me, one representing Wiesje, and one representing Axel. (To be fair, Axel doesn't really exist; it's the imaginary axolotl my tiny human has. My main human is afraid I'd eat Axel, so he's not allowed to actually get one. Pfft.)

Alright, so back to reading and writing files. Python's `json` module can encode (serialize) and decode (deserialize) data from Python to JSON or back again. This means that the JSON data is represented as a Python object (deserialized) or that the Python object is represented in a JSON format (serialized). Don't worry if you don't exactly understand what a Python object is yet; we'll dive into it in the next chapter. For now, you can think of them as dictionaries.

Let's use a smaller data object for the sake of the readability of this example:

```
import json

data = {
    "pet": "Zia",
    "toys": ["feather wand", "ball", "laser pointer"],
    "weight": 2.2
}

with open("pet_data.json", "w") as file:
    json.dump(data, file)
```

Here, we have a small dictionary. Then, we go ahead and open a file in write mode, and write that object in JSON format to it using the `json.dump()` method. If we open the file (`pet_data.json`), we can see the JSON object:

```
{
    "pet": "Zia",
    "toys": ["feather wand", "ball", "laser pointer"],
    "weight": 2.2
}
```

Now, we can do all sorts of things. If we wanted to read this file in Python later, that is one of the possibilities we have. Here's how to do that:

```
with open("pet_data.json", "r") as file:
    loaded_data = json.load(file)
    print(loaded_data["pet"])
```

We open the file in reading mode this time. There, we use the `json.load()` method to turn the JSON into a Python object. We can navigate it like we're used to doing for a dictionary, by using the key to get the value. In this case, we use the `"pet"` key, so we'll see the value `"Zia"` printed. By using the `json` module, we don't have to worry about splitting lines or doing complicated parsing on our own in order to interpret the JSON structure. Very handy indeed!

That doesn't mean nothing can go wrong, though. Let's talk about how to manage when things go wrong.

Handling errors and exceptions

Errors can always happen. For example, you may try to run this Python program:

```
print(age)
```

You'd get an output like this:

```
ERROR!
Traceback (most recent call last):
  File "<main.py>", line 1, in <module>
NameError: name 'age' is not defined
```

We get a `NameError` here (which would be really funny if the variable were called `name`). This is because we are trying to access a variable called age, which we don't have. Since it doesn't have that variable, Python can't print it. It would be like giving Wiesje a command we never taught her. What would a dog do if we told it to lemon?

The output shows the traceback, sometimes also called stacktrace. In this case, it's only one line. It could be multiple lines, and if so, then it shows the path through the code that happened before the error occurred. This helps in figuring out what went wrong. In this case, it's simple. It says that line 1 in our `main.py` file gave an error. After that, it specifies the precise error.

This particular error could have been avoided by writing better code. If we had defined the variable, we could have printed it:

```
age = 2
print(age)
```

No problem here, it's just outputting the value of `age` now.

When working with files, errors can happen too. Some of the errors can be avoided by writing better code. However, some errors are out of our control, such as the following:

- The file we try to read might not exist, or we might not have permission to open it
- The content of the file that we're trying to read has a surprising format, and we're trying to access keys or other structures that don't exist
- We might run out of disk space while writing or reading a file

Well, how about those? We can't make these problems go away by simply writing better code. What we can do is specify how to handle these errors when they do occur.

Handling errors is done with a `try-except` code block.

try-except blocks

In order to deal with possible errors, we can put the code that potentially gives an error in a `try` block. This `try` block is followed by an `except` block. In this `except` block, we specify how to respond when a certain error occurs. The code in the `except` block only runs if that error happens in the `try` block. Ideally, we don't get the error, and the code in the `except` block never runs. Here's an example of a basic `try-except` block:

```
try:
    print("Great job so far,", name)
except:
    print("Oh no, something went wrong")
```

If we run this code, we get the following output:

```
Oh no, something went wrong
```

In this code snippet, we say: try to execute the following code (in this case, printing a line). If we get an error, execute the code in the except block instead. Since the variable name has not been defined, we get `NameError`. That means that the code in the `except` block is executed. In this case, the `except` block is triggered for all sorts of errors. We could be more specific by writing the exact error just after the `except` clause.

That way, the `except` block only gets triggered for that specific error, like this:

```
try:
    print("Great job so far,", name)
except NameError:
    print("Oh no, something went wrong")
```

Clearly, this is a terrible practice. We should have just defined the `name` variable. We can also specify a block for when `try` does not result in any errors; that's where the `else` block comes in:

```
try:
    name = "Wiesje"
    print("Great job so far,", name)
except:
    print("Oh no, something went wrong")
else:
    print("Woohoo, all went well")
```

Now that we have defined `name`, our code will output the following:

```
Great job so far, Wiesje
Woohoo, all went well
```

If we want to run some code regardless of whether the `try` block executed with or without an error, we can write this code in a `finally` block. This can be used for cleaning up resources, such as closing files if you need to do so manually. Here's what that syntax looks like:

```
try:
    name = "Wiesje"
    print("Great job so far,", name)
except:
    print("Oh no, something went wrong")
finally:
    print("You'll see this message, error or not")
```

This outputs the following:

```
Great job so far, Wiesje
You'll see this message, error or not
```

Even if the preceding code resulted in an error, the `finally` block would execute, and the last line would have been printed. Alright, back to handling files. Here are two common errors we can get when working with files:

- `FileNotFoundError` happens if the file doesn't exist when opening in read mode
- `PermissionError` can happen if we don't have permission to read or write the file

To deal with these gracefully, we can wrap our file operations in a `try-except` block:

```
try:
    with open("secret_plans.txt", "r") as file:
        data = file.read()
        print(data)
except FileNotFoundError:
    print("No secret plans found. Perhaps they're locked away safely?")
```

Here, we try to open a file called `secret_plans.txt`. If this file cannot be found, we print the message that there are no secret plans found. If it gives `PermissionError`, we still get the ugly stacktrace. Let me show you how we can deal with multiple errors by adding additional `except` blocks:

```
try:
    with open("secret_plans.txt", "r") as file:
        data = file.read()
        print(data)
except FileNotFoundError:
    print("No secret plans found. Perhaps they're locked away safely?")
except PermissionError:
    print("You do not have permission to access these secrets.")
```

You can see that we now have two `except` blocks. If an error occurs, Python is going to look for an `except` block that deals with that specific error. This way, our program doesn't crash with a scary traceback when we get `FileNotFoundError` or `PermissionError`. Instead, it prints a friendly message if one of these errors happens. If the code in the `try` block encounters a different error, it will still show a traceback, as we didn't specify what to do in case of other errors.

Ensuring data integrity

One last note before we wrap up this chapter. Let's say that our program crashes halfway through writing to a file. This means that we might end up with half-written data. This can be problematic, especially if we're overwriting a file and end up losing important content.

One common safeguard is writing to a temporary file first. If that were successful, we would then rename it to the final file. That's a more advanced technique that you don't need to worry about at this stage of your coding career, but it's good to be aware of it for mission-critical data.

Quiz

1. What is the advantage of opening files with the `with` statement?

    a. It prevents accidental overwriting of content

    b. It automatically deals with errors

    c. It automatically calls the `close()` method when you exit the block

    d. If the file you're trying to open doesn't exist, it will create it for you

2. What does the `read()` method do when reading a file?

    a. It reads the file one line at a time

    b. It iterates over the lines of the file to handle one line at a time

    c. It reads the line of the file where the cursor is at

    d. It reads the entire file and returns it as a single string

3. What does the `readlines()` method return when reading a file?

    a. A list of all the lines in the file

    b. A string of all the lines in the file

    c. A `for` loop that iterates over each line in the file

    d. The length of the file

4. Which mode would you use to write an extra line of text to an existing `.txt` file?

    a. `"a"`

    b. `"w"`

    c. `"r"`

    d. `"y"`

5. When opening a file in `"wb"` mode, what happens?

    a. The file is opened for writing, and all existing content stays intact

    b. The file is opened for appending binary data without erasing existing content

    c. The file is opened for writing in backup mode, keeping a copy of the original file

    d. The file is opened for writing in binary mode, and any existing content is erased

6. What does CSV stand for?
    a. Cat supremacy verification
    b. Code syntax validator
    c. Comma-separated values
    d. Column-structured variables
7. What is a CSV file?
    a. A binary file that can contain an image
    b. A text file that stores tabular data
    c. A spreadsheet
    d. A file that can hold an object or list in JavaScript syntax
8. What does the first row of a CSV file typically contain?
    a. The filename
    b. The column headers
    c. Curly or square brackets
    d. Default values
9. What's JSON?
    a. A binary data format that can store images
    b. A programming language closely related to Python
    c. A text file format used to store tabular information
    d. A data format that can hold one object or a list in JavaScript syntax
10. How can you use JSON data in your Python project?
    a. Directly. The syntax of JavaScript objects is the same as Python dictionaries.
    b. By importing the `json` module and using the `load()` method.
    c. By importing the `json` module and using the `dump()` method.
    d. Only by using the `with` statement to open the `.json` file.
11. How do you handle errors and exceptions?
    a. By writing flawless code, so you never get any errors
    b. With a `try-except` block
    c. With a `try-catch` block
    d. With a `fly-accept` block

Exercises

For these exercises, we'll work with a few files. You can download them from our book's GitHub repository. So there's no need to type anything over by hand.

GitHub repository: `https://github.com/BrightBoost/python-illustrated`

If downloading these files isn't possible for you right now (or maybe you just don't feel like it), no problem. The full contents of all files are included in the *Appendix A* (page 333), so you can still follow along by recreating the files. That option does, however, involve typing. Quite a bit of it.

7.1 Reading a personal letter

In this exercise, you'll practice opening and reading a file using Python, as well as handling errors gracefully.

Here's what you'll do:

1. Download `letter.txt` from our Git repository. Alternatively, you can create your own `.txt` file in which you write a short, heartfelt letter to Wiesje or your own pet.
2. Write a Python script that opens `letter.txt` and reads and prints the entire content of the file at once.

3. Use a `try-except` block to handle cases where the file is missing. Think of a friendly error message that is printed when the file cannot be found.
4. Test your error handling, make the `letter.txt` file go missing, and run the script again.

7.2 Adding your name to the list

For this exercise, let's pretend you're helping me build a simple attendance list for my Python workshop. Every time someone runs the script, they'll be able to add their name to the file, without removing the names of others who've joined, obviously.

Your task is to write a program that does the following:

- Asks the user to enter their name
- Opens a file called `attendance.txt`
- Adds the name to the list
- Prints a welcome message to confirm that the user's name was added to the list

7.3 Note to self

I believe in the power of self-reflection. In this exercise, you'll create a file in which you write a few lines of empowering or meaningful advice for yourself. Once you've finished writing, read the file and display each line on the screen, numbered individually.

The following are the recommended steps:

1. Open and create a file named `note_to_self.txt`
2. Use the `write()` method multiple times to add several lines of empowering words to the file.
3. Read the file and print each line numbered individually. Make sure you use the right reading method for this.
4. Add error handling to manage any issues if the file can't be read.

Bonus challenge: Define a function in which you pick a random line from your file and display it. You can go wild with this. Work with user input, add `if` statements, combine everything you've learned so far, or keep it simple. Just write a funny program that acts a bit like an oracle. Purrfect for a quick dose of wisdom or encouragement!

7.4 Wiener dog races

Wiener dog races are a thing. I know, it sounds controversial, maybe a little weird, but everyone needs a hobby, right? Anyway, you're given a file, `wiener_dog_race_results.csv` (available from the book's GitHub repository), that holds the results of a wiener dog race. With this file, you're going to practice your CSV file handling skills.

Count the participants

First, you're going to write a function that counts how many participants took part in the race. Don't just open the file and count the names manually; use Python to do the work for you.

There are several solutions to this problem. Here are my recommended steps if you need a little guide:

1. Import Python's `csv` module.
2. Open the `wiener_dog_race_results.csv` file in read mode.
3. Use `csv.reader()` to read the contents of the csv file.
4. Convert the contents to a list using the built-in `list()` function.

5. Use the `len()` function to determine how many rows or participants were in the race file. Keep in mind that the first row of a CSV file represents the header of a table! There are multiple ways to deal with this. You could just subtract the total number of rows by 1, or see whether you can find a way to extract just the race data into a new list.
6. Up for a small challenge? Deal with possible empty rows in the list.

Add Wiesje's race results

Just when you thought no more dogs were going to cross the finish line... here comes Wiesje! She finishes with a time of 42.0 seconds. Your job is to add her race results to the CSV file.

The following are the suggested steps:

1. Open the `wiener_dog_race_results.csv` file in the correct opening mode for writing that does not overwrite the original content of the file.
2. Create a function that can be used to add new race results to `wiener_dog_race_results.csv`.
3. Use `csv.writer()` along with its `writerow()` method to add new results to the file.

4. Comment out the function call, so you don't keep adding Wiesje's results each time you try to run your code. Or, even better, make sure you can't add a new participant to the list if there's already a dachshund with the same name in the file. In the real world, you would probably work with race numbers to deal with duplicates, but we're keeping it simple here.

Rank the wieners

Now that all results are in, it's time to rank the dachshunds by speed. You need to write a function that sorts the dogs by their finish time, with the fastest dachshund at the top.

This exercise might be a bit of a hurdle, so take your time to really think it through.

Here's my advice:

1. Open the `wiener_dog_race_results.csv` file in reading mode.
2. Use the `csv.reader()` and `list()` functions to parse the content of the file to a list.
3. Store the participant data (excluding the header of the file) in a separate variable by creating a tactic slice.

4. Loop over the participant data and convert all finish times to floats using the `float()` function. This is necessary to be able to compare finish times.
5. Once you've converted the finish times to floats, the next step is to sort the list of dogs by their finish time, with the fastest (the smallest number) at the top. To do this, you'll need to compare each dog's finish time with every other dog's finish time. You'll use nested loops to do this. The outer loop picks a dog to compare, and the inner loop compares that dog's time with all the others that come after it in the list. If the dog in the outer loop has a slower time than the dog in the inner loop, you swap their places in the list. You can use swap syntax `data[i], data[j] = data[j], data[i]` to switch the positions of the two dogs. Alternatively, you can figure out how to use the `sorted()` function to sort this list of data.

Determine the wiener, uh, winner

Lastly, write a function to announce the winner. The output should look something like this:

```
"Dachshund [name] wins the race with an astonishing time of [time]
seconds!"
```

There are, again, multiple ways to do this. If you managed to create a file with sorted results, it should be pretty easy to find the results of the winner.

Play around

You've created quite a fun set of functions now. Play around and see what happens if you add more participants to your list. You could try and find ways to handle cases where an invalid finish time, or no time at all, was entered. Break your file or code on purpose and improve your error handling. Maybe refactor your code to see whether y ou can wrap repetitive pieces of code in functions. There's so much to practice!

7.5 Wood type catalog

Wood can be used for scratching posts, furniture, holding up entire buildings, and so much more. It's truly amazing. There are different types of wood, and each type has its own properties and use cases. For this exercise, you're given a digital wood catalog stored in a JSON file: `wood_types.json`. This file contains data about a few wood types: their name, hardness, color, and common uses.

You can download this file from the book's GitHub repository. Typing it over from the appendix could be a meditative practice, but it won't improve your skills.

Define a function to load the data

Start by creating a function called `load_woods()` that loads the data from `wood_types.json`. You'll use this function later whenever you want to read from the file.

Display all wood data

Take a good look at the structure of the JSON file and define a function, `display_woods()`, that prints all information of each wood type, separated by a blank line.

The output of `display_woods()` will look a little bit longer than this, but this is the format we're aiming for:

```
Name: Oak
Hardness: 9
Color: rich brown
Uses: furniture, flooring, barrels, architectural joinery

Name: Maple
Hardness: 8
Color: creamy white
Uses: kitchen cabinets, flooring, cutting boards, musical instruments

Name: Pine
Hardness: 4
Color: yellowish white
Uses: construction framing, interior paneling, furniture, millwork
```

Adding another type of wood to the encyclopedia

Great! Let's use Python to add another wood type to our `wood_types.json` file. Write a function, `add_wood()`, that handles this for you.

This is the wood type I want you to add:

```
{
    "name": "Dark Oak",
    "hardness": 8,
    "color": "dark brown",
    "uses": ["flooring", "furniture", "cabinets"]
}
```

Filter wood types

Define a function that takes one argument: a use case for wood (a string such as `"furniture"`). The function should search through the wood types and print the names of all woods that have this use in their uses list.

Example output:

```
Woods commonly used for furniture:
Oak
Pine
Birch
Cherry
Bamboo
Dark Oak
```

That's it. You've made it through the woods. However, there's always another log to load. I encourage you to think of other things you could do with this JSON file. Perhaps you can improve your `add_wood()` function so it doesn't allow duplicates, or sort the wood types by hardness. Keep challenging yourself. And if your code breaks or gets a little buggy? Remember, this is just an exercise. It's meant for practice, so it's okay to mess it up a little.

Summary

That's it for handling files and exceptions. I hope this chapter wasn't as boring to you as Wiesje predicted it would be. Even if it was a bit boring, you should now understand the importance of this topic. You learned that by storing data in files instead of just variables, you can keep your progress after a program has stopped running.

An important part of handling files is knowing where to find the files. This is why we dove into file paths. There are two kinds of paths: absolute and relative. An absolute path starts at the root directory of your system, and a relative path starts from the folder your program is currently in.

Paths work differently on different operating systems. This is where Python's `os.path` module comes to the rescue. It lets you deal with paths in a more platform-independent way.

We discussed several types of files that we can read, write, and update using Python code. The first thing you need to do when you want to do something with a file is open it. Pretty obvious, I know. When you're done, you have to close the file. You can open a file in different modes for different purposes: `"w"` for writing (and creating), `"a"` for appending, and `"r"` for reading. If it's binary data you're dealing with, you just add `"b"` after the letter of your opening mode.

We learned how to open and close files manually, but we also discovered an even more convenient way to do this: with the `with` statement! The `with` statement closes automatically once you exit the indented block. It looks like this:

```
with open("filename.txt", "r") as file:
    # Do something with file
```

There are a few ways to read a file, and which option is best depends on the size of the file and how you want to handle it:

- The `read()` method is an easy way to read files when they're not too large. It slurps up the entire content of a file as a single (multiline) string.
- The `readline()` method reads a single line every time it's called. You'd have to combine it with a loop that you break out of once there are no more lines to read. It's a better choice than `read()` if you're dealing with a large file, or if you want to deal with each line separately.
- With `readlines()`, we get a list of all the lines. This, like `read()`, processes the entire file at once, but still allows you to handle each line separately.
- You can also iterate over the file object in a `for` loop. This has the same advantages as the `readline()` method, but a slightly friendlier syntax.

The easiest way to write or append lines to a file is by using the `write()` method. The most crucial part of writing and appending is picking the right opening mode. Small reminder: `"w"` wipes out the original content of the file. So, if you just want to add something to an existing file without erasing it, use `"a"`. This is what adding an entry to a diary could look like:

```
with open("zia_diary.txt", "a") as file:
    file.write("Remember: never leave socks unattended.\n")
    file.write("Wiesje has claimed another victim.\n")
```

Writing and reading files is luckily not limited to diary entries and love letters to Wiesje. We can also work with different file formats, such as CSV and JSON.

CSV stands for **comma-separated values** and is a text-based format that's great for storing tabular data. With Python's `csv` module, we can read and edit these files. We studied how to use `csv.reader()` to read rows of data, and `csv.writer()` along with its `writerow()` method to add rows of data.

Like CSV, JSON is another format commonly used to store structured data. **JSON** stands for **JavaScript Object Notation**. We saw how the syntax of a JavaScript object is very similar to Python's dictionary syntax. A file in JSON format can represent data in a list or object. To use this JSON data in Python, it needs to be translated to a Python object. The `json` module allows us to convert data between Python objects and JSON format. The `json.load()` method turns the JSON into a Python object. The `json.dump()` method converts a Python object into JSON and writes it to a file.

Errors can happen sometimes, especially when handling files. You can't always prevent this by writing better code. However, you can write code that specifies how to deal with these errors. `try-except` blocks are your best friend here. You put the code that might give an error in the `try` block and specify how to respond to errors in the `except` block. An `except` block only runs if an error occurred in the `try` block. You can add multiple `except` blocks to deal with different errors. If something needs to happen, whether the code in the `try` block executed successfully or not, you can add a piece of code in a `finally` block. Here's an example of a `try-except` block in action:

```
try:
    with open("zia_diary.txt", "r") as file:
        print(file.read())
except PermissionError:
    print("Back off, Wiesje! Zia's diary is private!")
except FileNotFoundError:
    print("Zia's diary is missing...")
```

It might take a while to master the art of file handling in Python, or maybe you got it right away. Either way, you're making great strides! Remember that every bug you fix and every missing file you find brings you one step closer to becoming a Python pro. So, with that said, you're ready for the next chapter, on creating and using classes.

8

Creating and Using Classes

This is such a cool chapter. Up until now, we've been working in what is called a (mostly) procedural style: we have data structures such as lists and dictionaries, and we write functions to alter and use them. There's nothing inherently wrong with that. The procedural approach is fine for many scenarios.

But not for all! When we are working on programs that grow a little big, we might want a way to bundle data and behaviors together. And this is where classes come in. With classes, we define our own data types. We specify the data fields (attributes, sometimes called properties) and the methods for a type. Later, we can create instances of these classes (objects) to store specific data.

Working with classes allows us to move from procedural style programming to object-oriented programming. This chapter will introduce you to this concept to structure your code even more.

Introduction to Object-Oriented Programming (OOP)

OOP is not something that's specific to Python. All languages that support the creation of classes can be used to write code in the OOP style. The number one key building block to OOP is the concept of classes. This is not an easy concept, so please be patient and kind with yourself if you struggle to understand it at first.

Understanding classes and objects

A class can be seen as a blueprint for data, or a data type if you like. If we create a class, we specify two main things in there (don't worry about how to do that just yet):

1. Attributes (data fields): The data each object of that class holds
2. Methods (like functions): The actions or behaviors each object can perform

So, let's say we create a class for cat. It could have attributes such as name, age, energy level, and color. And it could have methods such as play, eat, demand cuddles, and sleep on a laptop. This class would be the blueprint of a cat, not an actual cat. It's a specification for the concept of a cat. A cat has said attributes and can perform the specified methods.

If you think of an actual cat, like me, this actual cat would be known as an instance of the class. We call instances of classes "objects." An object has specific values for attributes; for example, the name property for me would have the value Zia.

There's only one blueprint, but there can be many objects. I would be an object, and all my cat friends would be objects too. We exist separately from one another. If I perform my sleep method on my laptop, my friend Muchu's energy levels won't be restored, but mine will.

So, each individual "cat" is also known as an **object** (instance of a class). Zia, Muchu, Garfield, and Puss in Boots are all objects (instances) of the class cat. That means we share the same blueprint (such as having a name, an age, energy level, and a color), but each cat has its own specific values for those attributes (such as "Zia", 1, 85, "grey").

This class versus object distinction is usually hard for anyone new to OOP, so don't worry if it's hard for you too right now. Just review it again later. Let me summarize it like this:

- Class = blueprint, the high-level concept of a type (or thing if you like)
- Object = instance of a class, actual concrete "thing" of a type of that class

You can think of the concept (class) without having an object. For example, I can think of an axolotl without having a concrete axolotl friend. That is because my mind has a blueprint of an axolotl. However, I can't feed the concept of an axolotl a worm; in order to be able to do that, I'd need an actual axolotl object.

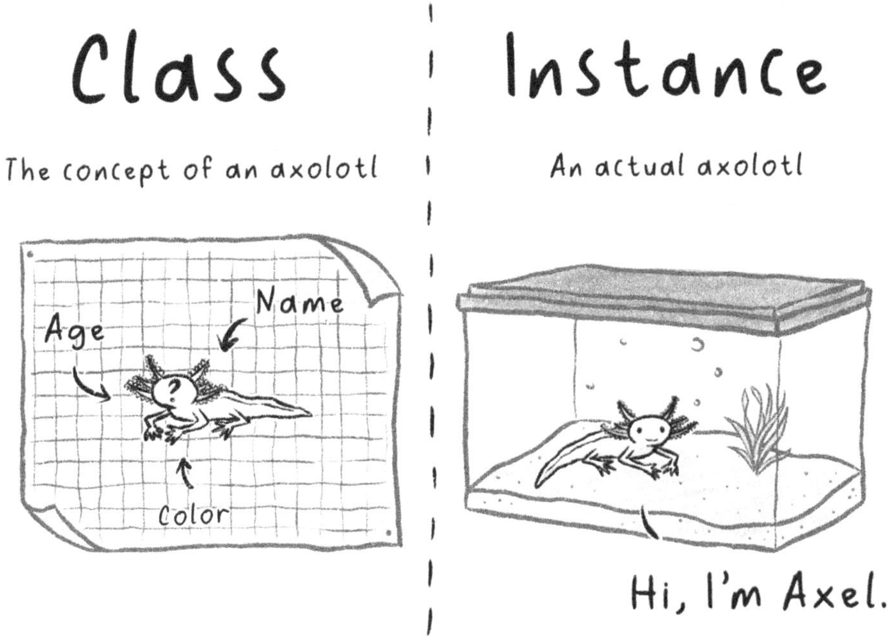

Disclaimer: This tank matches the book's minimalist style, not the authors' standards for real-life pet care.

Anything can be a type (which is a synonym for class in Python). Here are some random examples:

- Email
- User
- Product
- Invoice
- BlogPost
- Book

The main trick when thinking about classes is seeing that it's a way of reducing something (such as an email) to a set of attributes and methods. This is often hard to do when you're new to it, but with practice, it becomes a lot easier. For example, an email could have these attributes:

- Message body
- Date
- Sender
- Receiver
- Attachments

And these methods:

- Reply
- Forward
- Flag
- Delete

These types would represent core entities in our application, and they're typically easiest to understand, but classes can also be used for different purposes. Don't worry if this is too abstract still; it is something that you'll grow into if you use it more. Just to give you some more options for classes, I'll elaborate a little on it here.

You could have a service or manager class, such as EmailService or PaymentProcessor. There are also classes dedicated to connecting with the database. An example of that could be UserRepository or ProductRepository. If we create dynamic user interfaces (the visible layout the user interacts with) with Python, we can also have special classes for views, such as LoginForm or DashboardView. Configuration and helper classes are also a thing; classes such as AppConfig and MathUtils are not uncommon to encounter either. There's a lot to take in, but don't worry too much about it just yet.

Before we see how to do it in Python, let's make sure we understand why we bother grouping data and actions into these class blueprints at all.

Benefits of working with classes and objects

So far, we've worked with dictionaries to represent objects. There are risks with that. For example, look at these two objects:

```
cat1 = {
    "name": "Zia",
```

```
    "age": 1,
    "color": "grey",
    "energy_level": 85
}
```

And

```
cat2 = {
    "name": "Muchu",
    "age": 0,
    "colour": "grey",
    "energy_level": 99
}
```

You might have a great sense of detail and spot the difference right away. The first cat, `cat1`, has a `color` key and the second one has a `colour` key.

This can lead to bugs if you rely on the key being `color` in your code, because that key doesn't exist for `cat2`. By creating a class for cat, we bundle the attributes and methods in a single place. This way, we won't get bugs because of making typos on the keys, like in the previous example. It simply makes our code more coherent.

Also, if we want to specify functionality for a specific class, we don't have to manage matching functions for that data structure scattered across the program. Instead, we can have those defined in one logical location with direct access to the object itself (more on that soon).

Not only is there a smaller chance of introducing errors by forgetting keys or accidentally making typos in keys, but it is also a lot quicker to create multiple objects of a certain class. We call that reusability. By defining the class once, we can repeatedly use it in many places.

And lastly, by having classes, we give the type a name. The name should make clear what sort of category of things we contain in the instances of it. If we read code and see a `Pet` class, we have an idea about what that data type is and what it can do. This improves the readability of our code. Code that is easy to read is easier to debug and maintain later. This results in fewer headaches later, which is typically something worth striving for.

Alright, enough talking about the concepts and ideas. Let's see how to do all of this in Python!

Coding classes and objects

Before we can create objects, we need to define a class first. That's why it makes sense to go ahead and start by seeing how to define a class. After that, we'll use it to create some instances.

Class syntax in Python

Alright, finally! Let's define a basic Python class. A class is defined with the `class` keyword. After that, we specify the name of the class. It is a convention to capitalize class names. It looks like this:

```
class MyClass:
    pass
```

Here, we create a class called `MyClass` that currently does nothing. If we are writing code constructs such as classes and functions but have no implementation yet, we use `pass` to say "I've got nothing to put here yet." This won't break our code. However, leaving the classes or functions completely empty would break our code. So, the `pass` keyword is something you typically only see in work in progress.

Let's replace `pass` with some content!

Instance methods

Objects sometimes need to perform actions. For this to happen, the class needs functions. That's why a class can contain methods. Methods are just functions defined inside the class body. They typically take `self` as the first parameter. This `self` refers to the object, the instance of the class, that we're dealing with at that moment. If you go back to the example of thinking of an axolotl and actually feeding an axolotl, only one of these actions requires an actual axolotl (yes, it's the feeding). The `self` refers to the axolotl, the object it**self**, that we would be feeding.

Here's how we can define a method in our `Cat` class:

```
class Cat:
    def greet(self):
        print("Cat says: Meow!")
```

We create a method with the `def` keyword inside the class. The first parameter is always `self`.

If we want to specify other parameters, we can just add them, separated with commas, as we do for functions. Now that we've added the method, each cat can meow:

```
my_cat = Cat()
my_cat.greet()
```

With the first line, we create a new object of type `Cat` with `Cat()`. We'll talk about that in a little more detail soon. We store this cat object in `my_cat`. After that, we can use `my_cat` to call the `greet` method. It then outputs the following:

```
Cat says: Meow!
```

Let's see how we can add attributes too, which makes it even more interesting!

The __init__ method (constructor) and attributes

As mentioned previously, classes are blueprints that contain attributes. The main way to specify attributes is by adding a constructor. In a constructor, we specify attributes that all instances of that class should have.

A constructor is a special method called `__init__`. Python automatically calls this method each time we create a new instance. It's where we set up our object's initial attributes. Here's an example for a simple `Cat` class.

```
class Cat:
    def __init__(self, name, age, color):
        self.name = name
        self.age = age
        self.color = color
```

Inside the constructor (`__init__`), the `self` parameter refers to the instance being created. We assign the `name`, `age`, and `color` passed in by the caller to the instance's own attributes. An instance attribute is data that belongs to a particular object (such as `my_cat`). Hence, in our example, `name`, `age`, and `color` are instance attributes. Now, every time we make a `Cat`, it knows its name, age, and color.

When we do `my_cat.name` on an object representing me, we see `"Zia"`. Another cat instance might store `"Garfield"`. Now that we have attributes, we can use them inside our class – for example, in the `greet` method.

```
class Cat:
    def __init__(self, name, age, color):
        self.name = name
```

```
        self.age = age
        self.color = color

    def greet(self):
        print(f"{self.name} says: Meow!")
```

The `greet` method has been adjusted. Instead of always saying "Cat says," it now uses the `name` attribute of the object. The `greet` method knows about `self.name` because `self` refers to the instance, storing the cat's personal attributes. This can differ for each object. We've made our method a lot more dynamic. How cool is that! Now each cat can meow with its own name:

```
my_cat = Cat("Zia", 1, "grey")
my_cat.greet()
```

On the first line, we create a new cat in a different way. We specify the arguments that will become the attributes. When we then call the `greet` method, it is using the `name` attribute for the output, which will be as follows:

```
Zia says: Meow!
```

We can change the attributes after setting them, like this:

```
my_cat = Cat("Zia", 1, "grey")
print(my_cat.age)
my_cat.age = 2
print(my_cat.age)
```

This outputs the following:

```
1
2
```

First, the value of `age` is `1`, because that's what we specified. After that, we set the value to `2` and print it again. Let's talk about creating an instance in more detail now.

Creating an instance

We have already created two instances. Once with `Cat()` and once with `Cat("Zia", 1, "grey")`. As you can see, we use the name of the class, followed by parentheses. This is how we create a new instance. When we do call the name of the class, followed by parentheses with or without arguments, we are calling the constructor in the background. Quick reminder: the constructor is the `__init__` method.

You might wonder about this example:

```
class Cat:
    def greet(self):
        print("Cat says: Meow!")
```

Combined with how we created a new instance with `Cat()`, you might wonder where the `__init__` method is hiding in this case.

Well, great question! When we don't specify a constructor, Python generates one for us, one that doesn't take any arguments except `self`. This constructor that Python generates for us is called the default constructor. This default constructor ensures that there is always a constructor, and so it's always possible to create an instance.

If we specify arguments, these are used to specify the attributes of the class. Let's have a closer look at one:

```
my_cat = Cat("Zia", 1, "grey")
print(my_cat.name)   # This line outputs "Zia"
print(my_cat.age)    # This line outputs "1"
print(my_cat.color)  # This line outputs "grey"
```

This only works if we have class `Cat` with a constructor that takes three arguments, like this:

```
class Cat:
    def __init__(self, name, age, color):
        self.name = name
        self.age = age
        self.color = color
```

You might think this looks like four parameters, and you're actually right. The first one is the special `self` parameter, which refers to the object itself. It is the first parameter to all methods in a class, be they constructors or not. You will need to write it, but other than that, Python takes care of it. You can see I'm using `self` in the method to refer to the object's own attributes.

When we write `my_cat = Cat("Zia", 1, "grey")`, Python again calls `__init__` behind the scenes. In that constructor, Python is passing in the `my_cat` argument as `self`, and `"Zia"`, `1`, and `"grey"` for `name`, `age`, and `color`, respectively.

With this approach, `Cat()` no longer works. What if we want both of them to be possible? We cannot have more than one `__init__` method, but we can mark certain parameters as optional by providing a default value, like this:

```
class Cat:
    def __init__(self, name=None, age=None, color=None):
        self.name = name
        self.age = age
        self.color = color

    def greet(self):
        print(f"{self.name} says: Meow!")
my_cat1 = Cat()
my_cat1.greet() # None says Meow!
my_cat2 = Cat("Zia", 1, "grey")
my_cat2.greet() # Zia says Meow!
```

Here, we specify one constructor, but except for `self`, the parameters have a default value, `None`. We can then call the constructor with 0 arguments and with three arguments (and with 1 or 2 arguments). If we call it with 0 arguments (as in `Cat()`), the `name`, `age`, and `color` attributes are all set to `None`. If we specify arguments as we do for `my_cat2`, the attributes are set to `"Zia"`, `1`, and `"grey"`, respectively.

That's how to create instances! Let's talk about a different type of attribute that we haven't seen yet, class attributes.

Class attributes (shared data)

Let's, once more, go back to thinking about an axolotl and feeding an axolotl. We used these two actions to distinguish between the class and the instance. This distinction is important!

The attributes we have specified previously, the instance attributes, belong to the instance. We cannot think of the name of the axolotl without having a specific instance of an axolotl in mind. We cannot feed an axolotl without having a specific axolotl. But we can think about the concept of an axolotl, or the Latin species name, without having a specific instance. This is because this attribute doesn't belong to a single axolotl, but rather is part of the concept of axolotl, and all instances of axolotl share this attribute.

This is where class attributes come into play. When we want data that's shared by all instances, we define a class attribute. This is done by defining the attribute outside of `__init__`, at the class level, like this:

```
class Cat:
    species = "Felis catus"   # class attribute

    def __init__(self, name, age, color):
        self.name = name        # instance attribute
        self.age = age          # instance attribute
        self.color = color      # instance attribute
```

Here, `species` is the same for every cat object. It is a class attribute. If we were to change `Cat.species`, it updates for all cats. Meanwhile, `name`, `age`, and `color` remain instance-level because they are specified in the constructor.

That's it for class attributes. Let's talk about another concept that sounds more intimidating than it is: encapsulation.

Encapsulation in Python

So, what is encapsulation? If you think about the meaning, it's pretty much that something is wrapped around something. This is the case in coding as well. Encapsulation is the idea of hiding internal state (the value of the attributes) and requiring all interaction to be performed through an object's methods.

This is not just a Python concept; it's a universal concept. For Python, it works a little funky because true privacy is not strictly enforced in Python. Instead, we work with naming conventions we can follow to tell everyone who uses our code: "This is internal, please don't touch directly."

Here's how the naming conventions work.

Public versus private naming conventions

By default, everything is **public**. We can use a leading underscore (_) to indicate that a variable or method is **private**. For example, `_secret_attribute`. A double underscore (__) triggers some internal magic (more on that in the special method section that you'll see soon), so we're really only talking about a single underscore here. In general, Python relies more on social contracts than on strict privacy rules for working with encapsulation. Here's how we could mark `age` as private:

```
class Cat:
    def __init__(self, name, age, color):
        self.name = name # public
        self._age = age  # private
        self.color = color
```

You have to look closely to even see what is different. The names of the attributes in the parameter list are still the same. The difference is that we call the age attribute _age. We do this with `self._age = age`. This means that we mark the attribute as private.

But what's the point of having a private attribute, you might wonder. Isn't the point that we can access it? Well, let's talk about that next.

Getters and setters (when and why)

We can specify getter and setter methods. These methods are meant to retrieve the value of an attribute (the getter) or to change the value of an attribute (the setter). In many other languages, we might always define "getter" and "setter" methods to control how attributes are read or updated and enforce encapsulation everywhere. Python does not follow this approach. Python is more relaxed: we often think it's perfectly fine to let you do something such as `my_cat.name = "Garfield"` directly.

However, if we want extra checks or side effects, we can provide methods that behave as a getter or setter method. Here's how to do that:

```
class Cat:
    def __init__(self, name, age):
        self._name = name  # using underscore to hint it's 'private'
        self._age = age
```

```
    def get_name(self):
        return self._name

    def set_name(self, new_name):
        if len(new_name) > 0:
            self._name = new_name
        else:
            print("Invalid name!")
```

In this example, both `name` and `age` are private. We've specified a getter and a setter for `name`. The `get_name` method is used to get the value of the attribute name. We could specify more content, such as logging that someone accessed it to a log file, or setting a counter that updates how often the value of name has been retrieved.

The `set_name` method is used to change the value of the attribute name. There is some validation going on before doing that in `set_name`: we only set the name if the length of `new_name` is bigger than 0 (meaning it has characters). If `new_name` contains no characters, we don't change the value but print a message instead.

Python also has a neat feature called **property decorators** that can make getters and setters look like normal attribute assignments. We have not talked about decorators at all. So, let's see what that means next.

Decorators (Not as scary as they sound! Also, not related to parties as much as they sound)

Let's talk about something that sounds and looks a bit intimidating at first: decorators. To just get to it right away, here's what one looks like:

```
@some_decorator
def my_function():
    pass
```

I promise it's not a magical wizard spell, even though the @ symbol makes it look like one. It's actually a convenient, shorter way of achieving something. Decorators let us modify or enhance functions or methods in a very readable way. You'll encounter them a lot when you start to work with Python more, especially if you were to learn a framework such as Flask or Django (more on that in *Chapter 11*).

Back to decorators, we can think of them like this: we have a cake (which could be our method), and we want to decorate it with something – for example, sprinkles, frosting, or a tiny edible sculpture of Wiesje. Instead of rewriting the whole cake from scratch to add the decoration, we just say to Python: *"Put sprinkles on it!"* And just like that, our cake is now decorated.

The same thing goes for Python functions and methods. A decorator is something you "wrap around" a function to change how it behaves, or add some superpowers to it.

Let's break that down by showing how we can achieve the same thing **without** decorators. The `@some_decorator` that you can see in the preceding example is just a cleaner way of writing the following:

```
def some_decorator(func):
    def wrapper():
        print("Something happens BEFORE the function is called.")
        func()
        print("Something happens AFTER the function is called.")
    return wrapper

def my_function():
    print("Hello from my_function")

my_function = some_decorator(my_function)
my_function()
```

Keep breathing, I'll talk you through it. First, we specify the decorator function. Yes, decorators are just functions that go around another function. We pass the function that is wrapped – it is called `func` in the parameter list. Inside `some_decorator`, we call `func`, but we don't do just that; we decorate it with other behavior. In this case, something happens before and after calling `func`, but it could also have been only before or only after. It really depends on what we need. In this case, we just print a line before, and we print a line after. How do we know what `func` does? We don't! It just does whatever the function that's passed in does.

We use the decorator function on this line: `my_function = some_decorator(my_function)`. We overwrite the `my_function` definition with a call to the decorator function and pass in the original `my_function` definition. Then we call it on the line after. Here's what it prints:

```
Something happens BEFORE the function is called.
Hello from my_function
Something happens AFTER the function is called.
```

First, the BEFORE line is printed, then the original `my_function` runs (which outputs `"Hello from my_function"`), and after that, the AFTER print statement does its job. The same thing could have been achieved with this full code example that uses the decorator:

```
def some_decorator(func):
    def wrapper():
        print("Something is happening BEFORE the function is called.")
        func()
        print("Something is happening AFTER the function is called.")
    return wrapper

@some_decorator
def my_function():
    print("Hello from my_function")

my_function()
```

So, adding `@some_decorator` on top of the `my_function` definition is the equivalent of `my_function = some_decorator(my_function)`. If you know that this is essentially all it does, it's hopefully not so intimidating, but a little confusing and new at most.

We can use the decorator for multiple functions if we like. It will just add the print statement before and after the function's own actions. Clearly, this example is particularly useless. You might wonder when we would use this kind of decorator in real projects. Here are some examples:

- Logging (e.g., write when a function starts/stops to a file)
- Timing (how long does a function take?)
- Authorization (is the user allowed to run this function?)
- Caching (save the result so we don't compute it twice)
- Retrying (try again if it fails!)

And now that we know all this, let's talk about the property decorator.

The @property decorator

Alright, back to our topic. Let's zoom in on a decorator that's extremely useful when working with classes and talking about encapsulation: `@property`.

Remember when we talked about getters and setters just now. (Those methods that can retrieve or update private attributes.) In order to create those, we had to write methods such as `get_name()` and `set_name()`.

With `@property`, we are doing something similar but nicer. Someone developing Python was thinking: "Hmm, wouldn't it be nice if we could write `my_cat.name` and still have it go through a getter method without having to call `my_cat.get_name()`?" In order to achieve that, they built in an `@property` decorator. With `@property`, we call the attribute like a regular attribute, but secretly it goes through a method.

Let's look at an example using our favorite subject: cats.

```
class Cat:
    def __init__(self, name):
        self._name = name  # _ so it is marked as 'private'

    @property
    def name(self):
        return self._name
```

We defined a method called `name`, but by adding the `@property` decorator, we can now access it like it's a regular attribute:

```
my_cat = Cat("Zia")
print(my_cat.name)  # prints "Zia"
```

We call it like an attribute, but we're using a method under the hood. Beautiful! This only takes care of retrieving the name; let's also allow updating the name, but only if the new name has a length greater than 0:

```
class Cat:
    def __init__(self, name):
        self._name = name

    @property
    def name(self):
        return self._name

    @name.setter
    def name(self, new_name):
        if len(new_name) > 0:
            self._name = new_name
        else:
            print("Invalid name!")
```

We added another special built-in decorator: `@xxx.setter`. The `xxx` is replaced by the name of the property – in this case, `@name.setter`. This connects the `name` property to the setter and lets us change it using an attribute-like syntax:

```
my_cat = Cat("Zia")
print(my_cat.name)    # This calls the getter and prints "Zia"
my_cat.name = "Garfield" # This calls the setter
print(my_cat.name)    # This calls the getter and prints "Garfield"
my_cat.name = ""      # Prints "Invalid name!" and keeps the old one
```

Just like that, we've enforced encapsulation! We can also use this to add extra logic, such as logging, more validations, or side effects such as notifications. The code looks so clean – we can just access it like a regular attribute from outside.

Clearly, we could still access the private attribute directly from outside, like this:

```
cat._name = ""
```

That way, you could get around the validation and still set it to an empty string. But that's a bad practice! The `_` indicates the convention, and that means that this shouldn't be done. Often, it remains unknown from outside that there is an underlying private attribute, because it is not directly visible like it was with the `get_name` and `set_name` methods.

Let's talk about something that is magic: the magic methods!

Dunder (magic) methods

Python has special methods that determine how certain objects behave. We call these magic methods or dunder methods. They're called dunder methods because they start with a double underscore. Sounds like something we've just seen? Yes! One example of this is `__init__`. We won't go over all of these, but there are a few I'd like to point out.

__str__ dunder method

The first one on the menu is `__str__`. This method is responsible for displaying an object as text.

Let's say we do this (assuming we have a cat class).

```
cat = Cat()
print(cat)
```

We get something like this:

```
<__main__.Cat object at 0x7a3520c99430>
```

This is the default behavior of the built-in `__str__` dunder method. If we define our own version of the `__str__` method, we can return a human-readable string for `print()`:

```
class Cat:
    def __init__(self, name, age):
        self.name = name
        self.age = age

    def __str__(self):
        return f"{self.name} is {self.age} years old."


cat = Cat("Zia", 1)
print(cat)
```

Now, `print(cat)` says `"Zia is 1 years old."` This is because the `__str__` method is responsible for how to turn a cat object into a string, and that is what is used by the `print` method when printing objects. There are a few more to go over. The next one on our list is `__len__`. This one tells you how long a list is!

__len__(self) for counting

Remember the `len(some_list)` that we have seen? Here, we are actually relying on a dunder method. This dunder method is called when you use the built-in `len()` function on an object – for example, a list. In the case of a list, it counts the number of elements in the list. In the case of a string, it counts the number of characters in the string.

The dunder method that we are relying on is `__len__(self)`. By adding this dunder method to our own classes, we implement how to calculate the length of such an object. Here's an example to hopefully clarify this. Let's say we have a `ToyBox` class:

```
class ToyBox:
    def __init__(self, toys):
        self.toys = toys

    def __len__(self):
        return len(self.toys)
```

We have specified the `__len__(self)` dunder method. Now, we can do things like this:

```
box = ToyBox(["Mouse", "Laser pointer", "Catnip banana"])
print(len(box))
```

We have made our class something that can be counted! The preceding code outputs `3`. The `__len__(self)` method is set to count the number of elements in the list of toys with the `len()` method. So, whenever we ask for the length of a toybox, we get the length of the list of toys. This is an easy example, and it could be more difficult, of course. We only add this to our class when our class is storing something countable – for example, items, pages, or characters. In these cases, it makes sense to support `len()` by adding the `__len__(self)` dunder method so your class works naturally with Python's built-in functions.

__eq__(self, other) for comparing objects

How do we know if two objects are the same? We typically do this with something such as `object1 == object2`. By default, Python just checks if the two objects are the same instance in memory. However, typically, we are more interested in checking if the content is the same. If we want to override the behavior of determining equality, there is a dunder method to add! In this case, it's `__eq__(self, other)`. Here's how we can add that to a `Cat` class.

```
class Cat:
    def __init__(self, name, age):
        self.name = name
        self.age = age

    def __eq__(self, other):
        return self.name == other.name and self.age == other.age
```

This class is now no longer checking if it's the same instance in memory, but checking if both `name` and age are the same. If that is the case, it will say that they are equal. So now, say we have the following:

```
cat1 = Cat("Zia", 1)
cat2 = Cat("Zia", 1)
cat3 = Cat("Garfield", 5)

print(cat1 == cat2)
print(cat1 == cat3)
```

It will print this:

```
True
False
```

Right now, the first `print` statement will print `True`, because `name` and `age` of these objects are the same. The second statement will print `False`, because `name` and `age` are not the same. This is something that is really useful in many situations. Anytime we need to check for equality in tests, filter lists, or whenever our logic depends on the contents being the same, we will add this dunder method.

Just to make sure you got it, can you determine what this will output?

```
class Cat:
    def __init__(self, name, age):
        self.name = name
        self.age = age

    def __eq__(self, other):
        return True
```

And this?

```
cat1 = Cat("Zia", 1)
cat2 = Cat("Zia", 1)
cat3 = Cat("Garfield", 5)

print(cat1 == cat2)
print(cat1 == cat3)
```

Have a good look at the dunder method. What does it do? It always returns `True`, regardless of the object that is passed in. So, in this case, it will print `True` for both `print` statements, as it always returns `True`.

Let's look at the next dunder method – we're going to be doing some cathematics!

__add__(self, other) for adding objects

This dunder method is called when you use the + operator. That's one of the things I find very cool about Python! We get to define what it means to "add" our objects. We do this by adding the `__add__(self, other)` dunder method. Let's say that when we add two cats (`cat1` + `cat2`) we will get back a list with both cats. Here's how to do that:

```
class Cat:
    def __init__(self, name):
        self.name = name

    def __add__(self, other):
        return [self, other]
```

Having written this class, we can now add cats:

```
cat1 = Cat("Zia")
cat2 = Cat("Wiesje")
family = cat1 + cat2
print([cat.name for cat in family])  # ['Zia', 'Wiesje']
```

Let's say we have two cats, one named Wiesje and one named Zia.

If we add these two cat objects, they will turn into a list with these objects in it. We could have gone for a tuple as well; however, we chose a list here!

We are doing something special with that last line. This is an inline `for` loop. This is saying create a list entry using the `name` attribute of every cat in the family. This syntax might take some getting used to. But you will when working with Python, as it's actually not uncommon to see that quite a lot in real projects.

There are infinite options, really. We could also return a new custom object, such as `CatFamily`, or just a silly string – for example:

```
def __add__(self, other):
    return f"{self.name} + {other.name} = mischief"
```

If we had chosen this implementation of `__add__(self, other)`, the output of the Zia cat + the Wiesje cat would have been as follows:

```
Zia + Wiesje = mischief
```

As you can see, we are free to decide how we want to combine two instances. That's it for add!

We don't need to implement these dunder methods; we only need these if we want our objects to act like built-in types in these operations. It's almost time to wrap up this chapter. Just a few final notes before we go to the practice part.

Final notes on working with classes

At this point, you are acquainted with classes. There are a lot of details to discover later, when working with them in real life, but a few things should be mentioned before we move on to the next chapter.

Built-in classes and objects

Here's something that might blow your mind just a little: almost everything in Python is already an object. To be a little bit more precise (and hopefully without confusing you at this stage), there are many built-in objects that we have created already. Yes, things such as numbers, lists, and text are actually objects! For example, when we create a text value, under the hood, Python creates an instance of a text class.

So, let's say you write this:

```
message = "Hello!"
```

Python is secretly doing this:

```
message = str("Hello!")
```

That "Hello!" you see? It's not just text floating in the void. It's an object stored in memory. This object is an instance of the str (string) class. That means it has methods that are built-in too! For example, we can do something like this:

```
print(message.upper())
```

This snippet outputs the following:

```
HELLO!
```

The upper() method comes from the built-in str class. So, when we say that Python is object-oriented, we mean it all the way down to the smallest values.

The same goes for lists, integers, booleans, and so on. Even 42 is an object of class int, and it comes with its own methods and dunder magic. That's how we can add numbers and determine equality based on the value.

Keep classes focused (single responsibility principle)

Let's talk about a best practice that's not just true for Python but goes for all OO languages... It's called the single responsibility principle, and it's a fancy way of saying that each class should only do one thing.

If you have a `Cat` class, it should be about cats. Storing their name, age, color, maybe how much mischief they've been up to, and how many lives of their 9 lives they have left. That's all great for a `Cat` class.

But if you suddenly add in methods for logging errors, connecting to the internet, sending emails, or ordering sushi... well, you've created a cat that's doing too much.

There are some reasons to keep classes **narrow and focused**. By doing this, the code we write is more reusable, because it is less oddly specific. It makes our code more intuitive and easier to understand and update.

It's recommended to have lots of small classes instead of one big mega-class that can do it all.

When to use classes versus other structures

Lastly, you might wonder, when do I create a new class, and when do I use built-in structures? That's where it becomes a bit of an art and less of an absolute science. We probably do not need a class for everything.

If our data is extremely simple, a dictionary might suffice. But if you have related data plus specific behaviors that all belong together, a class is probably the better choice. This is something that, with experience, you'll develop a feeling for. Experiment with both approaches and discover the limitations of each to get the hang of it.

Quiz

1. Which of the following best describes a class in Python?

    a. A blueprint, the high-level concept of a data type

    b. A way to store a list of items

    c. A data type for multiple functions

    d. A group of objects that are instantiated from the same data type

2. True or false? You can create multiple different objects from the same class.

3. Which of the following is **not** an advantage of working with classes?

    a. The possibility of specifying functionality for a certain data type

    b. Improved performance for all types of programs

    c. Reduced chance of errors due to typos

    d. Easy creation of multiple objects from the same blueprint

4. Which keyword is used to define a class in Python?

    a. `def Class`

    b. `def`

    c. `Class`

    d. `class`

5. What is an attribute?

    a. A piece of data that belongs to an object

    b. A function that lives inside a class

    c. A decorative party prop

    d. A variable that can only be used inside an indented block

6. Which of the following in global scope displays a method call?

    a. `meow()`

    b. `my_dog.walk()`

    c. `len(dogs)`

    d. `class Dog`

7. What does `self` refer to inside a method?

    a. The method name

   b. The class itself
   c. The current instance of the object
   d. The action performed on the class

8. What is meant by the term class attribute?
   a. A parameter that is passed into the constructor method
   b. A piece of data that belongs to a single object.
   c. A value that is shared across all instances of a class
   d. A solution for when no constructor method is defined in a class.

9. What's the purpose of the `__init__` method in a class?
   a. It's the constructor that sets up an object's initial attributes
   b. It marks properties as private
   c. When called, it creates a class
   d. It controls how attributes are read or updated

10. How can you, by convention, mark an attribute as private when defining a class?
    a. By adding the word private before the attribute
    b. By putting it in a separate constructor for private attributes
    c. By defining it as a class attribute
    d. By using a single underscore

11. What are decorators on functions?
    a. Class-specific functions
    b. A way to define private attributes
    c. Functions that wrap around other functions
    d. Magic methods

12. What does the `@property` decorator do?
    a. It sets up initial attributes for class instances.
    b. It allows calling a getter method like a regular attribute.
    c. It overwrites values of private attributes when called.
    d. It turns methods into class attributes shared by all instances.

13. What are dunder methods?

    a. Methods that are imported from external libraries.
    b. Functions that are used to decorate other functions.
    c. Special methods with double underscores that define built-in behavior.
    d. Private methods that can't be accessed from outside the class.

14. What happens if you don't define any dunder methods in your class?

    a. Your code will run; weird things can happen when you try out any built-in operations such as `len()` or `print()` on your objects.
    b. Python throws an error at you when you create an instance of the class.
    c. Python crashes as soon as you use the constructor of your class.
    d. Your code won't run.

Exercises

8.1 Smoothie blender

Let's get ready for some healthy exercise! You're going to create a `Smoothie` class where you can add ingredients, print all ingredients in a smoothie, and even mix two smoothies together using `+`.

Add ingredients to taste:

- Define a `Smoothie` class and write a constructor (`__init__`) that takes in a list of smoothie ingredients. Mark the ingredients as private.
- Add a method to add ingredients to the ingredient list.
- Define a method that prints a description of the smoothie when called.
- Use a dunder method to deal with situations where we try to add different smoothies together. For example, adding a smoothie with strawberry and banana with another that has kale and orange should create a new smoothie with all four ingredients. Make sure your code deals with duplicate ingredients.
- Create a few instances of `Smoothie` and check if everything is working as it's supposed to.

8.2 Dress code: classy

Let's say we want to create a digital closet. We have different types of clothes in different sizes, colors, and made from all sorts of fabric types. There are several things you could do with these garments. You can wash them, wear them, let a cat take a nap on them, and you could even dye them to change the color, if you get a little crafty.

- Start out by building a `ClothingItem` class with the following attributes:
    - Type of garment
    - Size
    - Color
    - Fabric type
- Define a `dye()` method that changes the color of a `ClothingItem`.
- Define a `__str__`, so printing a `ClothingItem` results in something readable, such as:

```
"Green cotton shirt, size M"
```

- Define another dunder method that checks if two clothing items are equal based on garment type, color, and size.
- Add a `wear()` method that prints a simple message and keeps track of how many times a garment has been worn. Also, make it mark the item as dirty.
- If clothes get dirty, they're going to need to be washed. Add a `wash()` method that checks whether something needs washing and prints a fitting message.
- Create a fun feature that prints goofy messages when you add up two garments. You can go wild with this. Here are some possible outputs:

```
pink sweater + red trousers = fashion disaster
blue jeans + white shirt = basic, but cute
```

- Test this all out by creating a few instances of `ClothingItem`, wearing them, washing them, and combining them in odd ways.

8.3 Building a Plant class

You're going to write a simple Python program that helps take care of houseplants. Every plant has attributes and a couple of things it can do: get watered and die.

You'll define a `Plant` class that can create plants with a name, size, desired climate, and alive status. You'll also track how many plants have been created. Every time a new plant is created, the plant counter needs to be updated.

Here's what you need to do:

- Define a `Plant` class.
- Within this class, define a constructor that sets attributes for name, size, desired climate, and alive status. Every plant starts out alive.
- Define a `count` class attribute that keeps track of how many plants were created.
- Define a `water()` method for watering plants. Let's keep it simple: just print a message such as `"Watering your cactus"`.
- Add a `die()` method that prints a dramatic message when called and updates the status of your plant. Don't forget the plant count needs to be decreased by 1 when a plant dies. Add logic that prevents a plant from dying twice and notify the user when they try to water a plant that's already dead.
- When you try to print a plant using `print(your_plant)`, Python gives you something strange such as `<__main__.Plant object at ...>`. That's not very helpful. Define a dunder method that tells Python how to represent your plant as a string. Using `print(your_plant)` should print something like this:

```
Name: Fern | Size: Medium | Desired climate: Tropical | Alive: yes
```

- Test your code. Create a few plant instances and try things out. Water them using the `water()` method. Kill them off with `die()`. Try watering it after it has died and check if the plant count updates correctly. Use `print()` to see what the plant looks like now.

8.4 Logging logins

In this exercise, you'll build a simple user system. You'll define a `User` class to create user objects. You'll combine your newly gained knowledge on decorators with what you learned about file handling in the previous chapter to log login and logout attempts.

Define a User class

First, define a `User` class and set up a constructor that sets initial attributes: `name`, `password`, and `logged_in_status` (always starts as `False`). Mark all attributes as private.

Add getters and setters

Next, add getters and setters for each attribute. For the password, the setter should check if the new password is at least 8 characters long. For the name, make sure it isn't set to an empty string or just a bunch of spaces.

Define a login() method

Create a login method that takes in one parameter: a password. It should check if the entered password is correct, and if so, set `logged_in_status` to `True`. Handle cases where the user is already logged in with an informative `print()` statement.

Define a logout() method

If we're logging in, we'll also need to log out at some point. Add a method for that. If the user is already logged out, print a helpful message.

Create a decorator

Now for the fun part: you're going to create a decorator to log actions to a file.

- Let's start small by making a basic decorator that just prints a message before and after a method is called.
- Decorate your `login()` and `logout()` with it and test them.
- If your decorator needs to work on functions with different numbers of parameters, think of the variable-length arguments we discussed in *Chapter 6*.

If you've got the simple decorator working, it's time to upgrade it.

Make the decorator write logs to a file

It's time to write actual logs to a `.txt` file. We want the decorator to add lines to a file that tells us something about login attempts and whether or not they were successful. Typically, it's useful to have a timestamp in such logs.

Suggested format:

```
[timestamp]: [name] tried to call [method]. Result: [success]
```

Which could look like this:

```
2025-04-05 19:08:48.417932: Wiesje17 tried to call login. Result: Success
```

Okay, so here's what we'll need:

- The time of the login/logout attempt (remember there's a module in Python's standard library that can help with this)
- The user name
- The method that was called. Pro tip: use `func.__name__` to get a cleaned-up print of a function/method name.
- The result of that function: success, a wrong password, user was already logged in, and so on.

Test it!

Create several instances of `User` and try logging in and out. What happens if you enter the wrong password? Change the username! Is your `.txt` log file updating correctly after each login/logout attempt?

Summary

Before we move on to the next topic, let's quickly review what we learned in this chapter. We discovered the world of object-oriented programming: a way of structuring your code with objects. These objects are instances of classes, the blueprints of data types. Wiesje could, for example, be an instance of the `Dog` class. When creating a class, you specify attributes and methods. Methods are class-specific functions that an object can perform, and attributes are the data each object of that class holds.

By defining classes, instead of creating every object separately, you decrease the chance of errors with forgotten keys or accidental typos, and you give your data type a name. Also, it allows you to create multiple objects with a lot more ease (reusability), and you can specify functionality for a specific class using methods!

Okay, so classes are great. But how do you define one? Well, with the `class` keyword. It's pretty straightforward, but things get more complicated when you want to add attributes and methods.

To specify attributes, you need to add a constructor: the `__init__` method. Python calls this method automatically when you create a new instance to set up your object's initial attributes. This is what that could look like:

```
class Dog:
    def __init__(self, name, age, color):
        self.name = name
        self.age = age
        self.color = color
```

You don't pass in `self` explicitly when calling the constructor; Python does that for you. But it must be the first parameter in the method definition. The `name`, `age`, and `color` are what you would pass in when creating a class instance:

```
wiesje = Dog("Wiesje", 7, "brown")
```

Sometimes, attributes are not specific to a certain instance of a class, but relevant for all instances or the concept itself. This is why we have class attributes. To define a class attribute, you simply put it at the class level, so outside the constructor method or any other method in the class. Here's an example:

```
class Dog:

    annoying = True # Class attribute

    def __init__(self, name, age, color):
        self.name = name
        self.age = age
        self.color = color
```

With class attributes covered, we moved on to the subject of encapsulation. Encapsulation is the idea of hiding attributes and requiring all interaction with them to happen through an object's methods. You can mark attributes as private using a single underscore. However, true privacy is not strictly enforced in Python, and we need to rely on naming conventions to signal to ourselves and other developers that some values are not to be touched directly. Instead of modifying and reading values directly, we can specify getters and setters. Python doesn't require you to do so, but by using getter and setter methods, you can add extra checks or side effects.

Here's a simple example with a getter and setter method:

```
class Dog:
    def __init__(self, name):
        self._name = name # Name marked private with an _

    # Getter method
    def get_name(self):
        return self._name

    # Setter method
    def set_name(self, new_name):
        if not new_name.strip() == "": # Checks for valid new_name
            self._name = new_name
        else:
            print("Invalid name!")
```

So far, so good, but there are even better ways to do this. With decorators! Decorators are basically functions that wrap around other functions. You can use them to assign behavior that should happen before and after another function. Decorators can be recognized by their `@` symbol, and you can use them multiple times. You can create your own decorators for all sorts of things. Python comes with handy built-in decorators that let you access and update values without calling the method explicitly. I'm talking about `@property` and `@xxx.setter` here. I could try and explain it all word by word, but it's probably better if I just give you another code snippet:

```
class Dog:
    def __init__(self, name):
        self._name = name

    # Getter method decorated with @ property
    @property
    def name(self):
        return self._name

    # Setter method decorated with @name.setter
    @name.setter
    def name(self, new_name):
        if not new_name.strip() == "":
            self._name = new_name
```

```
            print("Name changed!")
        else:
            print("Invalid name!")

wiesje = Dog("Wiesje")

print(wiesje.name) # Calling the getter method like a regular attribute

wiesje.name = "Teun" # Calling the setter method to change Wiesje's name
```

After decorators, we looked at magic methods, also called dunder methods, because they start and end with a double underscore. These methods define how objects behave in common situations, such as printing, comparing, adding, and getting their length. For example, if you want to compare two dogs and have Python decide whether they're equal based on their name and age (instead of their location in memory), you can define the `__eq__` method:

```
class Dog():
    def __init__(self, name, age):
        self.name = name
        self.age = age

    def __eq__(self, other):
        return self.name == other.name and self.age == other.age

wiesje = Dog("Wiesje", 7)
other_wiesje = Dog("Wiesje", 7)
chewie = Dog("Chewie", 10)

print(wiesje == other_wiesje) # Outputs True
print(wiesje == chewie) # Outputs False
```

Without a defined `__eq__`, `wiesje == other_wiesje` would return `False`, even though they have the same values. This is because, by default, Python compares object locations in memory. Dunder methods let you change that behavior and define what equality, length, or addition means for your objects.

This was quite an informative chapter. If some parts felt tricky, that's a good sign. It means you're growing your skills. In the next chapter, we'll look at inheritance: a way for one class to absorb traits from another. Like a dog having puppies, but with fewer vet bills.

9

Understanding Inheritance

Now that we understand classes, this chapter is going to be a treat.

Python is about to get even cooler. So far, we've been building our classes from scratch. We created them, added constructors, attributes, and wrote methods... That is already pretty impressive. But what if I told you there's a way to reuse what we have already built, tweak it just a bit, and avoid writing the same thing over and over again?

That's where inheritance comes in. Inheritance is about how to take an existing class and extend it. We'll learn how to create new classes based on existing ones. This keeps our code clean and reusable, and we avoid duplicate code by reusing classes. And we can do it all while making room for even more animal friends.

Why inheritance?

Before we dive into how to do this, let's make sure we understand why we want to do it. The main reason is to avoid duplicate code. We don't want to have duplicate code, but write reusable code once instead.

Duplicate code and reusability

Let's talk about code reusability. In coding, we don't like repeating ourselves. There's even an abbreviation for it: **DRY**. That stands for **Don't Repeat Yourself**.

Imagine we already have a `Pet` class. It has attributes such as `name` and `age`, and methods such as `eat` and `sleep`. Now, let's say we want to create classes for `Cat`, `Dog`, and `Axolotl`. Should we just copy and paste all the code from `Pet` into each of those classes?

No!

Whenever you feel the need to copy and paste, there is typically something better that you should be doing. We've already seen functions; these are great for not repeating your code. We've seen classes, also great for not repeating your code. And now we'll see inheritance, which is ideal for avoiding duplicate code across classes.

With inheritance, we define the shared things once in a parent class (such as `Pet`), and then create child classes (such as `Cat`, `Dog`, or `Axolotl`) that inherit those features.

Let's pretend we don't have inheritance first, and we want to create a `Dog`, `Cat`, and `Rabbit` class.

They all would have a `name`, `weight`, and `age` attribute, and perhaps methods such as `eat`, `run`, `play`, and probably more. Of course, these classes could also have some custom methods that others don't have. As they are different classes, they can have different implementations for each method as well.

Here's what it could look like:

```
class Dog:
    def __init__(self, name, weight, age):
        self.name = name
        self.weight = weight
        self.age = age

    def eat(self):
        print(f"{self.name} is eating.")
```

```
    def run(self):
        print(f"{self.name} is running.")

    def play(self):
        print(f"{self.name} is playing.")
class Cat:
    def __init__(self, name, weight, age):
        self.name = name
        self.weight = weight
        self.age = age

    def eat(self):
        print(f"{self.name} is eating.")

    def run(self):
        print(f"{self.name} is running.")

    def play(self):
        print(f"{self.name} is playing.")

class Rabbit:
    def __init__(self, name, weight, age):
        self.name = name
        self.weight = weight
        self.age = age

    def eat(self):
        print(f"{self.name} is eating.")

    def run(self):
        print(f"{self.name} is running.")

    def play(self):
        print(f"{self.name} is playing.")
```

As you can see, there's a lot of duplicate code going on here. This is not good practice: imagine we want to give all of these classes a breathe method; we'd have to add it in three places. This is not efficient. And that's why we have inheritance.

Basic syntax of inheritance

If we think of cats, rabbits, and dogs, we can say that they have a common category: all of them are pets. Instead of creating three new classes from scratch, we can create a parent class called `Pet` and base the other classes on the `Pet` class:

```
class Pet:
    def __init__(self, name, weight, age):
        self.name = name
        self.weight = weight
        self.age = age

    def eat(self):
        print(f"{self.name} is eating.")

    def run(self):
        print(f"{self.name} is running.")

    def play(self):
        print(f"{self.name} is playing.")
```

You won't see anything special about this `Pet` parent class. The trick is done in the child classes. This is the general syntax for specifying that a class is a child of another class:

```
class ChildClass(ParentClass):
    # child class body
```

The name of the class is specified like we used to, but we point to the parent after the class name between the parentheses. This gives the child class all the attributes and methods of the parent class. And with that in mind, here's how to get the same functionality that we had before for the three classes:

```
class Dog(Pet):
    pass

class Cat(Pet):
    pass

class Rabbit(Pet):
    pass
```

As you can see, this looks a lot cleaner. The child classes are all a type of `Pet`. The `pass` means we're not adding anything (yet), but the class still exists and inherits everything from `Pet`. For example, we can create a `Cat` object, and it will already know how to eat, run, and play:

```
my_cat = Cat("Zia", 2.5, 1)
my_cat.eat()
```

This outputs the following:

```
Zia is eating.
```

So, to inherit the attributes and methods of a class, we specify the name of the parent class between parentheses. And just like that, the child has the attributes and methods of the parent class. If we want to add a method to all three of them, we only have to do it in `Pet`. For example, if we want to add a `breathe` method to all the pets, here's how to do that:

```
class Pet:
    def __init__(self, name, weight, age):
        self.name = name
        self.weight = weight
        self.age = age

    def eat(self):
        print(f"{self.name} is eating.")

    def run(self):
        print(f"{self.name} is running.")

    def play(self):
        print(f"{self.name} is playing.")

    def breathe(self):
        print(f"{self.name} is breathing.")
```

There are no changes required in the child classes. Because they inherit from `Pet`, they now also have access to the `breathe` method. And we can call it on the objects, like this:

```
my_dog = Dog("Wiesje", 2.5, 1)
my_dog.breathe()
```

And that's how simple it is to extend the functionality of the parent class and all the child classes. We can also add functionality to specific child classes only. Let's see how to do that next.

Adding methods to the child classes

If we want to add custom behavior to each child class, we can. It's actually very straightforward. We just add the method to the child class(es), like this:

```
class Dog(Pet):
    def fetch(self):
        print(f"{self.name} is fetching the ball!")

class Cat(Pet):
    def climb(self):
        print(f"{self.name} is climbing the curtain. Again.")

class Rabbit(Pet):
    def hop(self):
        print(f"{self.name} is hopping around happily!")
```

We're just adding methods like we would normally. But this way, not all pets can hop. Only the rabbit can hop.

Similarly, we can add specific attributes to child classes. Let's see how to do that.

Adding attributes and calling the parent constructor with super()

Let's say we want to add a new attribute to the `Cat` class only, for example, the number of lives left. This is slightly more complex to do. In that case, we'll need to add an `__init__` method to our `Cat` class. In there, we still want to make sure that the parent's `__init__` method gets called as well. Why? Well, because we also need to set `name`, `age`, and `weight`, and that's specified in the parent class.

Great news, we can still use the existing `__init__` method from `Pet` for `name`, `weight`, and `age`. We can do this with a special function called `super()`, which refers to the parent class; it gives us access to the methods there. Here's what it looks like:

```
class Cat(Pet):
    def __init__(self, name, age, weight, number_of_lives_left):
        super().__init__(name, age, weight)
        self.number_of_lives_left = number_of_lives_left

    def climb(self):
        print(f"{self.name} is climbing the curtain. Again.")
```

And boom! We reused the parent constructor and only added what was new in the `__init__` method of the `Cat` class. We can also overwrite functionality in the child class. That involves using `super()` sometimes as well. Let's see it next.

Overriding methods

What if you don't like how a method works in the parent class? That might seem like a problem, but it's not really a problem. You can just override it in the child class. Let's assume that Wiesje's kind doesn't agree with the standard eating but has her own way. Here's how we can specify that:

```
class Dog(Pet):
    def eat(self):
        print(f"{self.name} is eating from a marble bowl.")
```

If necessary, we can also call the original method with `super()`:

```
class Dog(Pet):
    def eat(self):
        super().eat()
        print("...from a marble bowl.")
```

This one first calls the functionality of the original `eat` method (which, for Wiesje, will say `"Wiesje is eating"`). After that, it adds another `print` statement that adds `"...from a marble bowl."`

Another common concept related to inheritance and various methods is polymorphism. It might sound intimidating, but I promise you that the core of it is actually quite simple.

Demonstrating polymorphism

So what is this polymorphism? Well, it's a Greek word that consists of two parts:

- *poly*, which means many
- *morph*, which means shapes or forms

So, many shapes, and that's exactly what it is about. Remember when I said that classes can also be called types? Some types can be more specific versions of other types, we call those subtypes. Thinking in terms of *types* and *subtypes* (instead of parent and child classes) often makes polymorphism easier to understand.

Let's take a non-code example: Wiesje.

Wiesje has many shapes.

And by that, I don't mean she's very flexible.

It means that I can refer to Wiesje with multiple terms. For example, I can say she is the following:

- Animal
- Pet
- Dog
- Dachshund

Why? Well, because these types are related. Any object that is of the Dog type is also of the Pet and Animal types. Let's see why:

- A dog is a pet
- A pet is an animal
- And therefore, a dog is an animal

Being able to refer to one thing using multiple types is polymorphism. You might be thinking: Well, sure, but why does this matter? This is actually very convenient. Let's say we have multiple pets, and we don't know the specific subtypes. But because we know the common category, we know things these pets have in common. All the methods and attributes specified in the `Pet` class will be available to them.

Let me show you some polymorphism in action. But first, let's look at what the classes for this example look like:

```
class Pet:
    def __init__(self, name, age):
        self.name = name
        self.age = age
    def speak(self):
        print(f"{self.name} makes a sound!")
    # Other shared attributes and methods omitted to keep it short

class Cat(Pet):
    def speak(self):
        print(f"{self.name} says: Meow!")
    # Other cat specific details omitted
class Dog(Pet):
    def speak(self):
        print(f"{self.name} says: Woof!")
    # Other dog specific details omitted

class Rabbit(Pet):
    def speak(self):
        print(f"{self.name} says: Squeak!")
    # Other rabbit-specific details omitted
```

As you can see, all of them have the `speak` method. In `Pet`, this is very generic. In each subtype, this has been overridden with specific behavior for that type. So, if we have a code snippet like this:

```
pets = [Cat("Zia", 1), Dog("Wiesje", 7), Rabbit("Ralph", 2)]
for pet in pets:
    pet.speak()
```

It will output the following:

```
Zia says: Meow!
Wiesje says: Woof!
Ralph says: Squeak!
```

This output shows each pet speaking in its own way. We have a list of pets; we don't know the exact subtypes, but that's irrelevant. And that, right there, is polymorphism in action.

We can call a method without worrying about it not being present in a subtype, and we know it has been implemented to meet the requirements of the subtype. That means that there could be custom implementations available depending on the exact subtype, much like the previous example.

Well, now you already have the basic knowledge of inheritance that you need to know! Let's talk about a few different types of inheritance, which are pretty much variations on what we've just seen.

Types of inheritance

We will discuss four different types of inheritance:

- Single inheritance (one parent, one child)
- Multilevel inheritance (a parent with a parent)
- Hierarchical inheritance (one parent, multiple children)
- Multiple inheritance (one child, multiple parents)

Let's start with single inheritance.

> So far, I've been talking about parent and child classes. There are multiple names for this that are acceptable. The parent class is sometimes called the base class, and the child class is called the derived class. Another one would be type (parent) and subtype (child).

Single inheritance

It's always a good idea to start with the easiest one. When we have one parent that has one child, we call this single inheritance. For example, this could be the hierarchy:

```
class Human:
    pass

class PetOwner(Human):
    pass
```

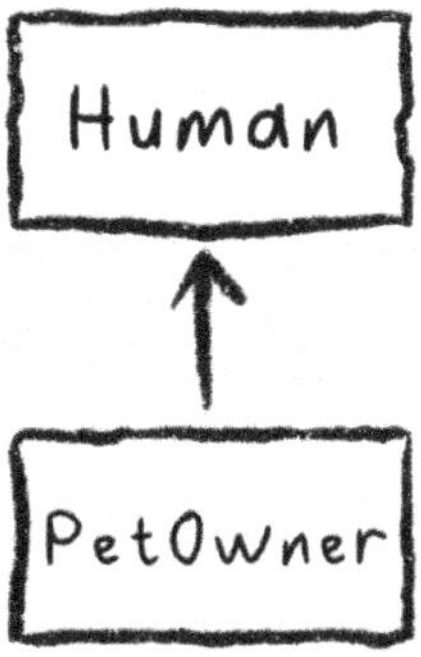

If we assume that `Human` doesn't have any other child classes, this is an example of single inheritance. We have one parent (`Human`) and one child (`PetOwner`). In this case, they have no content because I just want to illustrate what is meant by single inheritance.

Talking about illustrating, here's a diagram explaining single inheritance:

We can add more levels, and that would mean we'd go from single inheritance to multilevel inheritance. Let's talk about what that is next.

Multilevel inheritance

My human has tiny humans, and they are quite a fan of e-pets. Let's say that we want to have digital pets as a class as well. A digital pet, such as a `RoboCat` or `RoboDog`, inherits from a new class, `RoboPet`. And `RoboPet` is a `Pet` type, and therefore, it inherits from `Pet`. Here's how we do that:

```
class Pet:
    def eat(self):
        print("Nom nom nom")

class RoboPet(Pet):
    def charge(self):
        print("Charging...")

class RoboCat(RoboPet):
    def meow(self):
        print("Beep-meow!")
```

So first, we have the parent class, `Pet`. We then make a more specific class, `RoboPet`, which inherits from `Pet`. Then, we have `RoboCat`, which is a `RoboPet` type as it inherits from `RoboPet`. We have three levels here; we could have had more, and that makes it multilevel inheritance. Multilevel inheritance is also displayed as a diagram:

Hierarchical inheritance

You might wonder what we call the examples we've seen so far. Well, wonder no longer, it's called hierarchical inheritance. This means that we have one parent class that has more than one child class. Here is an example:

```
class Pet:
    pass

class Dog(Pet):
    pass

class Cat(Pet):
    pass

class Rabbit(Pet):
    pass
```

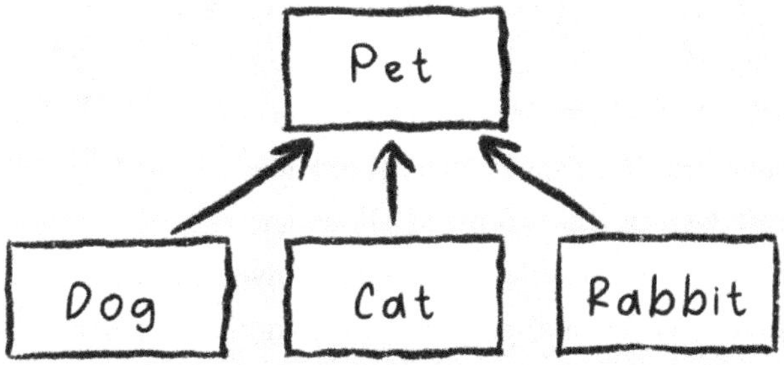

The parent here is `Pet`. And we have three child classes, namely, `Cat`, `Dog`, and `Rabbit`.

And yes, they can be combined! We can have multilevel and hierarchical inheritance. For example, if all of these three classes were `RoboPet` types, and we had the `RoboPet` layer in between, we would have multilevel inheritance between `Pet`, `RoboPet`, and the individual `RoboDog`, `RoboCat`, and `RoboRabbit`. And we would have hierarchical inheritance between `RoboPet` and the child classes: `RoboDog`, `RoboCat`, and `RoboRabbit`.

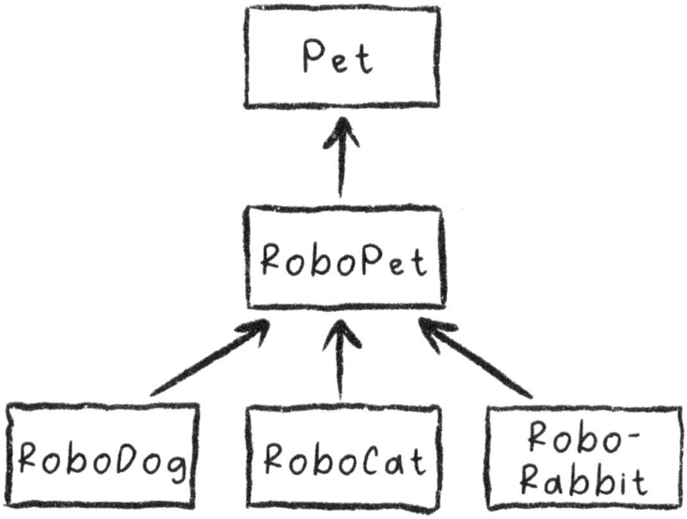

Let's see something that might be the most surprising in this list: multiple inheritance!

Multiple inheritance

In Python, we can do a type of inheritance that is a little special, as not all languages facilitate this. We can inherit from multiple parents. Let's imagine we're building a simple system for organizing conference speakers. Some speakers need to log in to a web portal to upload slides and check their schedule. So, we might have a class that deals with authentication, and another that handles speaker info.

Here's the setup:

```
class LoginUser:
    def login(self, username, password):
        print(f"Logging in as {username}...")
```

So, first, we have a `LoginUser` class. This class handles logging in. Maybe it talks to a database, checks credentials, and so on. We don't want this logic mixed in with other things. We are sticking to the single responsibility principle. That's why we also have a `Speaker` class to handle logic related to speakers at the conference:

```
class Speaker:
    def __init__(self, name, topic):
        self.name = name
        self.topic = topic

    def speak(self):
        print(f"{self.name} is speaking about {self.topic}.")
```

As you can see, this class contains attributes and behavior related to someone speaking at an event. Finally, let's make a child class that inherits from both these classes:

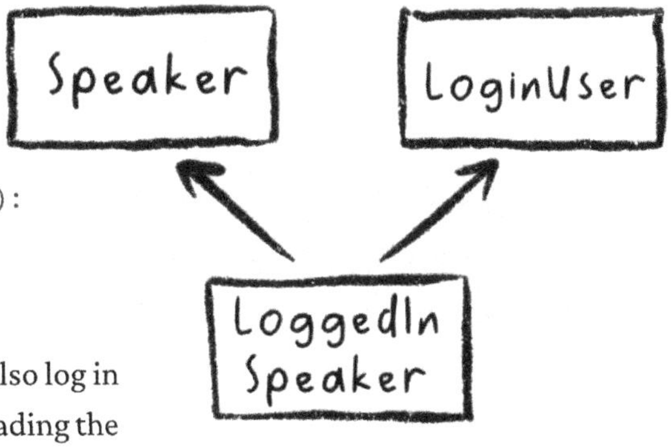


```
class LoggedInSpeaker(Speaker, LoginUser):
    def upload_slides(self, slides):
        pass
```

This works great! Now we have a speaker who can also log in to do tasks that require authentication, such as uploading the slides. And here's how we can use it:

```
s = LoggedInSpeaker("Dr. Zia", "Quantum Computing for Cats")
s.speak()
s.login("dr_zia", "Purrsecure123!")
```

This is a nice solution. By inheriting from both these classes, we avoid having unrelated logic in one supersize class.

Please note, multiple inheritance is often a code smell. A code smell is an indication of poor coding practices. We should only use multiple inheritance when the two parent classes serve different purposes, and neither is pretending to be a subtype of the other. For example, the following is a bad example. Can you tell why?

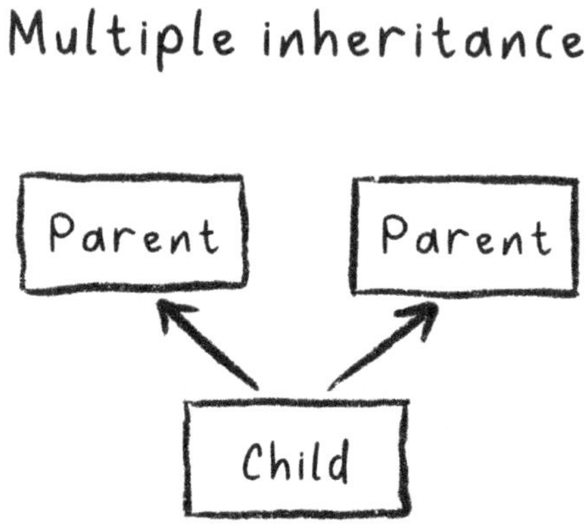


```
class Pet:
    def eat(self):
        print("Nom nom nom")

class RoboPet:
    def charge(self):
        print("Charging...")

class RoboCat(Pet, RoboPet):
    pass
```

It doesn't make a lot of sense to make `RoboCat` inherit from both classes, as `RoboPet` could very well be a child class of `Pet`. That's why multilevel inheritance is the better solution here. In this example, `RoboCat` should extend `Cat` and `RoboPet`.

Be careful, though! What do you think will happen if two parent classes define the same method? Well, Python uses a rule called the **method resolution order** (**MRO**) to decide which one to use. Let's illustrate this by adding to our example. Let's imagine both `LoginUser` and `Speaker` define a method called `welcome()`... but with different intentions:

```
class LoginUser:
    def login(self, username, password):
        print(f"Logging in as {username}...")

    def welcome(self):
        print("Welcome to the portal!")

class Speaker:
    def __init__(self, name, topic):
        self.name = name
        self.topic = topic
```

```
    def speak(self):
        print(f"{self.name} is speaking about {self.topic}.")

    def welcome(self):
        print(f"Welcome to the conference, {self.name}!")
```

In this example, both classes define a method called `welcome()`. One is from the tech platform perspective (`"Welcome to the portal!"`), and the other is more event-oriented (`"Welcome to the conference, Zia!"`).

No problem yet so far. The issue arises in the child class that's inheriting from both parents:

```
class LoggedInSpeaker(Speaker, LoginUser):
    pass
```

If we now instantiate `LoggedInSpeaker` and call `welcome()`, what do you think will happen? Which version of `welcome()` will be executed: the one in `Speaker` or the one in `LoggedInSpeaker`?

```
speaker = LoggedInSpeaker("Dr. Zia", "Quantum Computing for Cats")
speaker.welcome()
```

In this case, it outputs the following:

```
Welcome to the conference, Dr. Zia!
```

Why that one? Because of the MRO. Python looks at the order in which the parent classes are listed, and in this case, the `Speaker` class is listed first: `class LoggedInSpeaker(Speaker, LoginUser)`.

It searches for the `welcome()` method starting from its own class, then moving on to search in `Speaker` next. If it's not found, it will check `LoginUser`, then eventually, if it's still not found, it checks `object` (Python's base class for everything). It stops looking as soon as it has found one. So, the one in `Speaker` wins in this case.

If you want to specify which version of `welcome()` to use, you can call it directly:

```
LoginUser.welcome(speaker)
Speaker.welcome(speaker)
```

And this outputs the following:

```
Welcome to the portal!
Welcome to the conference, Dr. Zia!
```

If we want neither, we can even override it entirely in the child class:

```
class LoggedInSpeaker(Speaker, LoginUser):
    def welcome(self):
        print("Welcome, authenticated speaker! Enjoy the event and your
coffee.")
```

Now, let's say we do this:

```
speaker = LoggedInSpeaker("Dr. Zia", "Quantum Computing for Cats")
speaker.welcome()
```

It will print the following:

```
Welcome, authenticated speaker! Enjoy the event and your coffee.
```

And that's it for inheritance. To wrap up this chapter, let's go over two best practices you need to be aware of.

Inheritance best practices

Inheritance is a great tool, but like all tools, you should only use it when it's needed. Let's talk about what I mean by that.

Is-a versus has-a

First of all, there's an important distinction between *is-a* and *has-a* when it comes to inheritance. We use inheritance when there is an *is-a* relationship. When there is a *has-a* relationship, we give the class that has the *has-a* relationship an attribute to represent it. We call that **composition**.

Here are some examples:

- A cat *is a* pet
- A car *has an* engine (that should use composition, not inheritance)

Here are the code examples of both:

```
class Pet:
    def __init__(self, name):
        self.name = name
class Dog(Pet):  # Dog is-a Pet
    def bark(self):
        print(f"{self.name} says: Woof!")
```

We can use it like this:

```
dog = Dog("Wiesje")
print(dog.name)  # Inherited from Pet
dog.bark()       # Dog-specific behavior
```

This is a good usage of inheritance because a dog *is a* pet. Whenever there isn't an *is-a* relationship, we should not use inheritance. For example, don't use inheritance in the following situations:

- A pet *is a* robopet (all robotpets are pets, but not all pets are robopets!)
- A dog *is a* cat (they're not)
- An animal *is a* dog (wrong way around)

Let's illustrate composition (*has-a* relationships) as well. It's again one of those terms that sounds fancy, but it's actually not too hard.

Let's stick with the classic example of composition: we have `Engine` and `Car`. A car isn't a kind of engine. But a car does *have* an engine, so we use composition here:

```
class Engine:
    def start(self):
        print("Engine started.")

class Car:
    def __init__(self):
        self.engine = Engine()  # Car has-a Engine

    def drive(self):
        self.engine.start()
        print("Car is driving.")
```

And we can then use it like this:

```
car = Car()
car.drive()
```

This works because a car *has an* engine. It outputs the following:

```
Engine started.
Car is driving.
```

The `drive()` method calls the `start()` method in the instance of the `Engine` type. That's why we see both the lines printed.

We didn't use inheritance because a car is *not* a type of engine. It does contain one, though, which means there's a *has-a* relationship and, therefore, we use composition. As you can see, composition just means that it has that class type as an attribute.

So, to wrap up this best practice: don't force inheritance if it doesn't fit. If something doesn't make sense as a subtype of another, it probably isn't a use case for inheritance.

Avoiding deep inheritance chains

And the last note to make here: try not to go more than a couple of levels deep. Deep hierarchies can get messy. A common coding best practice is KISS.

KISS stands for **keep it simple, stupid**. This is used to say that simplicity is better than complexity, and that simple solutions are to be preferred. They are easier to understand, easier to debug, and therefore easier to modify later.

Losing that simplicity is exactly what can go wrong when inheritance chains get too deep. We might be looking at `class FancyRoboCat(RoboCat)` and have no idea where `fancy_dance()` is coming from. Is it in `RoboCat`? `Pet`? `SuperPet`? `Animal`? And as a result, when something breaks, it's harder to know where to look. You have to trace the error through a whole stack of classes. And also, because we have less oversight, it can be unpredictable as to what happens if we change something in the base class. It might break behavior several layers down, without us realizing it before it's too late. And lastly, having this long chain makes the code quite fragile. The more classes depend on each other in a chain, the greater the chance that something will break if one layer changes.

So what do we do instead? When things get too deep, we might want to favor composition over inheritance if it works for the use case. If that's not an option, we need to look at ways to flatten our design. If you find yourself writing `class ExtraUltraMegaSuperRoboAxolotl(UltraMegaSuperRoboAxolotl)`... it might be time to take a break, get some coffee, and rethink your latest decisions. Instead of having so many shared layers, we can extract shared behavior into helper classes instead of adding even more layers.

Let's make fun of some bad code here. Let's say we're building a virtual pet simulator. But instead of keeping it simple, we get a little carried away. Our brains might be all like, "Well, I need a flying version, and a swimming version, and one with lasers, and maybe a unicorn upgrade too..."

And before we know it, we've written code like this:

```
class Pet:
    def eat(self):
        print("Eating.")

class FlyingPet(Pet):
    def fly(self):
        print("Flapping wings...")

class SwimmingFlyingPet(FlyingPet):
    def swim(self):
        print("Splashing in the water...")

class LaserSwimmingFlyingPet(SwimmingFlyingPet):
    def shoot_lasers(self):
        print("Pew pew!")

class InvisibleLaserSwimmingFlyingPet(LaserSwimmingFlyingPet):
    def turn_invisible(self):
        print("Now you see me, now you don't.")

class
UnicornInvisibleLaserSwimmingFlyingPet(InvisibleLaserSwimmingFlyingPet):
    def sparkle(self):
        print("Magical sparkles everywhere!")
```

And now we try to use it:

```
pet = UnicornInvisibleLaserSwimmingFlyingPet()
pet.fly()
pet.swim()
pet.shoot_lasers()
pet.turn_invisible()
pet.sparkle()
```

We get the following output:

```
Flapping wings...
Splashing in the water...
Pew pew!
Now you see me, now you don't.
Magical sparkles everywhere!
```

Even though this is funny, it is bad design. We have six layers of inheritance. That's just too many. And we are not really using all these classes (even though they have proper *is-a* relationships) for code organization; we are using them to stack the superpowers. Our code becomes fragile; if `Pet.eat()` breaks, the `Unicorn` thing might stop eating altogether.

Instead of having this monster hierarchy, we could work with composition instead. It might look something like this:

```
class Pet:
    def eat(self):
        print("Eating.")

class Wings:
    def fly(self):
        print("Flapping wings...")

class Fins:
    def swim(self):
        print("Splashing in the water...")

class LaserEyes:
    def shoot_lasers(self):
        print("Pew pew!")

class Sparkles:
    def sparkle(self):
        print("Magical sparkles everywhere!")

class UltraMegaPet(Pet):
    def __init__(self):
        self.wings = Wings()
```

```
        self.fins = Fins()
        self.lasers = LaserEyes()
        self.sparkles = Sparkles()
```

As you can see, we still have a few classes, but without the long inheritance chain. In `UltraMegaPet`, we use composition to be able to work with all of these superpowers.

Quiz

1. What is inheritance?

    a. Copying and pasting code

    b. An instance of a class as an attribute of another class

    c. Default behavior

    d. Creating new classes based on existing ones

2. What kind of relationship does inheritance represent in Python?

    a. Has-a

    b. Must-have

    c. Is-a

    d. Platonic

3. If you have a `Book` class and an `AudioBook` child class, how would you access the constructor of `Book` in `AudioBook`?

    a. `self.Book()`

    b. `super().__init__()`

    c. `Book.__init__(self)`

    d. `super(Book).__init__()`

4. What does DRY stand for in programming?

    a. Don't Run Yet

    b. Don't Repeat Yourself

    c. Do Remember YouTube

    d. Define, Refine, and Yield

5. In which case is it better to opt for composition over inheritance?

    a. When you want to reuse code from a parent class without modifying it

    b. When you only want to reuse specific functionality from another class

    c. When you need one class to represent a type of another class

    d. When one class owns an attribute of another class.

6. What is meant by polymorphism?

    a. A method in the parent class that can be overridden in the child class
    b. Being able to refer to one thing by multiple types
    c. A function that can accept multiple types of arguments
    d. The ability to override a method in a child class

7. How do you apply composition in a class?

    a. By passing in a class in another's parentheses like this: `Car(Engine)`
    b. By creating an instance of a class in another's attributes
    c. By using the `super()` function to call the desired functionality from a class in another class
    d. By calling a class as a method in another

8. What happens when a regular method is called in a child class, but that method is not defined in that child class?

    a. Python throws an error at you immediately
    b. Python will look for that method in the parent class(es) first
    c. Nothing happens
    d. It will add the method to the class

9. What happens when a child class overrides a method in the parent class?

    a. The parent method is deleted
    b. The parent method is called before and after the new functionality
    c. The child class can't call the parent method anymore
    d. The parent method is ignored and never called

10. Which of the following describes multiple inheritance?

    a. One class inherits from multiple parent classes
    b. One class inherits from a parent class, which inherits from another parent class
    c. One parent class is inherited by multiple child classes
    d. One class has multiple other class instances as attributes

11. What is the MRO responsible for in Python?

    a. Deciding which constructor to call when creating an object

    b. Deciding the order of method resolution in multiple inheritance

    c. Defining the order of inheritance

    d. Deciding which attributes to pass between classes

12. What does the `super()` function do?

    a. Calls a method from the parent class

    b. Creates a new child class

    c. Deletes the parent class

    d. Overrides a method from the parent class

Exercises

9.1 Practicing inheritance with vehicles

1. Create a class hierarchy for different types of vehicles. Start with a `Vehicle` base class, and create child classes for `Car`, `Truck`, and `Motorcycle`.
2. Start by creating the `Vehicle` class with a constructor that initializes the `make`, `model`, and `year` attributes.
3. Add a `ride()` method that can be applied to every type of vehicle. Print a simple message such as `"[vehicle] is riding"`.
4. Define the `__str__` dunder method so that it returns a description of the vehicle in the format `"[year] [make] [model]"`, for example, `"2002 Fiat Multipla"`.
5. Create the child classes that inherit from `Vehicle`: `Car`, `Truck`, and `Motorcycle`. Add class-specific attributes. For example, add `has_sunroof` or `is_electric` (boolean) for `Car` and `payload_capacity` for `Truck`.
6. Extend or overwrite (your choice) the `__str__` method to print a more specific description of the vehicle per class.
7. Set a few class-specific methods for the child class. For example, set `rev_engine()` for `Motorcycle` or `can_carry()` for `Truck`, which checks whether a certain weight fits within the truck's payload capacity.
8. Create a list with one instance of each child class. Iterate over the list, printing each and calling the `ride()` method on each list item, and observe the differences.

9.2 Superheroes fighting crime with composition

In this exercise, you're going to compose your very own Superhero League. You'll create a `Superhero` class, and each instance of `Superhero` will have multiple powers or tools that an instance of `Superhero` can use to fight crime. You probably guessed it, but we'll be using composition for this. You'll create a `Superhero` class that will have attributes for `name`, `power`, and `gadget`. Each power and gadget will be simple classes with one method each, a `use()` method. You'll practice composition by giving the superhero a mix of powers and gadgets as attributes.

Here is a step-by-step guide:

1. Create a few power classes, such as `SuperStrength` or `Invisibility`, each with a `use()` method that prints `"Using super strength!"` or `"Becoming invisible."` Have fun with this; the choice of powers doesn't affect the quality of your solution for this exercise.
2. Create some gadget classes, such as `LaserBelt` and `Shield`, again with `use()` methods that print something like `"Using laser belt!"` or `"Activating shield!"`.
3. Now, create the `Superhero` class. Its constructor will initialize attributes for name, powers, and gadgets. When creating the instance of `Superhero`, you pass in a list of powers and gadgets. Add a nice `__str__` method that introduces the superhero.
4. Add a `fight_crime()` method that will randomly choose a power or gadget to call `use()` on. Since we declared a `use()` method for all gadgets and powers, the result of calling it will depend on which power or gadget was selected.

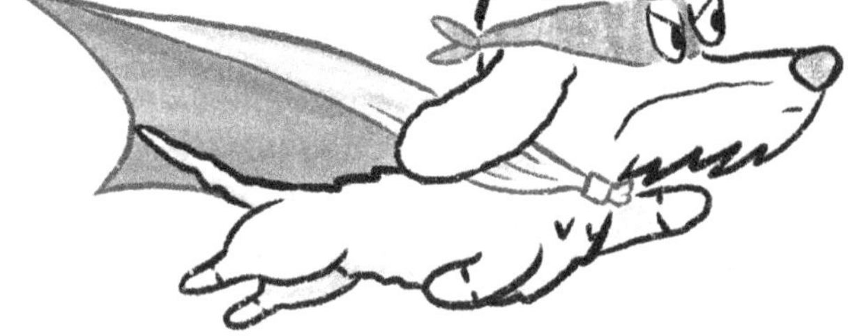

Summary

In short, inheritance is all about creating new classes based on existing ones. This helps keep your code clean, reusable, and compact. Reusability is popular in the programming world. We even have an abbreviation for it: DRY (short for *don't repeat yourself*). If you find yourself copying and pasting pieces of code, there's usually a better way. When working with classes, this is where inheritance shines. It lets one class pass on attributes and methods to the next.

For example, we saw how `Dog`, `Cat`, and `Rabbit` were all types of `Pet` and that they inherited everything from the `Pet` class. Quick reminder, this is what the class syntax looks like:

```
class Cat(Pet):
    pass
```

Here, the `Cat` class inherits everything from the `Pet` class simply by placing `Pet` inside the parentheses. You probably wouldn't create child classes unless you plan to add some custom behavior.

To add methods to the child classes, you just define them as you would otherwise. Adding custom attributes for child classes is a little bit more complicated. You write a new constructor for the child class, and inside, you reuse the parent's constructor using the `super()` function. Here is an example for demonstration:

```
class Cat(Pet):
    def __init__(self, name, age, weight, color):
        super().__init__(name, age, weight)
        self.color = color
```

The `super()` function calls the constructor of the parent class, which sets `name`, `age`, and `weight` attributes. Then, we add the `color` attribute, specific to the `Cat` class.

Sometimes, you might want to change how a method works in a child class. This is called overriding. One way to do this is by simply redefining the method you want to change in the child class. If you want to keep the functionality from the parent class's function, but add your own twist to it, you can again use the `super()` function.

You might not always exactly know what kind of subtype something is. Polymorphism is the ability to refer to one thing by multiple types.

There are different types of inheritance. Let's go over the ones we discussed once more:

- **Single inheritance**: One child inherits from one parent class
- **Multilevel inheritance**: A child class inherits from a parent class, and that parent class inherits from another parent class
- **Hierarchical inheritance**: One parent class has multiple child classes
- **Multiple inheritance**: A child class inherits from more than one parent class

Multiple inheritance can be tricky. It's important to make sure that parent classes serve different purposes and aren't secretly subtypes of each other. Things can get especially confusing when the two parent classes define the same method. Python then uses a rule called the method resolution order to decide which one to use. It's a good idea to be cautious when using multiple inheritance to avoid trouble.

Inheritance is a great tool, but it can be overused. Sometimes, it's better to use composition instead. In composition, one class has an attribute that is an instance of another class. This is useful when there is a *has-a* relationship between classes, rather than an *is-a* relationship.

For example, a car might have an engine, but a car is not a type of engine. Here's what composition looks like:

```
class Car:
    def __init__(self):
        self.engine = Engine()  # Car has-a Engine
```

As you can see, `Car` does not inherit from `Engine`. It uses composition by creating an instance of `Engine` as an attribute.

Composition can also be a solution to avoid deep inheritance chains.

Inheritance is a powerful solution for keeping your code clean. However, it can get fragile and hard to maintain if you're not careful. Deep inheritance chains can make things messy, especially when you're trying to change or debug stuff. It's all about balance. Use inheritance when there's a clear *is-a* relationship between classes, and go for composition (the *has-a* relationship) when you just want to combine functionality without tying everything together too tightly.

In the end, it's important to KISS (short for *keep it simple, stupid*). Don't overcomplicate things just because you can. When in doubt, go for clarity and choose your class designs with care. It'll save you a lot of headaches down the road.

10

Debugging Our Code

Let's talk about one of my favorite activities: catching bugs.

Unfortunately, I don't really mean catching physical bugs, but debugging our code. Bugs are mistakes in our code, and debugging means finding and solving them. Sometimes, they're obvious to catch. Other times, they can *bug* you for days. Having a structured approach to debugging helps. That's what this chapter is for. I'm going to show you several methods that we can use to find bugs in our code. There are different approaches, and often we don't need all of them. However, especially if you're stuck for longer, it can be nice to try different things to find the problem.

Throughout this chapter, we'll be using an example project: a pet shelter management system. It's a small program with functions for adding pets, feeding them, and checking whether they're eligible for adoption. Cats and dogs alike, everyone's welcome. Except bugs. Bugs are not welcome.

Why debugging matters

Imagine writing a program, running it, and then: bam! A wild error message appears. Or worse: no error, but the program does something wrong. That's where debugging comes in.

Debugging is the process of identifying, analyzing, and fixing problems in your code. It's not something to be ashamed of at all. Believe it or not, even the most experienced developers debug daily. In fact, becoming good at debugging is a huge part of becoming a better programmer.

There are different bugs we face on a daily basis. Let's talk about them.

Common types of bugs

Not all bugs are the same. We have some categories of usual suspects, though:

- **Syntax errors**: This happens when Python can't even run our code because we broke one of its grammatical rules, for example, missing colons, bad indentation, and unclosed quotes. All of these result in syntax errors.
- **Runtime errors**: These are problems that Python runs into when it can't handle something while your program is running, such as trying to divide by zero or access a list element that doesn't exist.
- **Logical errors**: These are the last on the list and usually the most difficult to find and solve. Why? Because these bugs are sneaky. Our code runs and it doesn't crash, but it does the wrong thing. These are the ones that hurt the most, especially if we don't notice that the code is doing the wrong thing at first.

In order to debug these problems, we need different skills. Let's start with the first two: syntax and runtime errors. The nice part about these bugs is that they display an error message. The number one skill necessary for solving them is being able to understand these error messages.

Understanding error messages

Let's look at a (fictional) part of our pet shelter program:

```
def add_pet(pets, name, age, species):
    pet = {"name": name, "age": age, "species": species, "fed": False}
    pets.append(pet)


add_pet(my_pets, "Zia", 2, "cat")
```

Oops. We get an error:

```
Traceback (most recent call last):
  File "shelter.py", line 5, in <module>
    add_pet(my_pets, "Zia", 2, "cat")
NameError: name 'my_pets' is not defined
```

Let's decode this traceback:

- `File "shelter.py"` tells us which file has the error.
- `line 5` is the line where the error occurred.
- `NameError` is the type of error.
- `name 'my_pets' is not defined` tells us where we have the actual problem.

Now we know: we forgot to define `my_pets` before using it. This means that the `my_pets` variable doesn't exist. In order to be able to successfully run the code, we need to create the list, like this:

```
def add_pet(pets, name, age, species):
    pet = {"name": name, "age": age, "species": species, "fed": False}
    pets.append(pet)


my_pets = []
add_pet(my_pets, "Zia", 2, "cat")
```

We have now defined `my_pets` as an empty list. And now, our program runs successfully.

Common errors in Python

By reading the tracebacks, there are a few more errors you're likely to meet (or have already met). Let's make formal acquaintances with them!

- `SyntaxError`: You wrote something Python can't parse, such as a missing `:`
- `NameError`: You used a variable that doesn't exist
- `TypeError`: You tried to do something with the wrong type (such as adding a string to a number)
- `ValueError`: You gave the right type but the wrong kind of value
- `IndexError`: You tried to access a list index that doesn't exist, typically a number that's higher than the number of elements you have in the list

I tried to make things easy here; typically, this is what they mean. Sometimes, you can have a somewhat deceiving message. What do I do when I can't figure it out myself?

Well, I Google the error. Or sometimes I ask some AI to explain what I did wrong. I like to combine these two approaches. Google is still my first go-to, but that might be an outdated approach soon. Whichever one you choose, make sure you understand what is going on and that you learn a little from the error. This will help to solve the problem a little faster the next time it happens.

That's it for the runtime and syntax errors. Let's move on to the more sneaky category of bugs: logical bugs.

Tools and techniques for debugging

Sometimes, our code runs but it's not giving the correct outcome. Well, it's up to us to discover why that's the case. It can be annoying and frustrating and drive us mad, wondering whether we can even code at all. Even my human, who's coding for 20+ years, breaks down crying on day five of trying to find a problem, occasionally.

What should you do? Well, take a break, get some fresh air, get some rest, eat some chocolate chip cookies or ice cream (optional step), and try again later. As you get more experienced, your faith in being able to find the bug eventually will grow stronger.

Let's talk about some steps you can take to find the bug.

Print statements

My first step is debatable. It's frowned upon by many, but I dare to claim that most of us do it as a first step. Just put a quick and dirty `print()` in to see what's going on. Let's say that we are adding three pets to a list (simulated with code here) and then try to feed one, but for some reason, it's not printing that the pet has been fed. Let's take a look at our code:

```
def add_pet(pets, name, age, species):
    pet = {"name": name, "age": age, "species": species, "fed": False}
    pets.append(pet)


def feed_pet(pets, name):
    for pet in pets:
        if pet['name'] == name:
            pet['fed'] = True
            print(f"{name} has been fed.")


my_pets = []
```

```
# This would be done with a user interface in real life
add_pet(my_pets, "Zia", 2, "cat")
add_pet(my_pets, "Wiesje", 7, "dog")
add_pet(my_pets, "Axel", 2, "axolotl")

feed_pet(my_pets, "wiesje")
# End of user interface simulation
```

Now, I'd expect that code to print the following:

```
Wiesje has been fed.
```

However, it doesn't print anything. Maybe you've already spotted what's wrong, but let's pretend we all don't see it. In this situation, I'd go in and add a quick print statement. The hardest part when you're new to coding is deciding where to add the print statement. This should not be random but a strategic choice. For example, by printing each pet's name during the loop, we can confirm the following:

- We are looping over the pets correctly
- Each item is indeed a dictionary
- We are checking against the correct variable name

I'll add the print strategically to `feed_pets`, like this:

```
def feed_pet(pets, name):
    for pet in pets:
        print(f"Checking pet: {pet['name']}")
        if pet['name'] == name:
            pet['fed'] = True
            print(f"{name} has been fed.")
```

Right now, our code will output the following:

```
Checking pet: Zia
Checking pet: Wiesje
Checking pet: Axel
```

From this, I can conclude that the looping is going well; I get all the names, so the items are indeed dictionaries, and the name of the variable is correct. But it doesn't indicate that there's a problem, and I might still not see what's wrong. So, my next step would be to place a print inside the block of the `if`. Technically, there is a print already, and we could conclude that it's simply not getting there. However, I will add an extra print to double-check:

```
def feed_pet(pets, name):
    for pet in pets:
        print(f"Checking pet: {pet['name']}")
        if pet['name'] == name:
            print(f"In if block: {pet['name']}")
            pet['fed'] = True
            print(f"{name} has been fed.")
```

If I run it again, it's *not* showing my latest print statement. Therefore, it's not getting into the `if` block. In order to get into the `if` block, the pet name needs to match the input name. So, this could be the moment I see the problem. Let's assume I haven't had my coffee yet. I'll modify the first print statement to output the value in the `name` variable, like this:

```
def feed_pet(pets, name):
    for pet in pets:
        print(f"Checking pet: {pet['name']} and {name}")
        if pet['name'] == name:
            print(f"In if block: {pet['name']}")
            pet['fed'] = True
            print(f"{name} has been fed.")
```

And now I get this output:

```
Checking pet: Zia and wiesje
Checking pet: Wiesje and wiesje
Checking pet: Axel and wiesje
```

Now, having had my coffee, I can see that we are comparing the lowercase `"wiesje"` to the capitalized `"Wiesje"`. And that's our problem. Sometimes all you need is a few print statements to see what's going on. Not very fancy, but it works.

So, let's change the line where we are feeding Wiesje:

```
feed_pet(my_pets, "Wiesje")
```

Now it is showing the following:

```
Checking pet: Zia and Wiesje
Checking pet: Wiesje and Wiesje
In if block: Wiesje
Wiesje has been fed.
Checking pet: Axel and Wiesje
```

Now that our code is working again, there is one very important last step, and that is to remove all the print statements that we added for debugging. Let's see another way we could have debugged this program.

Using a debugger in your IDE

Instead of using print statements, IDEs come with built-in debuggers. Let me walk you through how to do this in VS Code, but it's possible with most other IDEs as well. In VS Code, the first step is to go to our debug tab. This is the play icon with a tiny bug in the vertical menu on the very left (the fourth icon down from the top in the following screenshot).

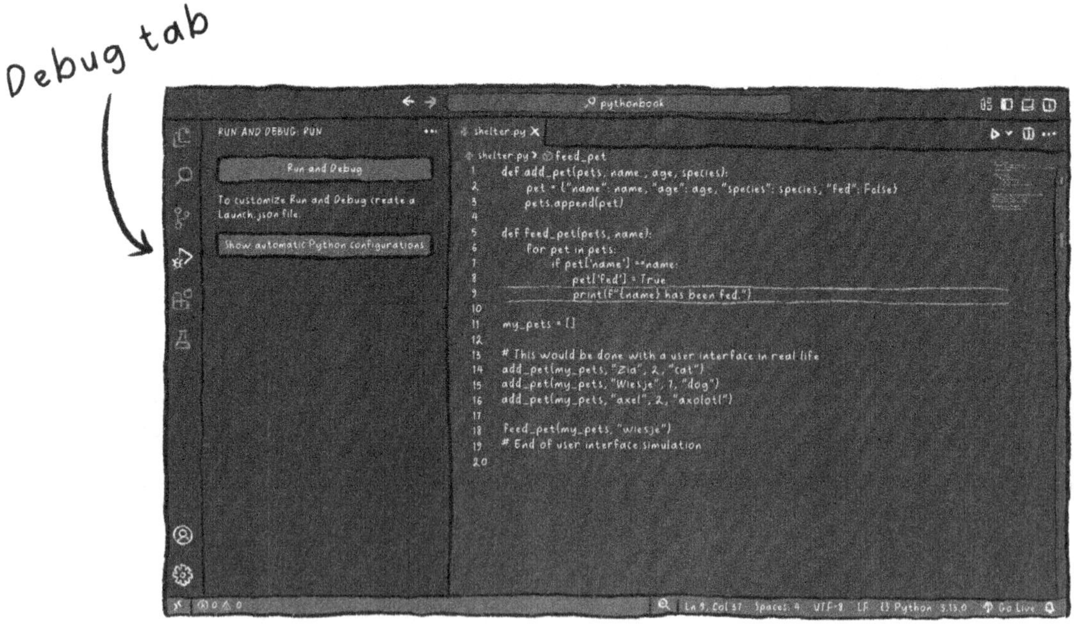

What we need to do next is add breakpoints to our code.

Breakpoints are places where we'd like to pause our code and see what is going on. This gives us the opportunity to check the values of variables, and if we want to, we can go through our code step by step from there. It's a little bit like being able to freeze time, and then being able to walk around yourself.

How do we add breaking points? Well, we click on the line that we want to have the breakpoint. It's important that you know where to click. In this case, I want the breakpoint on line 6. Then, we click a little to the left of the line number. At that spot, a red dot appears, indicating that the breakpoint has been set.

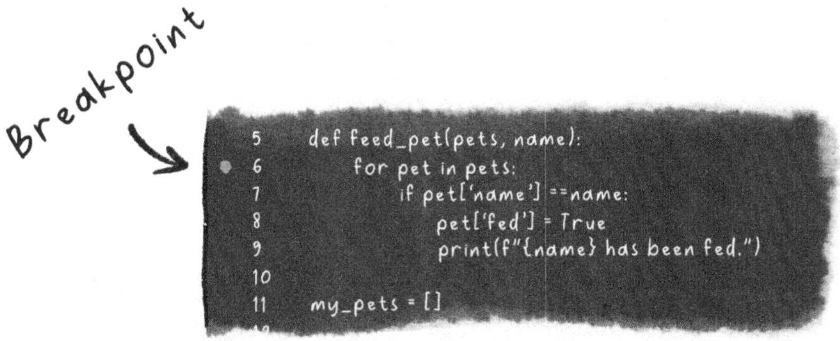

Now we need to run our code in debug mode. This is not done by clicking the regular play button.

Instead, we'll go for the **Run and Debug** button in the left pane, as shown here.

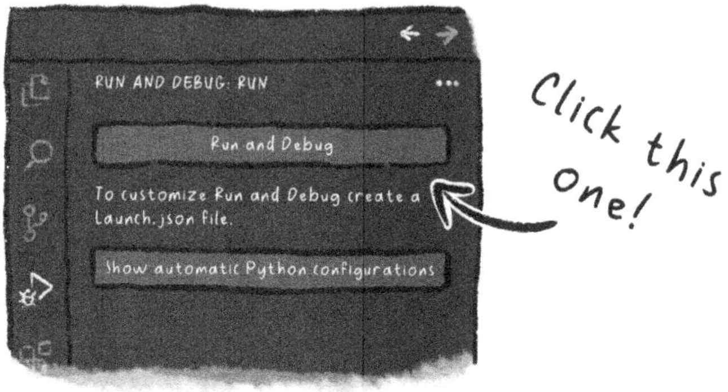

We are then prompted to select a debugger. I'm choosing **Python Debugger** here. Next, it asks for a debug configuration. We can set up all sorts of fancy things; for now, it's enough to choose **Python file**, because we just want to debug the current Python file. And that brings us to the paused execution of our code. This looks a little bit complicated, so we'll go over what is visible on the screen step by step:

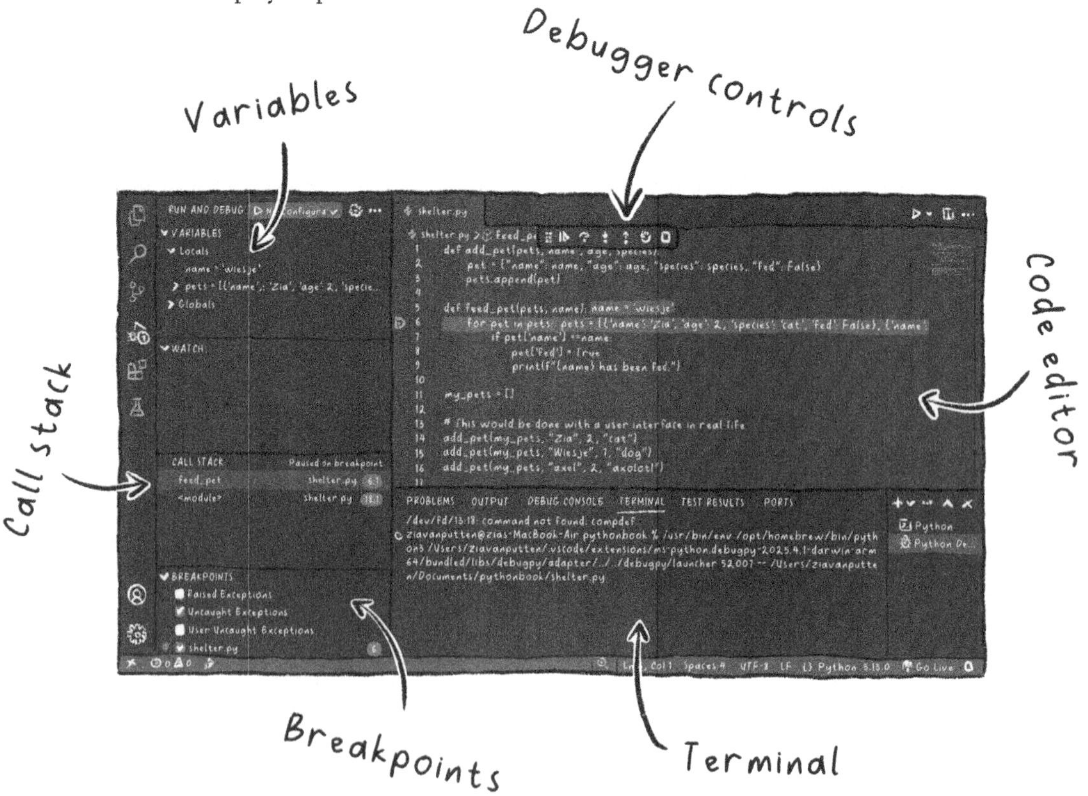

The code editor (middle panel)

Let's start with the center. In the middle panel, we see our code. We're looking at the `shelter.py` file. The line that we are currently paused on, line 6, is highlighted. The code execution is paused right before executing this line. This is because we've placed a breakpoint on line 6 (the red dot on the left). A breakpoint tells Python, *"Pause here, please, so I can inspect things."* So, right now, our program has paused inside the `feed_pet` function and is about to loop over the `pets` list. Before we talk about what's happening there and how to proceed, let's examine the rest of the screen.

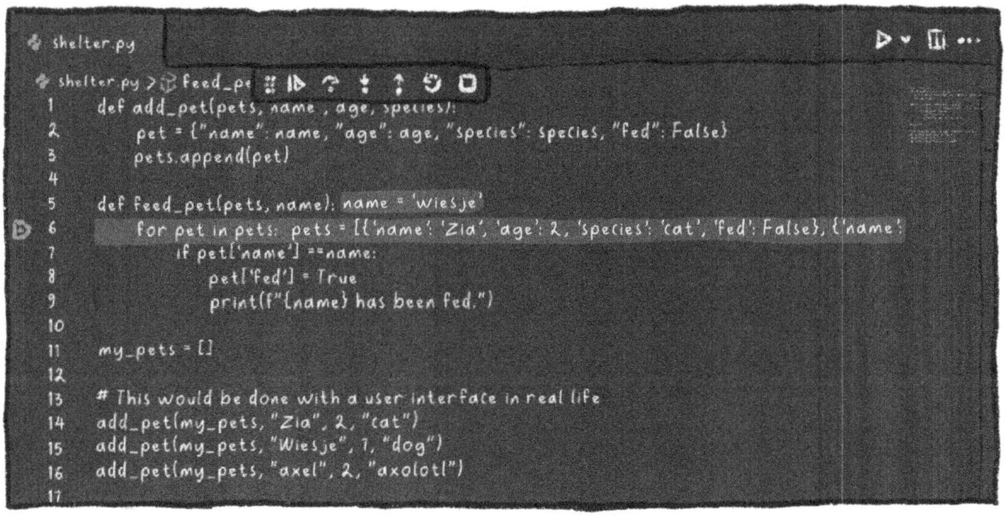

Breakpoints (bottom-left panel)

There's also a panel for breakpoints. This is the configuration for what elements to pause on. Currently, two boxes are checked. We are pausing for any breakpoints in `shelter.py`. It shows a 6 on the end, indicating that there's a breakpoint on line 6. The uncaught exceptions are also checked. This means that it will also take a break when an uncaught exception occurs. We have now only added one breakpoint, but we could set multiple breakpoints in our program to pause in more than one place.

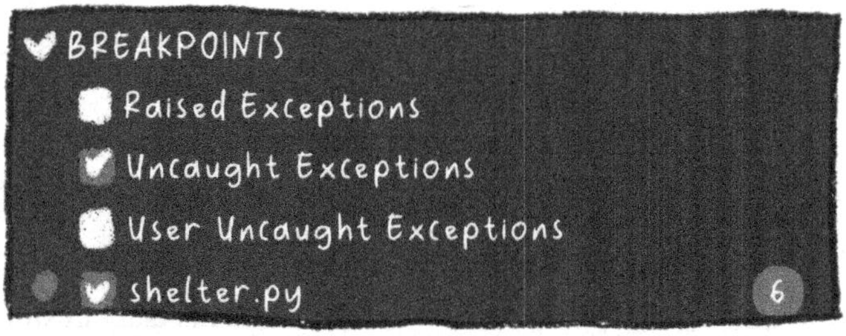

Call stack (left panel above the breakpoints)

A little above the breakpoints panel, we find the call stack panel. The call stack shows you where your program is currently "stacked" in terms of function calls. Right now, this is a small stack. If you have multiple functions (possibly across many modules) that are calling each other, the stack will be bigger. Right now, we're in the `feed_pet()` function at line 6. We can see that this function was called from line 18 in the main body of `shelter.py`.

This call stack is a trail showing how you got to where the code is currently paused.

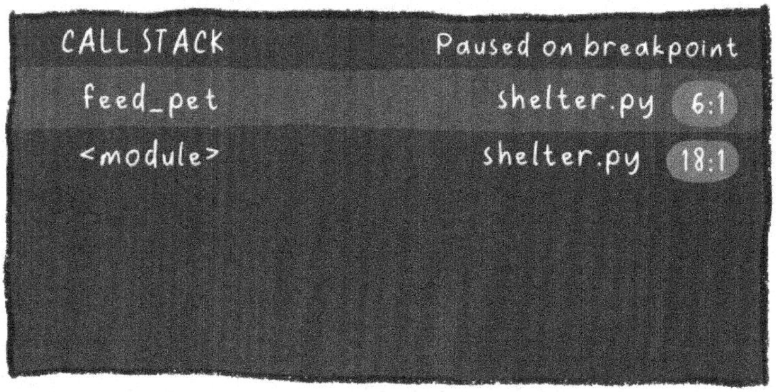

Variables (top-left panel)

Here's my favorite, the **Variables** panel on the top left. This panel is so incredibly helpful when debugging! We have two categories, **Locals** and **Globals**. In **Locals**, we can see all the variables in the current function. In here, we have the following:

- `name = 'wiesje'` tells us that the function is currently trying to feed my friend.
- `pets` is a list with the dictionaries of pets in it. You can open it up further by clicking on the > icon to see what exactly is in the list.

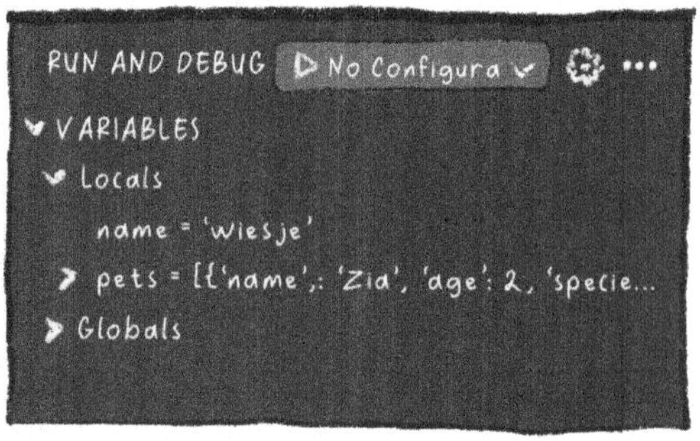

This panel lets you check whether the values are what you expect before and while stepping through the code. Since we haven't talked about stepping, let's see that next.

Debugger controls (top center, above the code)

It might just be me, but I always feel like I need to search for the debugger controls in VS Code. That is because they are floating. Currently, they are floating on the top center above the code, but you can move them to a more convenient location. For clarity, here they are:

That floating toolbar has the following buttons, from left to right:

- Continue (▷): Resume program execution until the next breakpoint
- Step over (↷): Run the current line and go to the next one, without stepping into any functions it might call
- Step into (↓): Enter any function call on the current line and pause on the first line of that function (if it isn't a function call, just go to the next line)
- Step out (↑): Finish the current function and return to the caller, and pause there
- Restart (↻): Restart the debug session
- Stop (□): Stop the debug session

Terminal (bottom-middle panel)

Lastly, we have the terminal at the bottom under the code. This terminal shows the shell running the Python script. If there were error messages, they would appear here. No error message is showing now, because the code hasn't failed. It's just paused. Also, if the program prints anything, you'll see it here too.

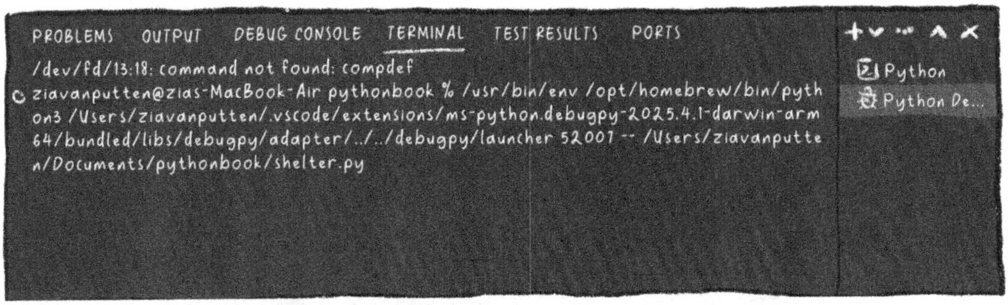

What's happening right now

Now that we've seen everything, let's go back to our current situation. We're inside the function call `feed_pet(my_pets, "Wiesje")`, and about to run the following:

```
for pet in pets:
```

Using the **Variables** panel, you can already see that the loop will first go over Zia. We can now step through the loop to see whether it correctly matches `pet['name']` with `"wiesje"`. This means it should not go into the `if` block, but back to `for pet in pets:`.

We are then trying to match `"Wiesje"` with `"wiesje"`. I can't show this in screenshots, but we can hover over variables and see their values appear. Here you can see the second pet we are looping over and that the name of that pet is Wiesje. If I hover over the name on the right-hand side of the `if` block, it shows `"Wiesje"`.

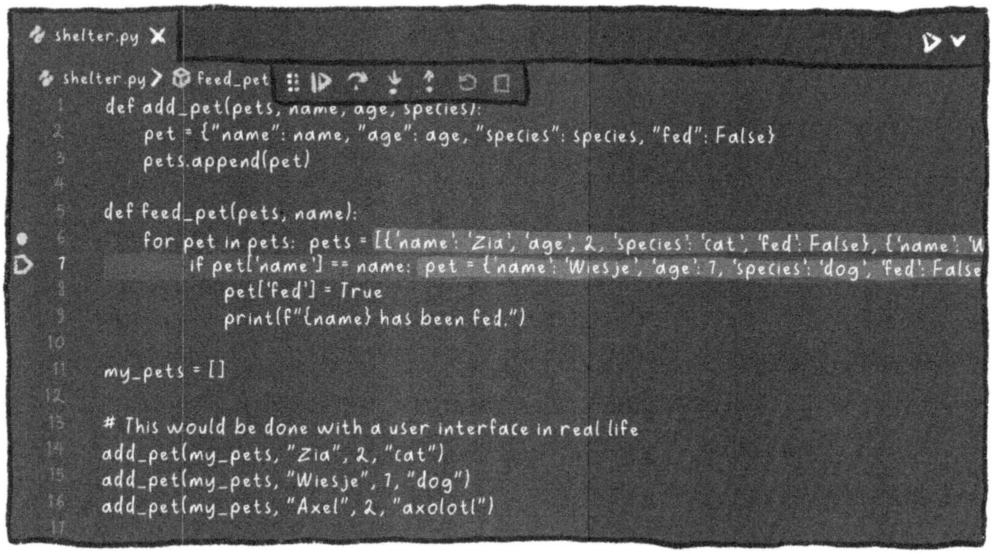

This is also visible in the **Variables** panel. That should give us an idea of what is going on.

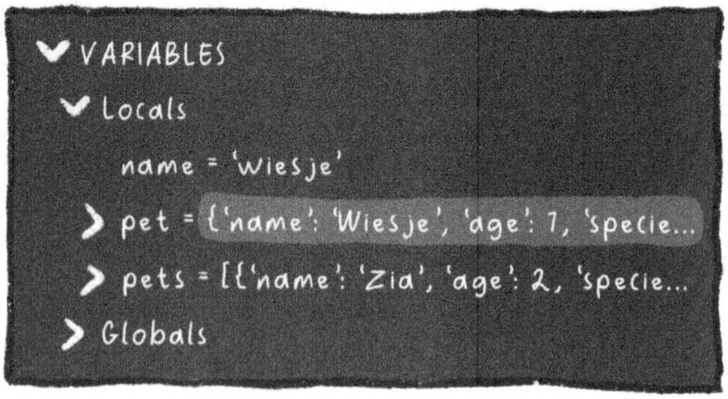

.If we somehow miss what is going on, we will find out something is up at this step when we click on the step-over button. Instead of going inside the `if` block, it goes back to the `for` loop. Then, if we restart the debugging session and pay more attention, we should be able to spot our typo.

The pdb module

If you want to do it via the terminal, you can take a different approach. To be honest, I don't recommend this for beginners. But this chapter would feel incomplete if I didn't at least briefly mention it. Python has a built-in debugger that we can call with `breakpoint()`. Where we'd like to pause our code, we can call `breakpoint()`.

Here's what the code would look like:

```
def add_pet(pets, name, age, species):
    pet = {"name": name, "age": age, "species": species, "fed": False}
    pets.append(pet)

def feed_pet(pets, name):
    breakpoint()
    for pet in pets:
        if pet['name'] == name:
            pet['fed'] = True
            print(f"{name} has been fed.")
```

```
my_pets = []

# This would be done with a user interface in real life
add_pet(my_pets, "Zia", 2, "cat")
add_pet(my_pets, "Wiesje", 7, "dog")
add_pet(my_pets, "Axel", 2, "axolotl")

feed_pet(my_pets, "wiesje")
# End of user interface simulation
```

We can then run the program and it will pause at that line. On my system, I can't run it with the play icon. Just like with the input function, it won't accept my input, and the next step is to type commands. So instead, I'll run it manually from the command line with the following command:

```
python3 shelter.py
```

This is assuming that you stored it in a file called `shelter.py` and that your command for running Python is `python3`. If that's different, you'd need a different command. Here's what my output looks like:

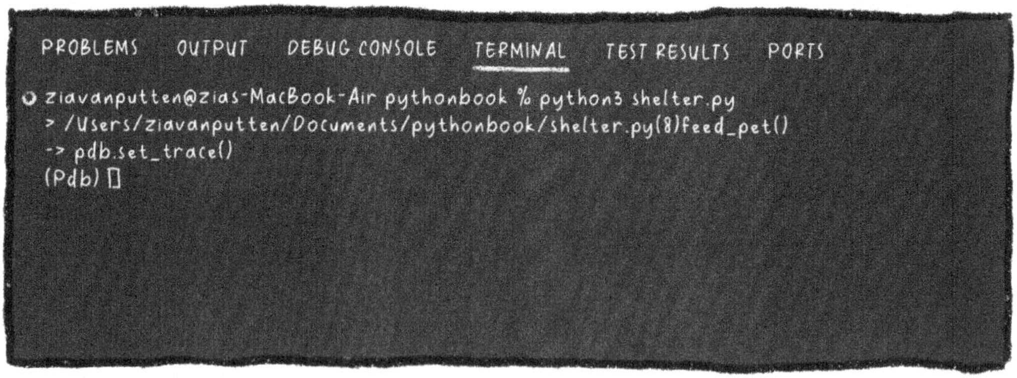

You can then type commands that are similar to the debugger controls (you know, those floating buttons), as follows:

- n: To go to the next line
- s: To step into a function
- c: To continue until a possible next breaking point or the end of the program
- l: To list current lines of code

- `locals()`: To get all the local variables
- `globals()`: To get all the global variables

Here's an example of me first going to the next line and then listing the current lines of code:

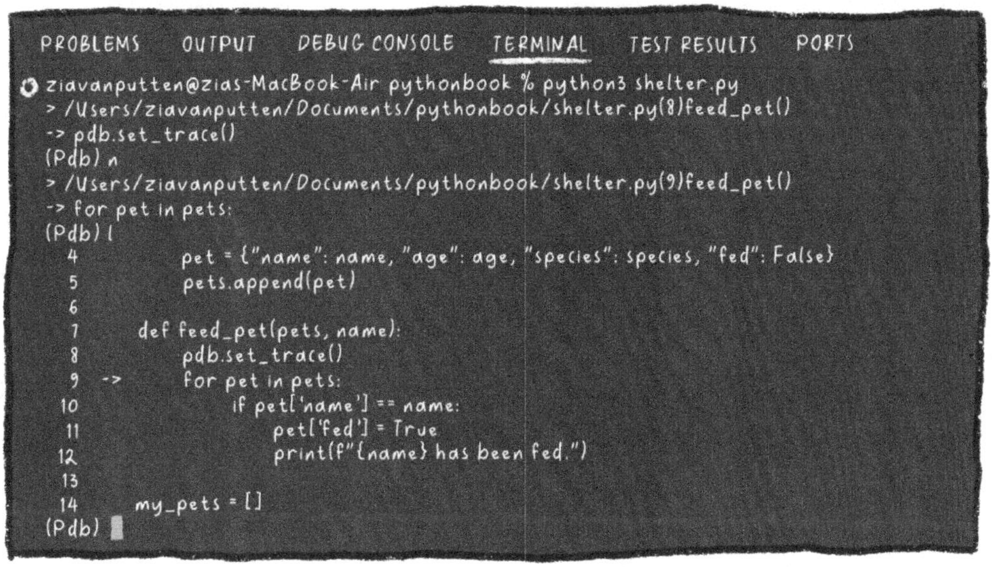

```
PROBLEMS    OUTPUT    DEBUG CONSOLE    TERMINAL    TEST RESULTS    PORTS

ziavanputten@zias-MacBook-Air pythonbook % python3 shelter.py
> /Users/ziavanputten/Documents/pythonbook/shelter.py(8)feed_pet()
-> pdb.set_trace()
(Pdb) n
> /Users/ziavanputten/Documents/pythonbook/shelter.py(9)feed_pet()
-> for pet in pets:
(Pdb) l
  4             pet = {"name": name, "age": age, "species": species, "fed": False}
  5             pets.append(pet)
  6
  7         def feed_pet(pets, name):
  8             pdb.set_trace()
  9  ->         for pet in pets:
 10                 if pet['name'] == name:
 11                     pet['fed'] = True
 12                     print(f"{name} has been fed.")
 13
 14         my_pets = []
(Pdb)
```

There is an arrow on line 9, which shows that I'm currently paused on the loop. Let's check out the local and global variables. These are two steps; here's how to do it and what it outputs on my system:

```
 14         my_pets = []
(Pdb) locals
{'pets': [{'name': 'Zia', 'age': 2, 'species': 'cat', 'fed': False}, {'name': 'Wiesje', 'age': 7, 'specie
s': 'dog', 'fed': False}, {'name': 'Axel', 'age': 2, 'species': 'axolotl', 'fed': False}], 'name': 'wies
je'}
(Pdb) globals()
{'__name__': '__main__', '__doc__': None, '__package__': None, '__loader__': <_frozen_im
portlib_external.SourceFileLoader object at 0x104d8d0d0>, '__spec__
ions__': {}, '__builtins__': <module 'builtins' (built-in)>, '__file__': '/Users
ocuments/pythonbook/shelter.py', '__cached__': None, 'pdb': <module 'p
mebrew/Cellar/python@3.13/3.13.0_1/Frameworks/Python.framework
/python3.13/pdb.py'>, 'add_pet': <function add_pet at 0x104c709a0>,
n feed_pet at 0x104ddb920>, 'my_pets': [{'name': 'Zia', 'age': 2, 'species'
, {'name': 'Wiesje', 'age': 7, 'species': 'dog', 'fed': False}, {'name': 'Axel',
olotl', 'fed': False}], '__pdb_convenience_variables': {'_frame': <fr
le '/Users/ziavanputten/Documents/pythonbook/shelter.py', line 9,
(Pdb)
```

I'll stop right here. As you can see, this is less intuitive. Whenever you have an IDE available, I'd recommend the debug options there. However, imagine if we had to SSH into an external Linux server (= connect to an external computer with sometimes no user interface other than the command-line interface). We could debug it there via the command line like this. Again, this is not for beginners, but I felt like I had to mention it.

Debugging workflow

Whatever tool we choose, there are a few steps we should take when we start to debug. If it's not our own bug, but a colleague or user indicates that there's a bug, the first step is always to reproduce it. Then again, I typically also do this when it's my own bug.

Reproducing the bug is not necessarily difficult. It means running the code again and seeing whether you indeed get the same wrong output. If you don't, it's important to make sure that you are running the code in the same way as when you or your colleague got the problem.

Then the next step is to hypothesize the cause of the bug. What could possibly be causing this error to occur? Depending on the problem, the steps are different. If you have a traceback, you start by reading that and going over the type of error and the line on which it went wrong. If you don't see it there, you can look at the line that was called before that and go back until you find the issue.

If it's a logical error or you still don't see what's going wrong with the traceback, you might want to work with the print statements or debugger to see what is going on.

Then, once you have an idea of what might be going on, you test the hypothesis by trying to solve the problem. If the error is gone (or you get a new problem), congratulations, you've solved that bug. If it's not gone, you'll have to undo the change (unless it's part of a series of changes that you need to make) and come up with a new hypothesis of what is causing the problem.

If you have a new problem, you just start the debugging workflow again after cleaning up and verifying that your hypothesis was correct. If you added print statements or debug prints, make sure to remove them again. Also make sure to verify edge cases; your program might work for this exact input, but what happens if there are variations? For example, if we input a name and a list, it works. But what happens if we input an empty string, an empty list, and so on? Lastly, make sure the rest of the code still works as expected. If it does, you're done debugging this problem.

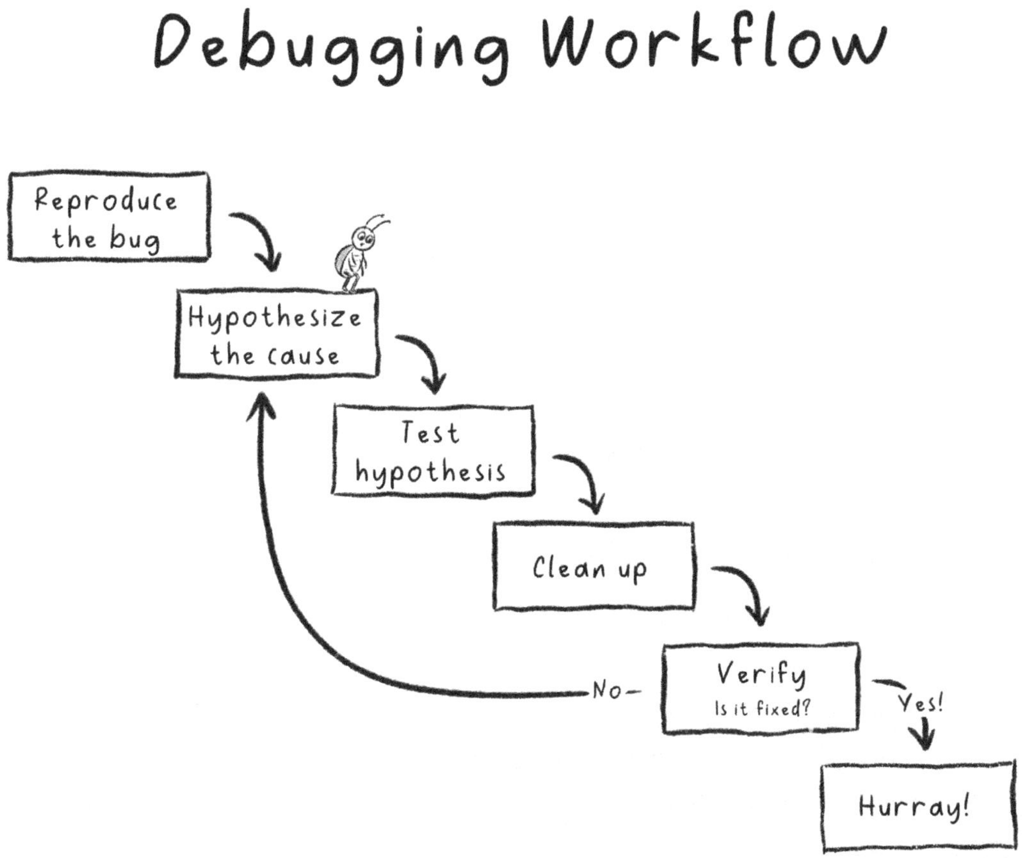

Quiz

1. What is a traceback, and where does it appear?

    a. A list of comments that developers usually put at the top of their script
    b. A log of successful runs, shown in the debugger window
    c. A detailed error message that appears in the terminal when your code crashes
    d. A form of version control that you can find in the **Source Control** panel

2. What's a common way to debug a logical error?

    a. Turning your device off and on again
    b. Using print statements
    c. Reading Python's error messages carefully
    d. Deleting everything and starting over

3. What happens when your code hits a breakpoint?

    a. Python skips that line and keeps running
    b. The code pauses and allows you to inspect variables and step through the code
    c. Your program exits the current loop and moves on
    d. An error message appears

4. What's the first step of the debugging workflow?

    a. Reproducing the bug
    b. Cleaning up unnecessary code snippets
    c. Hypothesizing what's causing the problem
    d. Adding breakpoints

5. Which of the following best describes a syntax error?

    a. The program fails to run because you tried to access a variable that doesn't exist
    b. The program pauses so you can inspect variables
    c. The program crashes because of a typo or formatting mistake
    d. The program runs, but the result is incorrect

6. What's the purpose of the red dot in VS Code?

    a. It highlights syntax errors in your script

    b. It marks a line where an error occurs

    c. It's a laser pointer feature included for developer cats

    d. It tells the debugger to pause at that line so you can check what your code is doing

7. What do you see in the call stack when debugging in VS Code?

    a. A list of error messages that shows you how your program crashed

    b. A list of files saved in your project folder

    c. A list of all function calls that led to the current line of code

    d. A list of variables and their current values

8. We've created a program to calculate the average time for a lap in a wiener dog race. The program runs without errors, but it always prints `"Average time: 0.0"`, which doesn't seem right. What print statement would be most helpful to debug this?

```
def average_time(laps):
    time = 0
    for lap in laps:
        lap += time
    return time / len(laps)

laps = [60, 62, 58]
print("Average time:", average_time(laps))
```

    a. Printing the values of `lap` and `time` after the function call

    b. Printing the values of `lap` and `time` in the loop, before and after the addition

    c. Printing the value of `laps` at the top of the `average_time` function

    d. Printing the length of `laps` using `len(laps)` outside the function

Exercises

For this chapter's exercises, you will again be working with existing files. I have a special talent for writing buggy code, and I've created just the right snippets for you to practice your debugging skills with. Each exercise includes its code right here. But I'm not going to ask you to debug it by staring at it. That was never a debug technique we discussed. That's why I recommend downloading the files from our GitHub repository. By now, I trust you know where to find it.

10.1 Buggy cat naps

We've written a program to calculate the total time your cat sleeps in a day. But something seems off... The total that our function returns doesn't match the actual time the cat spent napping:

```
def nap_time(hours_list):
    total = 0
    counter = 1
    while counter < len(hours_list):
        total += hours_list[counter]
        counter += 1
    return total

cat_naps = [2, 3, 1.5, 4]
print("Total nap time:", nap_time(cat_naps))
```

Even if you spot the error in this code right away, practice using print statements, a breakpoint, or the traceback log to figure out what's wrong and what kind of bug we're dealing with. Also, fix the problem so that the function returns the correct total nap time.

10.2 Museum tickets

You're helping a local museum set up a ticket machine. You've written a Python program for it: the visitor enters their age, and the machine prints the kind of ticket they get. The logic is simple:

- Kids under 12 get free access
- Teens under 18 get a youth discount
- Adults under 65 pay full price
- People aged 65 and older get a senior discount

```
def ticket_type():
    age = input("Enter your age: ")
```

```
    if age < 12:
        print("You get in for free. Lucky you!")
    elif age < 18:
        print("You get a youth discount!")
    elif age < 65:
        print("That's a full-price ticket for you.")
    else:
        print("You get a senior discount!")

ticket_type()
```

The preceding code might look fine, but when you test it, your program crashes. Can you figure out why? And, more importantly, can you fix the bug so that the machine runs smoothly, no matter what the visitor types in?

10.3 How much does your cat meow?

Imagine you've written this program to calculate how often your cat meows on average per waking hour. You've kept a log of how much they've meowed and how much they've slept each day. You've rounded the nap times. After all, you're a software developer, not a pharmacist. Everything in your code seems to look perfectly fine. But guess what? The program crashes anyway.

Time to debug!

Use the traceback, print statements, and/or breakpoints to figure out what's causing the crash and what type of bug you're dealing with. Think of a smart way to modify the code so it doesn't crash anymore:

```
def average_meows(logs):
    total_meows_per_hour = 0

    for log in logs:
        nap_hours = 0
        for nap in log["naps"]:
            nap_hours += nap
        awake_hours = 24 - nap_hours
        total_meows_per_hour += log["meows"] / awake_hours

    return total_meows_per_hour / len(logs)
```

```
logs = [
    {"day": "Monday", "naps": [1, 2, 5], "meows": 90},
    {"day": "Tuesday", "naps": [4, 3, 2], "meows": 75},
    {"day": "Wednesday", "naps": [8, 6, 9, 1], "meows": 9},
    {"day": "Thursday", "naps": [1, 1, 5, 7], "meows": 38},
    {"day": "Friday", "naps": [3, 3, 2, 8], "meows": 94},
    {"day": "Saturday", "naps": [4, 8, 3], "meows": 64},
    {"day": "Sunday", "naps": [3, 3, 2, 8], "meows": 37}
]

print("Average meows per awake hour:", average_meows(logs))
```

10.4 Trailing bugs

You're writing a program that calculates the total distance of a trail. The data is flexible, and each trail segment is passed as a tuple that consists of the distance and the unit. The function should print the total of all those segments. The program runs without crashing, but something about that total feels off... Use debugging techniques to find out what's wrong with this code and fix the bug:

```
def total_distance(*segments):
    total = 0

    for length, unit in segments:
        if unit.lower() == "M":
            total += length
        elif unit.lower() == "km":
            total += length / 1000

    print("Total distance:", total, "meters")

total_distance(
    (2.5, "km"),
    (400, "M"),
    (1.0, "km"),
    (800, "m"),
    (1.3, "KM"),
    (900, "m "),
    (1.1, "km")
)
```

10.5 None to say

We're almost through with the book. So let's start decorating for a little party. You've written a piece of code that involves classes and a decorator. There is an `Animal` class and `Cat` and `Dog` classes that extend it. Each animal has a `speak()` method that returns what sound it makes. This method is decorated with a decorator that announces the animal before it says something. The output of this code is, however, not as you intended. Use print statements or breakpoints to figure out why the code is misbehaving and fix the program so that it functions properly:

```
def log_call(func):
    def wrapper(self):
        print(f"{self.name} is about to speak...")
        func(self)
    return wrapper

class Animal:
    def __init__(self, name):
        self.name = name

    @log_call
    def speak(self):
        return "..."

class Dog(Animal):
    @log_call
    def speak(self):
        return "Woof!"

class Cat(Animal):
    @log_call
    def speak(self):
        return "Meow!"

dog = Dog("Cliff")
cat = Cat("Muchu")

print(dog.speak())
print(cat.speak())
```

Summary

Sooner or later, your code will do things you don't expect. Probably sooner. This chapter was about what to do when that happens. Debugging is the process of identifying, analyzing, and fixing problems in code. We looked at different types of bugs and ways to deal with them.

Syntax and runtime errors come with helpful error messages. If you can read a traceback (and don't get too intimidated by the red letters), Python is often telling you exactly what went wrong.

Logical bugs are trickier. That's when your code runs without errors but still doesn't behave as you intended. It's this detective work that makes debugging fun. Sometimes a simple cup of coffee is all it takes to spot the issue. But when that doesn't help, print statements can come to the rescue. They may be frowned upon, but they work. If you want more control, a lot of IDEs (including VS Code) also have a built-in debugger. That's where the little red dot comes in: you set a breakpoint, and your program will pause there so you can inspect what's happening step by step.

A helpful way to approach any bug is by following a debugging workflow. You always start by reproducing the problem. Then, you form a hypothesis about what might be going wrong. You test it by adjusting parts of the code to try to fix the problem. Next, you clean up any temporary code, such as print statements. Lastly, verify whether you've solved the problem. If not, you go back and try a new hypothesis.

Remember, it is completely normal to get stuck on a bug. It doesn't mean you're failing; it means you're programming. The key is not giving up.

By now, you've built a strong foundation in Python: enough to start building and breaking projects of your own or to keep learning in whatever way works best for you. In the next chapter, we'll look at where you can go from here.

11

Next Steps

You've made it!

You've worked your way through the fundamentals of Python. And that cannot have been easy! Now that you've come so far, you might wonder about what next steps you can take. Well, I've got you. There are so many fun next topics to explore, but let's discuss what makes the most sense for you to be your next topic.

We've split up this chapter into two parts. The first part relates to general topics that you should consider to learn if all this feels quite challenging still. The second part relates to the next big topics to explore, depending on what you aspire to do with Python.

General good advice

There are a few things that will help with whatever you plan to do with Python. The first is to build your own small projects and build a portfolio. Whether you are planning on using Python professionally or just for your own hobby, building more projects will be great for improving your Python skills. Coding is one of those things you can't learn by just reading a book.

Hands-on experience

I mean, don't get me wrong, books do help. But eventually, you need to put in the time behind the keyboard. Write a lot of Python, make (a lot of) mistakes, debug them, get a better understanding of what is going on, and repeat. That's how you learn!

If you don't know what to build next, the internet is full of great ideas to build your portfolio. You can build your own command-line tools, command-line games even, data analysis scripts, web apps, and so much more.

Another great way to get some hands-on experience, although this is a little more advanced, is to contribute to open source projects. You can import third-party modules into your Python programs. And these modules are built by other people. This is typically purely voluntary, and the creators most likely needed the code and functionality themselves at one time and then decided to share it for free and maintain it.

However, at some point, things can get out of hand, and continuing to maintain it can take a lot of time. That's why there might be open feature requests and more that you could work on. You can look for these projects (for example, on GitHub) and see whether you can implement features for the owners of the project. Experience like this looks great on your resume. The reason it looks great is that it's not easy. The code will have to be of high quality, and you will need to know how to work with Git and GitHub to manage it.

Topics everybody benefits from

If you want to do more with Python, whether it's for a career, research, or automating a light show in your Christmas tree, there are a few core concepts and tools that will level you up, no matter what your goal is. Here's a list of universal next steps for getting better at working with Python.

Git and GitHub

Git is a version control system. It helps you track changes in your code and (very importantly) roll back when you mess things up. GitHub is a platform that lets you share your code with others, collaborate, and even show off your work. There are alternatives to GitHub that you can opt for as well (they are all similar to work with to some extent), such as GitLab and Bitbucket.

Here are a few basic things you want to learn how to do:

- Mark a project as tracked by Git by initializing a Git repo (`git init`).
- Commit your changes (`git commit -m "added brilliance"`).
- Push to GitHub (`git push`).
- Handle branches and pull requests (especially when collaborating). This is a difficult one!

Writing tests

Coders typically code special methods in special files that are meant to test the functionality of the rest of their code. This way, they detect breaking changes to their code base automatically. Good tests test the requirements. And if some new change breaks an old requirement, your tests will tell you.

Writing tests might not sound very exciting, but it's like brushing your teeth. You have to do a little bit every day to avoid a problem. Future-you will thank you. Tests help you verify that your code still works after changes, and that definitely saves you time in the long run.

You'll want to explore the following:

- `unittest` or `pytest`
- Writing simple unit tests for your functions
- Testing edge cases and catching bugs before users do

Trust me, learning how to write tests will not be a waste of time.

Working with APIs

Every now and then, we want to get our data from an external source, send data to an external source, or use an external source to do some sort of calculation. For all this, it's great to be able to consume APIs. **API** stands for **application programming interface**. This is a way to connect your program with another program. It doesn't matter what language the other program is written in.

Very often, we work with REST APIs.

REST means that the API is sticking to certain conventions and that you can expect it to behave in a certain way. I won't dive into it here, but being able to consume APIs with Python is a great skill, and it opens up your application to communicating with other applications as well. It's a great way to connect your code to real-world data and make things feel more dynamic.

Using virtual environments and pip

When our projects start growing, we'll need to manage their dependencies (the external libraries/modules we use). Virtual environments allow us to isolate these dependencies so they don't mess with our other projects. It's like giving each project its own little environment instead of having one big environment for all the projects.

You'll want to learn what it means and how to do the following:

- Create virtual environments (`python -m venv env`)
- Activate them (`source env/bin/activate` or `env\\Scripts\\activate` on Windows)
- Install packages with `pip`
- Use a `requirements.txt` file

And that's it for the general topics that would be great to learn. Let's start talking about some adventure-specific topics to learn.

Path-specific advice

Let's move on to the second part of this chapter: which of the bigger topics should you explore based on what you want to do with Python? Well, there are actually a lot of things you can do with Python. So, there is quite a list of different paths you might take and what you should explore for each. Let's get started with my personal favorite: software developer.

Software developer

Software developers build all sorts of applications and programs. These range from small command-line utilities to elaborate web applications such as banking portals. They pretty much turn ideas into working products.

Python helps here by being the language that these software developers can write their apps in. Python offers frameworks, readability, and tons of third-party packages.

Is that what you want to be? Well, if you want to go into software development, you'll have to take your Python skills to the next level. Being able to do Python at an advanced level will be required to work with the tools you will need. After that, it depends a little on what you want to do.

If you want to make desktop tools or command-line apps, learn to work with libraries such as `tkinter` or `argparse`.

Being able to work with new libraries and understand what is going on is a skill in itself, and is something that I'd classify as "advanced Python." This is also important if you want to build websites and apps that live on the internet. If that's you, you are aspiring to be a web developer.

If you've ever used a blog, a store, or a dashboard in your browser, this is a web app, and someone built that! Is that what you'd love to do? Well, you're in luck! Python is actually used for many of the web's backends. The backend means that it's not what you see in your browser, but the logic beneath the surface that's built in Python, such as saving new comments to a post to a database.

Here are some next steps recommended for anyone who wants to get into web development:

- **Build a CRUD app**: **CRUD** stands for **Create, Read, Update, and Delete**. These are the basics of almost every web app.
- **Learn about Flask, FastAPI, or Django**: These web frameworks are the most common choice for building backends for web applications. You will need to write less code and get more done. Sounds too good to be true? There's a catch. Learning your first framework is not easy, but I promise you, it's worth it.
- **Learn about APIs, authentication, and deployment**: Learn how apps communicate, how to keep them secure, and how to publish your code to the end users.
- **Explore frontend basics**: The frontend is what you see in the browser. The basics of this consist of some HTML, CSS, and JavaScript. This will definitely be useful if you want to get into web development.

The fun part about being a software developer is that the learning never stops. There's always the next new thing or movement that you'll have to learn about. This keeps us sharp and ensures that our applications are meeting the modern standards.

Data analyst or data scientist

These roles are all about extracting insights from data. Analysts help businesses and researchers make decisions based on patterns they manage to find in the data.

And that's where Python comes in. Python is perfect for finding these patterns because of its rich data libraries.

Your next steps are as follows:

- Make sure that you can work with venv and `pip`, so that you can set up separate environments for each project.
- Get comfy with pandas, NumPy, and Matplotlib. These are your best friends for data wrangling and visualization.
- Learn how to clean, filter, and visualize real data. Practice by using public datasets or real business data to tell stories with charts.
- Explore Jupyter Notebook. This is a little bit like an IDE, but more. These interactive notebooks are perfect for presenting your analysis step by step while also writing your analysis.

Machine learning/AI engineer

Currently, a very popular role is a machine learning engineer. They are also called AI engineers. These engineers build models that can recognize faces, detect forbidden actions of pets (such as jumping on the kitchen counter when the human is away from home), suggest songs, or drive cars. The job is part math, part engineering, and a lot of experimentation.

Python is the main language for machine learning. This is partly because people love Python, but definitely because of its ecosystem.

So, let's say this is your dream profession. These would be your logical next steps:

- Understand data preprocessing. Learn how to prepare datasets for training machine learning models.
- Explore scikit-learn, then TensorFlow or PyTorch. These libraries help you build everything from simple models to deep neural networks.
- Also, try basic machine learning models. Start with classification, regression, and clustering.

Once you have the basics, you can specialize! For example, in **natural language processing (NLP)**, computer vision, or recommendation systems.

DevOps or automation engineer

DevOps and automation engineers are secret heroes, really. You might not notice their work, but they keep systems running and automate a lot of important work, such as making applications available to end users. Python is excellent for writing scripts that automate tasks, including DevOps tasks. And you chose well if this is what you want to do.

So, what are your next steps?

- Learn scripting for system tasks. This includes how to rename files, schedule backups, or generate and monitor logs.
- Explore setting `cron` jobs and working with networking tools. This is important for automating tasks that run on a schedule and working with logs or services.
- Learn how to use Python with Bash and Docker. This combination gives you pretty much superpowers for managing servers and deployments.

This path can lead to expertise in, for example, deployment pipelines, cloud infrastructure, and system monitoring.

Cybersecurity specialist or ethical hacker

If you're into security, this might be for you. These roles are all about protecting systems, responding to breaches, finding vulnerabilities first, and testing digital defenses. Ethical hackers are experts in breaking into systems, but they use their skills for good.

Python is a great language to help here. It gives you low-level access and fast prototyping power. There are also a bunch of ready-to-use tools in Python that you can work with for testing the security of systems.

These could be your next steps:

- Learn how to parse and inspect logs. That way, you can spot anomalies and patterns.
- Learn how to use libraries such as `socket`, `os`, and `scapy`. These libraries let you interact with networks and filesystems.
- Experiment with building simple pentesting tools. You can think of port scanners or brute-force testers (ethically, of course).

From here, you can explore digital forensics, malware analysis, or security automation.

QA engineer/tester

Testers make sure that the software works and keeps working after updates. Testers build systems that catch bugs before real users ever see them. In order to do this, they typically need to write code as well. And one of the languages that you can use for that is... You've guessed it: Python.

There are different ways you can use Python for testing. Exploring the next topics will definitely set you up for success:

- Learn `unittest` and `pytest`. These testing libraries help you write and organize automated tests. It's a good first step to take, and it will make you understand how to actually write code for testing.
- Explore Playwright or Selenium. Where you typically only test small chunks with `unittest` and `pytest`, you can automate browser tests to simulate user clicks and inputs with Playwright or Selenium. It's not that `unittest` and `pytest` are better than Playwright or Selenium; typically, an application is tested with both.

Another important skill for a tester is to have a good understanding from a product point of view. This will make you extra valuable for a company, as you have domain and product knowledge that is hard to find elsewhere.

Researcher/academic

Python is very popular in the academic world and among researchers of all kinds. Researchers use Python to analyze data, run simulations, and share their findings. If that's what you want to use Python for, no problem. Here are some next steps you could take:

- Start working with Jupyter Notebook. This is great for experiments and step-by-step documentation.
- Learn how to use the SciPy, SymPy, and `statsmodels` libraries. These are great for scientific computation, symbolic math, and statistical analysis.
- And lastly, if you need to use Excel, you can use Python to automate Excel work. With Python, you can convert spreadsheet chaos into elegant Python-powered reports that are managed in terms of version by Git. Of course, you'll have to dive into figuring out how to do this.

This paves the way for publishing results, collaborating on research, or creating educational tools.

Python as a gateway language

And lastly, maybe the only reason you picked up this book is that you wanted to learn how to code. Well, great choice! Python makes a great gateway language. After learning the fundamentals of Python, every other language is now easier to learn.

It's hard to give you the exact next steps here since there are so many opportunities, but here are some things you can do:

- Try building the same project in another language (such as Java, C#, JavaScript, Go, or whatever you want, really!)
- Explore algorithms and data structures using Python to understand computer science fundamentals
- Start learning about completely new ecosystems, such as web, AI, scripting, gaming, and more
- Explore advanced Python features such as decorators, generators, and context managers

Final words

From `print("Hello, world!")` to classes that inherit from one another containing complex data structures... that's not something small. That's an achievement! And the fact that you can do this means that you can do so much more.

Are you paralyzed choosing the best next step? If you know something you actually want to build, let that guide your learning. And if you don't, go for advanced Python, followed by Flask. Why those? Well, if you don't know, it doesn't matter. These are great choices in general, doable for most people (though still challenging), and now you're no longer stuck.

Take a break, and then continue learning.

You’ve got this. Keep going. And whenever you’re stuck, reach out. I’m rooting for you.

Get this book's PDF version and more

Scan the QR code (or go to `packtpub.com/unlock`). Search for this book by name, confirm the edition, and then follow the steps on the page.

UNLOCK NOW

Note: *Keep your invoice handy. Purchases made directly from Packt don't require an invoice.*

Appendix A: Exercise Files

Exercise 7.1

letter.txt:

```
Dear Wiesje,

You can be stubborn, a little cynical, and sometimes you act like you run
the place. But honestly, I love you just the way you are. Your little
grumbles and loud barks are what make you so special.

You're also doing an amazing job learning how to code! I'm so proud of how
far you've come. You might not get it all yet, but you're getting better
every day, and that's all that matters.

Keep being you, Wiesje. Don't change a thing.

With love,

Zia
```

Exercise 7.4

wiener_dog_race_results.csv:

```
Name,Finish time (seconds)
Java,12.1
Frank,8.9
Herman,10.0
Pippa,9.1
Rowdy,8.7
Tony,10.6
Tim,9.6
```

Exercise 7.5

wood_types.json:


```
[{"name": "Oak", "hardness": 9, "color": "rich brown", "uses":
["furniture", "flooring", "barrels", "architectural joinery"]}, {"name":
"Maple", "hardness": 8, "color": "creamy white", "uses": ["kitchen
cabinets", "flooring", "cutting boards", "musical instruments"]}, {"name":
"Pine", "hardness": 4, "color": "yellowish white", "uses": ["construction
framing", "interior paneling", "furniture", "millwork"]}, {"name":
"Birch", "hardness": 6, "color": "pale yellow", "uses": ["plywood",
"veneers", "furniture", "doors"]}, {"name": "Walnut", "hardness": 7,
"color": "dark chocolate brown", "uses": ["fine furniture", "gunstocks",
"cabinetry", "veneer"]}, {"name": "Cherry", "hardness": 6, "color":
"reddish brown", "uses": ["furniture", "cabinetry", "paneling",
"flooring"]}, {"name": "Cedar", "hardness": 5, "color": "reddish pink",
"uses": ["outdoor furniture", "decking", "closets", "shingles"]}, {"name":
"Bamboo", "hardness": 7, "color": "light tan", "uses": ["flooring",
"cutting boards", "furniture", "paneling"]}, {"name": "Ebony", "hardness":
10, "color": "deep black", "uses": ["musical instruments", "cabinetry",
"tool handles", "decorative inlays"]}, {"name": "Teak", "hardness": 9,
"color": "golden brown", "uses": ["boat building", "outdoor furniture",
"flooring", "laboratory benches"]}]
```

Appendix B: Quiz Answers

Chapter 1

1. b
2. a
3. d
4. c
5. False
6. An Integrated Development Environment, a special application meant for coding that offers features such as syntax highlighting, code completion, and debugging tools.

Chapter 2

1. b
2. False
3. `# like this, using the # symbol`
4. `snake_case`, with words in lowercase, separated by underscores
5. a
6. d
7. Age is stored as a string, and not as an integer. That's why Python can't multiply correctly and just repeats the string 7 times: `"28282828282828"`.
8. A hard-coded value is a value that is directly written in the code and can't be changed unless the code itself is updated.

Chapter 3

1. d
2. False
3. a
4. c
5. d

6. a
7. True
8. It inverts boolean values.
9. b
10. Yes

Chapter 4

1. d
2. b
3. d
4. c
5. a
6. a
7. False, the `get()` method returns `None` if the specified key is not found and no other default value has been provided.
8. b
9. a
10. c

Chapter 5

1. b
2. A `for` loop
3. d
4. b
5. c
6. True
7. a
8. c
9. False

Chapter 6

1. b
2. c
3. d
4. c
5. c
6. True
7. c
8. a
9. b
10. d

Chapter 7

1. c
2. d
3. a
4. a
5. d
6. c
7. b
8. b
9. d
10. b
11. b

Chapter 8

1. a
2. True
3. b
4. d
5. a

6. b
7. c
8. c
9. a
10. d
11. c
12. b
13. c
14. a

Chapter 9

1. d
2. c
3. b
4. b
5. d
6. b
7. b
8. b
9. d
10. a
11. b
12. a

Chapter 10

1. c
2. b
3. b
4. a
5. c
6. d
7. c
8. b

Appendix C: Exercise Solutions

Chapter 1

1.1 Getting familiar with VS Code

Creating the main folder

- Open VS Code.
- From the menu, choose **File** > **Open Folder**
- Select the location on your computer where you want to keep the exercises, and create a new folder named "python-illustrated".
- Open this newly created folder in VS Code.

Creating the first subfolder

- In the **Explorer** (the left sidebar), right-click the empty space below your project name.
- Select **New Folder** and type `chatper-1`.
- Hit *Enter*.

Alternatively, click the folder-plus icon (at the top, right next to the main folder name), with the desired location selected.

Renaming the folder

Right-click the folder chapter-1 and choose **Rename**. Then type the correct name: `chapter-1`, and press *Enter*.

Creating another subfolder

You don't want to accidentally create this folder inside chapter-1. To avoid that, first make sure the python-illustrated folder is selected. You can tell it's selected when the entire Explorer panel on the left has a blue border. Then again, right-click, select **New Folder** (or click the folder-plus icon at the top), name it `chapter-2` and hit *Enter*.

Creating a Python file

- Right-click the chapter-1 folder, select **New File.** Or, with the chapter-1 folder selected, press the file-plus icon at the top right of the Explorer panel.

- Type `exercise1.py` and press *Enter*.

Writing some code

- Click on **exercise1.py** to open it.
- Paste or type the line: `print("Hey, I can create folders and files in VS Code!")`

Saving the file

Save the file by hitting *Ctrl* + *S* (Windows/Linux) or *Cmd* + *S* (Mac). Or through the menu: **File** > **Save**, but the shortcut is much quicker.

Running the code

There are several ways to run your program:

1. Through the terminal:
   Open your terminal. Navigate to the location of your file using `cd` (change directory). For example, I personally stored my python-illustrated on my Desktop, which means I first use `cd Desktop` to step into my desktop. Then, I check what's inside with `ls` (macOS and linux) or dir (Windows). I saw my python-illustrated folder listed here. To step directly into the chapter-1 folder, I use the path: `cd python-illustrated/chapter-1`. Finally: `python3 exercise1.py` (macOS and Linux) or `python exercise1.py` (Windows) to run the program.

The quicker options are:

2. With the VS Code Runner Extension (if installed):
   If you have the VS Code Runner extension installed, the process is much quicker: you can simply click the **play** button at the top right of your editor, and a terminal window will open in VS code.
3. With VS Code's built-in option:
   Right-click anywhere inside your Python file in your code editor, and choose **Run Python file in terminal**

Closing your file and tidying up

Close the file tab for exercise1.py. You can also use the shortcut: *Ctrl* + *W* (Windows and Linux), or *Cmd* + *W* (Mac).

In the explorer, click the small arrow next to the chapter-1 folder to collapse it.

1.2 A chat with the terminal

Opening the terminal

- On Windows, you can open the command prompt with the shortcut *Windows button* + *R*. Or you type "cmd" in the search box in the start bar. If you prefer PowerShell, search for "PowerShell" instead.
- On Linux, you can use the shortcut *Ctrl* + *Alt* + *T*. If that doesn't work, you can open the application menu (sometimes called Activities) and look for the applications.
- On Mac, it's easy to hit *Cmd* + *Space*, and type "Terminal" to look for it.

Check your current location

To see which folder ("working directory") you are in, use the command `pwd`. On Windows, you can see the directory by looking at the terminal window. It tells you where you are.

Hopping into python-illustrated

Use commands to move into it. If you know where it is, you can use the full path to get there directly. If you're not sure, you explore it step by step using `ls` (macOS and Linux) or `dir` (Windows) to see which files can be found at your current location. Use cd <path> to change directory. For example, `cd Desktop/python-illustrated`. Or first `cd Desktop`, `ls` or `dir` to check if you can find your folder here, and then `cd python-illustrated`.

Navigate to the chapter-1 folder

Now that you're already in python-illustrated. Getting into chapter-1 is easy. Just use the command: `cd chapter-1`

Listing all files

Use `ls` on Linux/macOS or `dir` for Windows.

Running the code in exercise1.py

While located in the chapter-1 folder, run `python3 exercise1.py` or `python exercise1.py` (depending on your system).

Moving up in the folder hierarchy to go into chapter-2

If you want to go "up" to the parent folder of the folder you are currently in, you can use the `..` path. You can do it in two steps: first `cd ..`, then `cd chapter-2`, or at once: `cd ../chapter-2`. To check if there are any files in this directory, you can use `ls` or `dir`.

Bonus challenge

The command to create a new file on Mac and Linux is `touch`. So to create a file using the terminal, you would first navigate to the place where you want to create the file and then type a command like `touch bonus-challenge.py`.

The commands for Windows are a bit different.

- In Command Prompt: type `nul > bonus-challenge.py`
- In PowerShell: `New-Item bonus-challenge.py -ItemType File`

Chapter 2

2.1 Creating variables

```
name = "Imke"
cat_person = False
cookies_eaten_today = 3

print(name)
print(cat_person)
print(cookies_eaten_today)
```

2.2 Escape characters in action

```
joke = "Why did Wiesje sit in the shade?\nBecause she didn't want to be a
\"hot dog\"!"
print(joke)
```

2.3 How long will Wiesje's food supply last?

```
# Food in Wiesje's cupboards (in grams)
food_in_cupboards = 1500

# Wiesje's food intake per day (in grams)
food_per_day = 65  # But we all know it's more...

# Calculate how many full days the food will last using integer division
days_left = food_in_cupboards // food_per_day

# Print the result
print("Wiesje's food will last for", days_left, "full days.")
```

2.4 Adventure time for Wiesje

```
# Create a variable for the current day of the month
current_day = 12  # You can change this number to test different days

# Use modulo to check if it's an adventure day (divisible by 5)
adventure_day = current_day % 5 == 0

# Print whether it's an adventure day or not
print("Adventure day?", adventure_day)
```

2.5 Manipulating strings

```
fun_fact = "I love cat milk"

# Use Python to find out how many characters are in your fun fact. Print
the result.
length = len(fun_fact)
print(length)

# Create another variable that holds your fun fact in all lower case.
fun_fact_lower_case = fun_fact.lower()

# Alter the original variable and convert it to all uppercase letters.
fun_fact = fun_fact.upper()
```

Chapter 3

3.1 Even or odd?

```
# Step 1: Store a number in a variable
number = 7

# Step 2: Check if the number is even or odd using if/else
if number % 2 == 0:
    print(number, "is even.")
else:
    print(number, "is odd.")

# Bonus Challenge: Use ternary operator
result = "even" if number % 2 == 0 else "odd"
print(number, "is", result + ".")
```

3.2 Dachshund weight classification

```
# Step 1: Store the dachshund's name
name = "Wiesje"

# Step 2: Store the weight in kilograms
weight_kg = 2.5

# Step 3: Convert weight to pounds
weight_lbs = weight_kg * 2.2

# Step 4: Classify the dachshund's size
if weight_lbs < 12:
    classification = "Kaninchen"
elif 12 <= weight_lbs <= 16:
    classification = "Miniature"
else:
    classification = "Standard"

# Step 5: Print the result
print("With a weight of", weight_kg, "kgs,", weight_lbs, "lbs, dachshund",
name, "is classified as:", classification + ".")
```

3.3 Password checker

```
stored_password = "whiskers123"
input_password = "whiskers123"  # Pretend this is user input

if input_password == stored_password:
    print("Access granted.")
else:
    print("Access denied.")


# Bonus challenge
input_password = "whiskers123"
stored_password = "whiskers123"

input_username = "Zia the Cat"
stored_username = "Zia the Cat"

if input_password == stored_password and input_username == stored_
username:
    print("Access granted.")
else:
    print("Access denied.")
```

3.4 Grading system

```
score = 85

if score >= 90:
    grade = 'A'
elif score >= 80:
    grade = 'B'
elif score >= 70:
    grade = 'C'
elif score >= 60:
    grade = 'D'
else:
    grade = 'F'

print("Your grade is:", grade)
```

3.5 Fun activities for humans per weekday

```
weekday = "Wednesday"
match weekday:
    case "Monday":
        activity = "Go hiking"
    case "Tuesday":
        activity = "Take your dog to the park"
    case "Wednesday":
        activity = "Learn Python"
    case "Thursday":
        activity = "Knit a sweater"
    case "Friday":
        activity = "Go to the beach"
    case "Saturday":
        activity = "Go skate"
    case "Sunday":
        activity = "Watch a movie"
    case _:
        activity = "Go on an unknown adventure"

print("On " +  weekday + ", you should: " + activity)
```

Chapter 4

4.1 Favorite animals

```
# Create list of favorite animals and print it
favorite_animals = ["dachshund", "toy poodle", "cat", "turtle", "axolotl"]
print(favorite_animals)

# Print how many favorite animals you have
print("I have", len(favorite_animals), "favorite animals.")

# Use the first favorite animal in a sentence
print("The", favorite_animals[0], "is my first favorite animal.")

# Use the last favorite animal in a sentence
print("The", favorite_animals[-1], "is the last favorite animal on my
list.")
```

4.2 Favorite nap spots

```
fav_nap_spots = ["window", "cardboard box", "human's lap", "luxurious cat
bed"]

# Remove the luxurious cat bed from the list (last item)
fav_nap_spots.pop()

# Add "keyboard" as first item on the list
fav_nap_spots.insert(0, "keyboard")

# Insert "sunbeam on the floor" as third item on the list
fav_nap_spots.insert(2, "sunbeam on the floor")

# Add "Wiesje's bed" to the end of the list
fav_nap_spots.append("Wiesje's bed")

# Check if "Check for "human bed" and add if needed"
if "human bed" not in fav_nap_spots:
    fav_nap_spots.append("human bed")

# Slice the top three nap spots
top_three_nap_spots = fav_nap_spots[0:3]
print(top_three_nap_spots)

# Bonus challenge: Swap elements on a list
fav_nap_spots[1], fav_nap_spots[3] = fav_nap_spots[3], fav_nap_spots[1]

# Update top three after swapping items
top_three_nap_spots = fav_nap_spots[0:3]

print(fav_nap_spots)
print(top_three_nap_spots)
```

4.3 Phone book

```
# Create the dictionary with names as keys and phone numbers as values
contacts = {
    "John": "123-456-7890",
```

```
    "Jane": "987-654-3210",
    "Mike": "555-123-4567"
}

# Add a new contact
contacts["Imke"] = "123-978-6543"

# Check if "Maaike" exists in the dictionary, and if not, add her
if "Maaike" not in contacts:
    contacts["Maaike"] = "444-555-6666"

# Delete one of the contacts
contacts.pop("Imke", None)

# Print all the names in the dictionary
print("Names in contacts:", list(contacts.keys()))
```

4.4 Combining data types for a library database

```
library = {
    "Jane Eyre": {
        "author(s)": [{"name": "Charlotte Brontë", "birth_year": 1816,
"nationality": "British"}],
        "page_count": 659,
        "publication_year": 1847,
        "genres": ["Victorian fiction", "Bildungsroman", "Historical"],
        "rating": 4.6,
        "available": True,
        "borrowed_by": None
    },
    "Python Illustrated": {
        "author(s)": [{"name": "Zia van Putten", "birth_year": 2024,
"nationality": "Dutch"}, {"name": "Maaike van Putten", "birth_year": 1991,
"nationality": "Dutch"}, {"name": "Imke van Putten", "birth_year": 1997,
"nationality": "Dutch"}],
        "page_count": 432,
        "publication_year": 2026,
        "genres": ["Informative", "Education"],
        "rating": 5,
        "available": False,
```

```
        "borrowed_by": "Jacob",
    },
    "If Cats Disappeared From The World": {
        "author(s)": [{"name": "Genki Kawamura", "birth_year": 1979,
"nationality": "Japanese"}],
        "page_count": 144,
        "publication_year": 2012,
        "genres": ["Literary Fiction", "Magical Realism", "Philosophical
Fiction"],
        "rating": 4.2,
        "available": False,
        "borrowed_by": "Wiesje",
    }
}

# Print all book titles (The keys of the library dictionary)
print(list(library.keys()))

# Check and see if Python illustrated is a romance
if "Romance" in library["Python Illustrated"]["genres"]:
    print("Romance is a genre of Python Illustrated")
else:
    print("Romance is not a genre of Python Illustrated")

# Print the nationality of the author of Jane Eyre
print(library["Jane Eyre"]["author(s)"][0]["nationality"])

# Update values when Wiesje returned a book
library["If Cats Disappeared From The World"]["available"] = True
library["If Cats Disappeared From The World"]["borrowed_by"] = None

# Check whether Python Illustrated is available and print who borrowed it
if it isn't
if library["Python Illustrated"]["available"]:
    print("Python Illustrated is available!")
elif library["Python Illustrated"]["borrowed_by"]: # checks if borrowed_by
is not None before using its value
    print("Python Illustrated is not available and currently borrowed
by:", library["Python Illustrated"]["borrowed_by"])
```

Chapter 5

5.1 Summing numbers

```
total = 0

for number in range(1, 11):
    total += number

print("The sum is:", total)
```

5.2 Greeting a list of friends

```
names = ["Zia", "Wiesje", "Muchu"]

for name in names:
    print("Hello,", name + "!")
```

5.3 Infinite squirrel chasing?

```
# Infinite squirrel chasing
while True:
    print("Wiesje chases the squirrel!")
# Control + C in terminal to stop infinite loop
# Remove or comment out this infinite loop before continuing

# Squirrel chasing while wiesje has energy
wiesje_energy = 10

while wiesje_energy > 0:
    print("Wiesje chases the squirrel!")
    wiesje_energy -= 1

print("Wiesje is too tired and gives up.")

# Bonus challenge
wiesje_energy = 5
squirrel_energy = 100

while wiesje_energy > 0 and squirrel_energy > 0:
```

```
    print("Wiesje chases the squirrel...")
    wiesje_energy -= 1
    squirrel_energy -= 1

if squirrel_energy == 0 and wiesje_energy == 0:
    print("Wiesje catches the squirrel just before collapsing!")
elif squirrel_energy == 0:
    print("Wiesje caught the squirrel!")
else:
    print("Wiesje is too tired and gives up.")
```

5.4 Team up for game night

```
friends = ["Max", "Louise", "Jacob", "Sam", "Farah", "Selim"]
team_a = []
team_b = []

for index in range(len(friends)):
```

```
    if index % 2 == 0: # Using modulo to select even indices
        team_a.append(friends[index])
    else:
        team_b.append(friends[index])

print("Team A:")
for friend in team_a:
    print(friend)

print("\nTeam B:") # \n to create a line of whitespace between the two
teams
for friend in team_b:
    print(friend)
```

5.5 Factorial calculation

```
number = 5
factorial = 1

if number < 0:
    print("Factorials are only defined for non-negative integers.")
else:
    for i in range(number, 0, -1): # there are more ways to do this
        factorial *= i
    print(f"{number}! = {factorial}")
```

5.6 Secret pet gym

```
workouts = {
    "Zia": {
        "bench_press": {"weight": 5, "sets": 3, "reps": 10},
        "bicep_curls": {"weight": 2, "sets": 3, "reps": 10},
        "box_jumps": {"weight": 0, "sets": 2, "reps": 10},
        "deadlifts": {"weight": 10, "sets": 2, "reps": 1},
        "kettle_bell_swings": {"weight": 2, "sets": 3, "reps": 10},
        "lateral_raises": {"weight": 1, "sets": 3, "reps": 10},
        "stair_climber": {"minutes": 10}
    },
    "Wiesje": {
        "bench_press": {"weight": 5, "sets": 1, "reps": 1},
        "leg_extension": {"weight": 1, "sets": 2, "reps": 5},
        "planking": {"minutes": 5},
        "zoomies": {"minutes": 2}
    }
}

# Loop through the workouts dictionary for each gym member
for member, exercises in workouts.items():
    print(f"{member}'s workout:")
    # Loop through each exercise of the current member
    for exercise, details in exercises.items():
        if "minutes" in details:
```

```
            print(f"- {exercise}: {details['minutes']} minutes")
        else:
            print(f"- {exercise}: weight {details['weight']}kg,
{details['sets']} sets of {details['reps']} reps")
    print()

# Loop through the workouts dictionary for each gym member
for member, exercises in workouts.items():
    total_weight = 0  # Initialize the total weight to 0 for each member

    # Loop through each exercise of the current member
    for exercise, details in exercises.items():
        if "weight" in details: # Only add up the weight if the exercise
involves lifting weight (if it has a "weight" key)
            total_weight += details["weight"] * details["sets"] *
details["reps"]

    print(f"Total weight lifted by {member}: {total_weight}kg")
```

Chapter 6

6.1 Temperature conversion

```
def convert_temperature(temp_value, mode="CtoF"):
    """
    Convert temperatures between Celsius and Fahrenheit.

    Parameters:
    temp_value: The temperature to be converted.
    mode: The conversion mode, either "CtoF" for Celsius to Fahrenheit or
"FtoC" for Fahrenheit to Celsius. Defaults to "CtoF".

    Returns the converted temperature.
    """
    if mode == "CtoF":  # Celsius to Fahrenheit
        return (temp_value * 9/5) + 32
    elif mode == "FtoC":  # Fahrenheit to Celsius
        return (temp_value - 32) * 5/9
```

```
# Test cases
print(convert_temperature(99))  # Default: 99°C → Fahrenheit
print(convert_temperature(77, "FtoC"))  # 77°F → Celsius
print(convert_temperature(0))  # 0°C → Fahrenheit
print(convert_temperature(100, "CtoF"))  # 100°C → Fahrenheit
```

6.2 Tricky treat tracker

```
remaining_treats = 200

def print_treats_left():
    print(f"You have {remaining_treats} treats left.")

def eat_treats(remaining, eaten_treats):
    print(f"Ate {eaten_treats} treats.")
    return remaining - eaten_treats  # Return the updated value

print_treats_left()
remaining_treats = eat_treats(remaining_treats, 50)  # Update the global 
variable
print_treats_left()

# Using the global keyword would work too:
remaining_treats = 200

def print_treats_left():
    print(f"You have {remaining_treats} treats left.")

def eat_treats(eaten_treats):
    print(f"Ate {eaten_treats} treats.")
    global remaining_treats
    remaining_treats -= eaten_treats  # Directly modify global variable

print_treats_left()
eat_treats(50)
print_treats_left()
```

6.3 Packing lunch boxes

```
def pack_lunchbox(**items):
    print("You packed your lunchbox:")

    # Print packed items
    for category, item in items.items():
        print(f"{category}: {item}")

    # Print reminder for snack if necessary
    if not "snack" in items:
        print("Better pack a snack!")

# Example usage:
pack_lunchbox(main="sandwich", snack="cookie", drink="juice")
print("")
pack_lunchbox(main="salad")
print("")
pack_lunchbox(main="pasta", snack="chips", fruit="apple", drink="water")
```

6.4 Sorting hat

```
import random

def sorting_hat():
    houses = ("Slytherin", "Gryffindor", "Ravenclaw", "Hufflepuff")
    house = random.choice(houses)
    print(f"You belong in... {house}")

sorting_hat()

# bonus challenge
import random
import time

def sorting_hat():
    houses = ("Slytherin", "Gryffindor", "Ravenclaw", "Hufflepuff")
    print("The sorting hat is thinking...")
```

```
    time.sleep(2)
    house = random.choice(houses)
    print(f"You belong in {house}!")

sorting_hat()
```

6.5 Dachshund fetch simulator

```
import random

def fetch(name, item):
    responses = [
        f"{name} fetched the {item}!",
        f"{name} ignored you.",
        f"{name} went after the {item}, but never brought it to you.",
        f"{name} got distracted!",
        f"{name} goes after the {item}, but halfway there, decides to take
a nap."
    ]
    result = random.choice(responses)
    print(result)

fetch("Wiesje", "ball")
```

6.6 Shopping cart checkout tool

```
def checkout():
    """Asks the user for the number of items and their prices, then prints
the total cost."""
    num_items = int(input("How many items are you buying? "))
    total = 0

    for i in range(1, num_items + 1):
        price = float(input(f"Enter price of item {i}: "))
        total += price

    print(f"Total: ${total}")

checkout()
```

6.7 Rock-paper-scissors against the computer

```
import random

# Function to get the winner of the round
def determine_winner(player_choice, computer_choice):
    if player_choice == computer_choice:
        return "It's a tie!"
    elif (player_choice == 'rock' and computer_choice == 'scissors') or \
        (player_choice == 'scissors' and computer_choice == 'paper') or \
        (player_choice == 'paper' and computer_choice == 'rock'):
        return "Player wins!"
    else:
        return "Computer wins!"

# Function to play the game
def play_game():
    choices = ('rock', 'paper', 'scissors')
    player_score = 0
    computer_score = 0

    while player_score < 5 and computer_score < 5:
        # Get player's input and validate it
        while True:
            player_choice = input("Enter rock, paper, or scissors:
").lower()
            if player_choice in choices:
                break
            else:
                print("Invalid choice, please enter rock, paper, or
scissors.")

        # Random computer choice
        computer_choice = random.choice(choices)

        # Display choices
        print(f"\nYou chose: {player_choice}")
        print(f"The computer chose: {computer_choice}")
```

```
        # Determine the winner of this round
        result = determine_winner(player_choice, computer_choice)
        print(result)

        # Update the score based on the result
        if result == "Player wins!":
            player_score += 1
        elif result == "Computer wins!":
            computer_score += 1

        # Display current score
        print(f"Score - Player: {player_score} | Computer: {computer_
score}\n")

    # Announce the overall winner
    if player_score == 5:
        print("Congratulations! You win the game!")
    else:
        print("Sorry, the computer wins the game!")

    # Ask if the player wants to play again
    play_again = input("\nDo you want to play again? (yes/no): ").lower()
    if play_again == "yes":
        play_game()
    else:
        print("Thanks for playing!")

# Start the game
play_game()
```

Chapter 7

7.1 Reading a personal letter

```
try:
    with open("letter.txt", "r") as file:
        content = file.read()
        print(content)
except FileNotFoundError:
    print("Oops, the letter can't be found.")
```

7.2 Adding your name to the list

```
# Ask the user to enter their name
name = input("What's your name? ").strip()

# Open attendance file
with open("attendance.txt", "a") as file:
    # Add name to the list
    file.write(f"{name}\n")

# print a success message
print(f"Welcome, {name}! You've been added to the list.")
```

7.3 Note to self

```
# For bonus challenge
import random
import time

# Open and create a file named note_to_self.txt
with open("note_to_self.txt", "w") as file:
    # Write a few lines of empowering words
    file.write("Curiosity rarely kills a cat.\n")
    file.write("Just keep purring.\n")
    file.write("Be patient with yourself.\n")
    file.write("Take a break, but don't quit.\n")
    file.write("If all fails, blame Wiesje.\n")

# Read the file and print each line numbered individually
```

```
try:
    with open("note_to_self.txt", "r") as file:
        lines = file.readlines()
        for index, line in enumerate(lines):
            print(f"{index + 1}. {line.strip()}")
except:
    print("Something went wrong trying to read the file.")

# Bonus challenge: A function for a random piece of advice
def ask_oracle():
    intros = [
    "Nine lives taught me this:",
    "I gazed into the void between naps and found this:",
    "With a flick of my tail, I reveal:",
    "I have knocked over the mug of fate. Here's what spilled out:"
]
    in_need_of_advice = input("Do you need advice? ")
    if in_need_of_advice.lower() == "yes":
        try:
            with open("note_to_self.txt", "r") as file:
                lines = file.readlines()
                advice = random.choice(lines)
                time.sleep(1)
                print("Hmm...")
                time.sleep(2)
                print(random.choice(intros), advice.strip())
        except:
            print("Something went wrong trying to find my wisdom")
    elif in_need_of_advice.lower() == "no":
        print("Are you sure?")
        ask_oracle()
    else:
        print("I'm sorry, I only understand \"yes\" and \"no\"")
        ask_oracle()

# Calling the function
ask_oracle()
```

7.4 Wiener dog races

```
import csv

# Count the participants
def count_participants():
    try:
        with open("wiener_dog_race_results.csv", "r") as file:
            content = csv.reader(file)
            data = list(content)[1:] # Takes the rows of content as a list
but skips the header by starting at index 1

            # Determine the amount of participants using the len()
function
            print(f"{len(data)} dachshunds participated in this race.")

            # Dealing with empty rows in the list
            counter = 0
            for row in data:
                if len(row) >= 2 and row[0].strip() and row[1].strip():
                    counter += 1
            print(f"{counter} dachshunds participated in this race.")
    except FileNotFoundError:
        print("Could not find file with race data")

# Calling the function
count_participants()

# Function to add new results
def add_results(name, time):
    name_exists = False
    results = [name, time]

    # Check if name is already in results
    try:
        with open("wiener_dog_race_results.csv", "r") as file:
            content = csv.reader(file)
            for row in content:
```

```
                if len(row) and row[0] == name:
                    name_exists = True
                    break

        # if name does not exist in file, add results
        if not name_exists:
            with open("wiener_dog_race_results.csv", "a", newline="") as
file:
                content = csv.writer(file)
                content.writerow(results)
        else:
            print(f"{name} is already in the file")
    except FileNotFoundError:
        print("Could not find file with race data")

add_results("Wiesje", 42.0)

# Rank the wieners
def rank_the_wieners():
    try:
        with open("wiener_dog_race_results.csv", "r") as file:
            content = csv.reader(file)
            data = list(content)[1:] # Skip the header
            data = [row for row in data if len(row) >= 2 and row[0].
strip() and row[1].strip()] # This makes sure you only sort valid entries

            for i in range(len(data)): # For each item in the data list...
                data[i][1] = float(data[i][1]) # convert the time to float
(to enable comparison)

            for i in range(len(data)):
                for j in range(i + 1, len(data)):
                    # compare finish times and swap rows if they are in
the wrong order
                    if data[i][1] > data[j][1]:
                        data[i], data[j] = data[j], data[i]

        # save the sorted race results to a new file
```

```
        with open("wiener_dog_race_results_sorted.csv", "w", newline="")
as file:
                writer = csv.writer(file)
                writer.writerow(['Name', 'Finish Time (seconds)'])  #
Write the header
                writer.writerows(data)  # Write the sorted data rows

    except FileNotFoundError:
        print("Could not find file with race data.")

rank_the_wieners()

# Determine the winner
def determine_winner():
    try:
        # open the file with sorted results
        with open("wiener_dog_race_results_sorted.csv", "r") as file:
            content = csv.reader(file)
            data = list(content)
            winner = data[1] # take the second row of the file, just below
the header, which contains the dachshund with the fastest time.
            print(f"Dachshund {winner[0]} wins the race with an
astonishing time of {winner[1]} seconds!")
    except FileNotFoundError:
        print("There is no file with sorted race results found.")

# Call the function
determine_winner()
```

7.5 Wood type catalog

```
import json

# Define a function that displays each wood type
def load_woods():
    try:
        with open("wood_types.json", "r") as file:
            woods = json.load(file)
            return woods
```

```
    except FileNotFoundError:
        print("Hmm... Couldn't find the wood encyclopedia.")

def display_woods():
    woods = load_woods()
    for wood in woods:
        # create a string with use cases
        uses = ""
        for i in range(len(wood["uses"])):
            uses += wood["uses"][i]
            if i < len(wood["uses"]) - 1:
                uses += ", "

        print(f"Name: {wood["name"]}")
        print(f"Hardness: {wood["hardness"]}")
        print(f"Color: {wood["color"]}")
        print(f"Uses: {uses}")
        print("\n")

display_woods()

def add_wood(name, hardness, color, uses):
    new_wood = {
        "name": name,
        "hardness": hardness,
        "color": color,
        "uses": uses
    }

    woods = load_woods()
    woods.append(new_wood)

    with open("wood_types.json", "w") as file:
        json.dump(woods, file)

# add_wood("Dark Oak", 8, "dark brown", ["flooring", "furniture",
"cabinets", "architectural trim"])
```

```
def filter_wood(use):
    woods = load_woods()
    print(f"Woods commonly used for {use}:")
    for wood in woods:
        if use in wood["uses"]:
            print(wood["name"])

filter_wood("furniture")
```

Chapter 8

8.1 Smoothie blender

```
# Define a class Smoothie
class Smoothie:
    # constructor
    def __init__(self, ingredients):
        self._ingredients = [ingredient.lower() for ingredient in
ingredients] # Puts all ingredients in lower case for consistency

    # @property decorator to deal with private attribute
    @property
    def ingredients(self):
        return self._ingredients

    # and a setter decorator
    @ingredients.setter
    def ingredients(self, new_ingredients):
        self._ingredients = new_ingredients

    # a method to add an ingredient
    def add_ingredient(self, ingredient):
        ingredient = ingredient.lower()
        self.ingredients.append(ingredient) # using append because
ingredients is a list

    def describe(self): # If you used __str__, good job!
        print(f"A delicious smoothie with: {', '.join(self.ingredients)}")
# a fancy way to create a beautiful stringified display of a list
```

```
    def __add__(self, other):
        # temporary empty list
        combined = []
        # Looping over all ingredients
        for ingredient in self.ingredients + other.ingredients:
            # only adding each ingredient once to the ingredients list
            if ingredient.lower() not in combined:
                combined.append(ingredient)
        return Smoothie(combined) # a new smoothie with combined
ingredients

# Test it
drink1 = Smoothie(["strawberry"])
drink2 = Smoothie(["banana", "kale", "apple"])

drink1.add_ingredient("apple")

drink1.add_ingredient("apple")

drink3 = drink1 + drink2

drink3.describe()
```

8.2 Dress code: classy

```
class ClothingItem():
    def __init__(self, garment_type, size, color, fabric):
        self.garment_type = garment_type.lower() # all values set to lower
case for consistency
        self.size = size.lower()
        self.color = color.lower()
        self.fabric = fabric.lower()
        # Setting initial attributes that are the same for all instances
at first
        self.dirty = False
        self.times_worn = 0
```

```
    # A method to wear the item and set it to dirty after it has been
worn.
    def wear(self):
        self.times_worn += 1
        print(f"Wearing {self.color} {self.garment_type}...")
        self.dirty = True

    # A method to check if an item needs washing and wash it if needed
    def wash(self):
        if not self.dirty:
            print(f"Hmm... I don't think this {self.color} {self.garment_
type} needs washing")
        else:
            print(f"This {self.garment_type} is all clean again!")
            self.dirty = False # Not dirty anymore

    # A method to change the color of the garment
    def dye(self, new_color):
        self.color = new_color.lower()

    # To take care of clean prints:
    def __str__(self):
        return f"{self.color.capitalize()} {self.fabric} {self.garment_
type}, size {self.size.capitalize()}"

    # Let's mix and match with __add__
    def __add__(self, other):
        combo = f"{self.color.capitalize()} {self.garment_type} + {other.
color} {other.garment_type}"
        # Silly conditions for fashion verdicts
        if self.garment_type == other.garment_type:
            verdict = "I don't think you need two of those"
        elif self.color == other.color:
            verdict = "matchy-matchy"
        elif self.garment_type == "jeans" and other.garment_type ==
"shirt" or self.garment_type == "shirt" and other.garment_type == "jeans":
            verdict = "basic, but cute"
        elif self.color in ["pink", "red"] and other.color in ["pink",
```

```
"red"]:
            verdict = "fashion disaster"
        else:
            verdict = "you do you"
        return f"{combo} = {verdict}"

    # Checking if two items are the same based on type, color, and size
    def __eq__(self, other):
        return self.garment_type == other.garment_type and self.color ==
other.color and self.size == other.size

# Creating a few items for our digital closet
shirt = ClothingItem("shirt", "M", "pink", "cotton")
jeans = ClothingItem("jeans", "M", "red", "linen")
jacket = ClothingItem("jacket", "L", "black", "denim")
copy_shirt = ClothingItem("shirt", "M", "pink", "cotton")

# Let's print a few
print(shirt)       # Pink cotton shirt, size M
print(jacket)      # Black denim jacket, size L

# Wearing and washing
print("\n-- Wardrobe in use --")
shirt.wear()
shirt.wear()
print(f"Worn {shirt.times_worn} times.")

shirt.wash()       # Should wash
shirt.wash()       # Should say it's already clean

# Dyeing
print("\n-- Getting crafty --")
jeans.dye("purple")
print(jeans)    # Purple linen trousers, size M

# Equality check
print("\n-- Are these the same item? --")
```

```
print(shirt == copy_shirt)   # True
print(shirt == jeans)      # False

# Fashion verdicts
print("\n-- Fashion analysis --")
print(shirt + jeans)
print(shirt + jacket)
print(shirt + copy_shirt)
```

8.3 Building a Plant class

```
# Define a class Plant
class Plant():
    # A class attribute to keep track of the number of live plants
    count = 0

    # Define a constructor
    def __init__(self, name, size, desired_climate):
        self.name = name
        self.size = size
        self.desired_climate = desired_climate
        self.alive = True # Every plant starts out alive

        Plant.count += 1 # Updating the plant count

    def water(self):
        if not self.alive:
            print(f"There's no use... the {self.name.lower()} is no
more.")
        else:
            print(f"Watering the {self.name.lower()}")

    def die(self):
        if not self.alive:
            print(f"The {self.name.lower()} is already dead.")
        else:
            print(f"The {self.name.lower()} withered away.")
            self.alive = False
```

```
            Plant.count -= 1 # decrease plant count when plant dies

    # The dunder method to fix weird print messages
    def __str__(self):
        return f"Name: {self.name} | Size: {self.size} | Preferred
climate: {self.desired_climate} | Alive: {'yes' if self.alive else 'no'}"

# Test it!
plant_1 = Plant("Cactus", "Small", "Dry")
plant_2 = Plant("Monstera", "Large", "Tropical")
plant_3 = Plant("Fern", "Medium", "Tropical")

print(f"Plant count: {Plant.count}")

plant_1.water()
plant_1.die()

print(f"Plant count: {Plant.count}")

plant_1.water()

print(plant_2)
print(plant_1)
```

8.4 Logging logins

```
from datetime import datetime

# Decorator function
def log(func):
    # Wrapper takes in an unknown amount of arguments
    def wrapper(self, *args):
        # determine time for log
        now = datetime.now()
        # Save the result of the method call in a variable while calling
the function
        result = func(self, *args)
        # Write the login/logout attempt to the file.
```

```
        with open("logs.txt", "a") as file:
            file.write(f"{now}: {func.__name__} was called on {self.name}.
Result: {result}\n")
        return result
    return wrapper

class User():
    # Define a constructor
    def __init__(self, name, password):
        self._name = name
        self._password = password
        self._logged_in = False

    @property
    def name(self):
        return self._name

    @name.setter
    def name(self, new_name):
        if not new_name.strip() == "":
            self._name = new_name
        else:
            print("Invalid name")

    @property
    def password(self):
        return self._password

    @password.setter
    def password(self, new_password):
        # verifying password length
        if len(new_password) >= 8:
            self._password = new_password
        else:
            print("Password should at least be 8 characters long.")

    @property
```

```
    def logged_in(self):
        return self._logged_in

    @logged_in.setter
    def logged_in(self, bool):
        self._logged_in = bool

    # With @log decorated login method
    @log
    def login(self, entered_password):
        # No need to log in if you're already logged in
        if self.logged_in == True:
            print(f"{self.name} is already logged in.")
            # return statements for result in logs.txt
            return "Already logged in"
        # Only set logged_in to true if password is correct.
        if self.password == entered_password:
            self.logged_in = True
            print(f"{self.name} successfully logged in")
            return "Great success"
        else:
            print("Wrong password. Try again")
            return "Wrong password"

    # With @log decorated logout method
    @log
    def logout(self):
        # No use in logging out if you're not logged in
        if self.logged_in == False:
            print(f"{self.name} is already logged out.")
            return "Already logged out"
        else:
            self.logged_in = False
            print(f"{self.name} is logged out")
            return "Success"

user1 = User("Maaike91", "RightPassword!")
```

```
user2 = User("Imke97", "CorrectPassword?")

user1.login("RightPassword!")
user2.login("WrongPass")
user1.login("LoggingInAgain")
user1.logout()

user1.name = "MaaikeVanP"
user1.password = ""

user1.login("")
```

Chapter 9

9.1 Vehicles

```
class Vehicle():
    def __init__(self, make, model, year):
        self.make = make
        self.model = model
        self.year = year

    def ride(self):
        print(f"{self.make} {self.model} is riding")

    def __str__(self):
        return f"{self.year} {self.make} {self.model}"

class Car(Vehicle):
    def __init__(self, make, model, year, has_sunroof, is_electric):
        super().__init__(make, model, year)
        self.has_sunroof = has_sunroof
        self.is_electric = is_electric

    def __str__(self):
        return f"{'Electric ' if self.is_electric else ''}{super().__str__
()}, with{'out' if not self.has_sunroof else ''} sunroof"
```

```
class Truck(Vehicle):
    def __init__(self, make, model, year, payload_capacity):
        super().__init__(make, model, year)
        self.payload_capacity = payload_capacity

    def can_carry(self, weight):
        return self.payload_capacity >= weight

    def __str__(self):
        return f"{super().__str__()}, Payload Capacity: {self.payload_
capacity} tons"

class Motorcycle(Vehicle):
    def __init__(self, make, model, year, engine_type):
        super().__init__(make, model, year)
        self.engine_type = engine_type

    def do_wheelie(self):
        print("Popping a wheelie.")

    def rev_engine(self):
        print("Vroom vroom")

    def __str__(self):
        return f"{super().__str__()}, Engine: {self.engine_type}"

my_car = Car("Fiat", "Multipla", 2002, False, False)
my_truck = Truck("CAT", "735", 2021, 32)
my_motorcycle = Motorcycle("Harley-Davidson", "Sportster", 2017, "twin
engine")

my_list = [my_car, my_truck, my_motorcycle]

for vehicle in my_list:
    print(vehicle)
    vehicle.ride()
```

9.2 Superheroes

```
import random

# Power Classes
class NineLives:
    def use(self):
        print("Revived.")

class SuperStrength:
    def use(self):
        print("Using super strength!")

class Invisibility:
    def use(self):
        print("Becoming invisible!")

class SuperBark:
    def use(self):
        print("Using a high pitched bark!")

class MezmerMeow:
    def use(self):
        print("Using a mezmerizing meow to confuse enemy!")

# Gadget Classes
class LaserWhiskers:
    def use(self):
        print("Using laser whiskers!")

class Shield:
    def use(self):
        print("Activating shield!")

class TeleportationCollar:
    def use(self):
        print("Using collar gadget for teleportation! Got away safely.")
```

```
class SpeedBoots:
    def use(self):
        print("Using speed boots to run fast as light!")

# Superhero Class
class Superhero:
    def __init__(self, name, powers, gadgets):
        self.name = name
        self.powers = powers  # List of power objects (composition)
        self.gadgets = gadgets  # List of gadget objects (composition)

    def fight_crime(self):
        # Randomly use a power or gadget
        all_tools = self.powers + self.gadgets
        random_tool = random.choice(all_tools)
        random_tool.use()  # Use the tool (power or gadget)

    def __str__(self):
        return f"{self.name} is ready to fight crime!"

# Create instances of powers and gadgets
strength = SuperStrength()
invisibility = Invisibility()
nine_lives = NineLives()
super_bark = SuperBark()
mezmer_meow = MezmerMeow()

laser_whiskers = LaserWhiskers()
shield = Shield()
collar = TeleportationCollar()
speed_boots = SpeedBoots()

# Create superheroes with lists powers and gadgets
zia = Superhero("Captain Code", [nine_lives, mezmer_meow], [laser_
whiskers, shield, speed_boots])
wiesje = Superhero("Super Sausage", [super_bark, strength, invisibility],
[shield, collar, speed_boots])
```

```
# Fight crime by using a random tool (power or gadget)
print(zia)  # Print superhero's info
zia.fight_crime()  # Use a random tool (power or gadget)

print(wiesje)
wiesje.fight_crime()
```

Chapter 10

10.1 Buggy cat naps

A way to approach this:

1. Run the code and observe the output: hmmm, total is 8.5 instead of expected 10.5.
2. Use `print` statements to see what values are being added or add a breakpoint in the `while` loop to inspect `counter` and `total` values:
    - Print the `counter` value
    - Print the value being added each iteration
3. Notice that the first nap (2 hours) is never added.
4. Identify the bug: `while` loop starts at `counter=1`, skipping index 0.

Fix in the `while` loop OR use a `for` loop to eliminate indexing issues entirely (even cleaner solution).

```
def nap_time(hours_list):
    total = 0
    # BREAKPOINT at the original while loop: Step through to see which
values get added
    # Why: This reveals that index 0 is skipped (counter starts at 1)
    for nap in hours_list:
        total += nap
    return total

cat_naps = [2, 3, 1.5, 4]
print("Total nap time:", nap_time(cat_naps))

# Expected output: 10.5
# Bug was: while loop with counter starting at 1 skipped first element
# Fix: Used for loop to iterate through all elements
```

10.2 Museum tickets

A way to approach this:

1. Run the code and enter an age, oh dear, program crashes with `TypeError`.
2. Read the traceback: "`TypeError: '<' not supported between instances of 'str' and 'int'`".
3. Identify the issue: `input()` returns a string, not an integer.
4. The comparison `'age < 12'` tries to compare string to int, which fails.
5. Solution: Convert input to int with `int()`
6. Add `try-except` to handle cases where user enters non-numeric input.
7. Bonus: Add validation for negative ages.

Alternative debugging approach:

- Add `print(type(age))` after input to see it's a string.
- Set breakpoint before first `if` statement to inspect `age` variable type.

```
def ticket_type():
    # BREAKPOINT HERE (in original buggy code): Inspect type(age) to see
it's a string
    # Why: Reveals that age is str, not int, explaining the TypeError
    while True:
        try:
            age = int(input("Enter your age: "))
            break # Only break if conversion succeeds
        except ValueError:
            print("That didn't work. Please enter a whole number.")
    if age < 0: # Bonus validation for negative ages
        print("That can't be right. Come back when you're born.")
    elif age < 12:
        print("You get in for free. Lucky you!")
    elif age < 18:
        print("You get a youth discount!")
    elif age < 65:
        print("That's a full-price ticket for you.")
    else:
        print("You get a senior discount!")
```

```
ticket_type()

# Bug was: input() returns string, can't compare string to int
# Fix: Convert to int with int(), wrap in try-except for non-numeric input
# Bonus: Added negative age validation
```

10.3 How much does your cat meow?

A way to approach this:

1. Run the code, whoopsie, it crashes with `ZeroDivisionError`.
2. Read traceback: `"ZeroDivisionError: division by zero"` at line with `awake_hours` calculation
3. Add print statement:

   ```
   print(f"Day: {log['day']}, Awake hours: {awake_hours}")
   ```

4. Discover: Wednesday has 24 hours of naps (8+6+9+1=24), making `awake_hours = 0`
5. Solution: Check if `awake_hours == 0` before dividing
6. Use `continue` to skip days with no awake time
7. Track `valid_days` to calculate accurate average
8. Handle edge case: all days are full sleep (return `None` to avoid another division by zero)

Alternative debugging approach:

- Set breakpoint inside the `for` loop
- Step through each day's calculation
- Watch `awake_hours` variable, it will be `0` on Wednesday

```
def average_meows(logs):
    total_meows_per_hour = 0
    valid_days = 0

    for log in logs:
        nap_hours = 0
        for nap in log["naps"]:
            nap_hours += nap
        awake_hours = 24 - nap_hours
        # BREAKPOINT HERE: Watch awake_hours, it becomes 0 on Wednesday
        # Why: Reveals the division by zero condition when cat sleeps all
day
```

```
        if awake_hours == 0:
            print(f"{log['day']} was a full snooze day! Skipping...")
            continue
        total_meows_per_hour += log["meows"] / awake_hours
        valid_days += 1

    # Handle edge case: all days were full sleep
    if valid_days == 0:
        print("Your cat slept through the whole week. No data to average")
        return None

    return total_meows_per_hour / valid_days

logs = [
    {"day": "Monday", "naps": [1, 2, 5], "meows": 90},
    {"day": "Tuesday", "naps": [4, 3, 2], "meows": 75},
    {"day": "Wednesday", "naps": [8, 6, 9, 1], "meows": 9},
    {"day": "Thursday", "naps": [1, 1, 5, 7], "meows": 38},
    {"day": "Friday", "naps": [3, 3, 2, 8], "meows": 94},
    {"day": "Saturday", "naps": [4, 8, 3], "meows": 64},
    {"day": "Sunday", "naps": [3, 3, 2, 8], "meows": 37}
]

print("Average meows per awake hour:", average_meows(logs))

# Bug was: Wednesday has 24 hours of naps, causing division by zero
# Fix: Check if awake_hours == 0, skip that day with continue
# Improvement: Track valid_days for accurate average, handle all-sleep
edge case
```

10.4 Trailing bugs

A way to approach this:

1. Run the code, it executes but... `total_distance` seems wrong (should be around 8000m, not a tiny number).
2. Add `print` statements inside the loop:

   ```
   print(f"Segment: {length} {unit}, Current total: {total}")
   ```

3. Observe:
    - Some segments aren't being added (case sensitivity issue).
    - Kilometers are divided by 1000 instead of multiplied (math error).
    - Some segments with trailing spaces don't match (whitespace issue).
4. Identify 3 bugs:
    a. `unit.lower() == "M"`, lowercase `"m"` never equals uppercase `"M"`.
    b. `total += length / 1000`, should multiply to convert km to meters.
    c. Trailing whitespace in `"m "` doesn't match `"m"`.
5. Fix all three: use `.lower().strip()` and correct the multiplication.

Alternative debugging approach:

- Set breakpoint inside `for` loop.
- Step through each segment.
- Watch which `if/elif` branches execute.
- Notice some segments are skipped entirely.

```
def total_distance(*segments):
    total = 0

   # BREAKPOINT HERE: Step through to see which condition executes for
each segment
    # Why: Reveals that some segments don't match either condition due to
case/whitespace
    for length, unit in segments:
       # Print for debugging: print(f"Processing: {length} {unit}")
        if unit.lower().strip() == "m": # Fixed: added .lower() and
.strip()
            total += length # Meters - add directly
        elif unit.lower().strip() == "km": # Fixed: added .lower() and
.strip()
            total += length * 1000 # Fixed: multiply by 1000, not divide

    print("Total distance:", total, "meters")

total_distance(
```

```
    (2.5, "km"),    # Was being divided instead of multiplied
    (400, "M"),     # Uppercase M wasn't matching lowercase "m"
    (1.0, "km"),
    (800, "m"),     # This one worked in original
    (1.3, "KM"),    # Mixed case wasn't matching
    (900, "m "),    # Trailing space wasn't matching
    (1.1, "km")
)

# Three bugs fixed:
# 1. Case sensitivity: unit.lower() == "M" never matched, added .lower()
to both conditions
# 2. Wrong conversion: divided by 1000 instead of multiplying, changed to
* 1000
# 3. Whitespace: "m " didn't match "m", added .strip() to both conditions
# Expected output: Total distance: 8000.0 meters
```

10.5 None to say

A way to approach this:

1. Run the code, it prints the log messages but then prints `"None"` for both animals.
2. Expected output:

   ```
   Cliff is about to speak...
   Woof!
   ```

   But getting:

   ```
   Cliff is about to speak...
   None
   ```

3. Add print statement in wrapper to see what `func(self)` returns:

   ```
   result = func(self)
   print(f"DEBUG: func returned {result}")
   ```

4. Realize: The decorator calls `func(self)` but doesn't return the result.
5. The `speak()` method returns a string, but the wrapper doesn't pass it through.
6. Fix: Add `return` before `func(self)` in the wrapper.

Alternative debugging approach:

- Set breakpoint in the wrapper function.
- Step through and watch the return value of `func(self)`.
- Notice that the wrapper has no `return` statement.
- The decorated function's return value is lost.

```
def log_call(func):
    def wrapper(self):
        print(f"{self.name} is about to speak...")
        # BREAKPOINT HERE: Step through to see func(self) returns a value
        # Why: Reveals that we're calling func but not returning its
result
        # The value is lost because wrapper doesn't return anything
        return func(self) # Fixed: Added 'return' to pass through the
result

    return wrapper

class Animal:
    def __init__(self, name):
        self.name = name

    @log_call
    def speak(self):
        return "..."

class Dog(Animal):
    @log_call
    def speak(self):
        return "Woof!"

class Cat(Animal):
    @log_call
    def speak(self):
        return "Meow!"

dog = Dog("Cliff")
```

```
cat = Cat("Muchu")

print(dog.speak())
print(cat.speak())

# Bug was: Decorator's wrapper function called func(self) but didn't
return the result
# Fix: Added 'return' statement in wrapper to pass through the function's
return value
# Expected output:
# Cliff is about to speak...
# Woof!
# Muchu is about to speak...
# Meow!
```

Unlock Your Exclusive Benefits

Your copy of this book includes the following exclusive benefits:

DRM-Free PDF Version

Download DRM-free PDF and ePub copies of this book.

7-Day Packt Library Access

Get 7-day unlimited access to 8,000+ books and videos. No credit card required.

Available for first-time Packt+ trial users only.

Next-Gen Reader Access

Read this book on Packt Reader with progress sync, dark mode and note-taking.

Follow the guide below to unlock them. The process takes only a few minutes and needs to be completed once.

Unlock this book's free benefits in 3 easy steps

Step 1

Keep your purchase invoice ready for *Step 3*. If you have a physical copy, scan it using your phone and save it as a PDF, JPG, or PNG.

For more help on finding your invoice, visit `https://www.packtpub.com/en-us/unlock?step=1`.

> **Note:** If you bought this book directly from Packt, no invoice is required. After *Step 2*, you can access your exclusive content right away.

Step 2

Scan the QR code or go to `packtpub.com/unlock`.

On the page that opens (similar to *Figure U.1* on desktop), search for this book by name and select the correct edition.

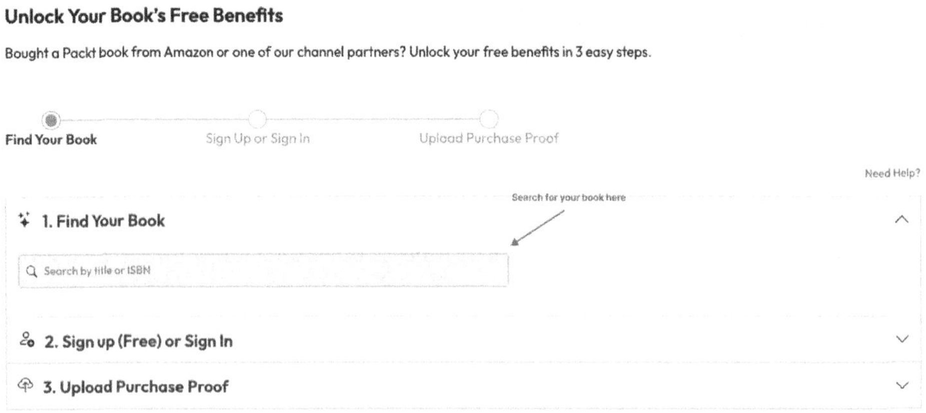

Figure U.1: Packt unlock landing page on desktop

Step 3

After selecting your book, sign in to your Packt account or create one for free. Then upload your invoice (PDF, PNG, or JPG, up to 10 MB). Follow the on-screen instructions to finish the process.

Need Help

If you get stuck and need help, visit `https://www.packtpub.com/unlock-benefits/help` for a detailed FAQ on how to find your invoices and more. This QR code will take you to the help page.

Note: If you are still facing issues, reach out to customercare@packt.com.

Other Books You May Enjoy

If you enjoyed this book, you may be interested in these other books by Packt:

Modern Python Cookbook – Third Edition

Steven F. Lott

ISBN: 9781835466384

- Master core Python data structures, algorithms, and design patterns
- Implement object-oriented designs and functional programming features
- Use type matching and annotations to make more expressive programs
- Create useful data visualizations with Matplotlib and Pyplot
- Manage project dependencies and virtual environments effectively
- Follow best practices for code style and testing
- Create clear and trustworthy documentation for your projects

Expert Python Programming – Fourth Edition

Michał Jaworski, Tarek Ziade, None Ziadé

ISBN: 9781801071109

- Explore modern ways of setting up repeatable and consistent Python development environments
- Effectively package Python code for community and production use
- Learn modern syntax elements of Python programming, such as f-strings, enums, and lambda functions
- Demystify metaprogramming in Python with metaclasses
- Write concurrent code in Python
- Extend and integrate Python with code written in C and C++

50 Algorithms Every Programmer Should Know – Second Edition

Imran Ahmad

ISBN: 9781803247762

- Design algorithms for solving complex problems
- Become familiar with neural networks and deep learning techniques
- Explore existing data structures and algorithms found in Python libraries
- Implement graph algorithms for fraud detection using network analysis
- Delve into state-of-the-art algorithms for proficient Natural Language Processing illustrated with real-world examples
- Create a recommendation engine that suggests relevant movies to subscribers
- Grasp the concepts of sequential machine learning models and their foundational role in the development of cutting-edge LLMs

Packt is searching for authors like you

If you're interested in becoming an author for Packt, please visit `authors.packt.com` and apply today. We have worked with thousands of developers and tech professionals, just like you, to help them share their insight with the global tech community. You can make a general application, apply for a specific hot topic that we are recruiting an author for, or submit your own idea.

Share your thoughts

Now you've finished *Python Illustrated*, we'd love to hear your thoughts! Scan the QR code below to go straight to the Amazon review page for this book and share your feedback or leave a review on the site that you purchased it from.

`https://packt.link/r/183664633X`

Your review is important to us and the tech community and will help us make sure we're delivering excellent quality content.

Index

Symbols

A

B

C

V

W

Made in United States
North Haven, CT
12 November 2026

22198994R00239